ARGUING THE JUST WAR IN ISLAM

ARGUING
THE JUST WAR
IN ISLAM

JOHN KELSAY

HARVARD UNIVERSITY PRESS
Cambridge, Massachusetts & London, England ·· 2007

Library of Congress Cataloging-in-Publication Data

Kelsay, John, 1953–

Arguing the just war in Islam / John Kelsay.

p.   cm.

Includes bibliographical references and index.

ISBN-13: 978-0-674-02639-1 (alk. paper)

ISBN-10: 0-674-02639-X (alk. paper)

1. War—Religious aspects—Islam.   2. Jihad.   3. Just war doctrine.

4. Islam and politics.   I. Title.

BP190.5.W35K434   2007

297.5′6242—dc22   2007011930

to my parents

CONTENTS

Introduction   1

1. Sources   8

2. Shariʿa Reasoning   43

3. Politics, Ethics, and War in Premodern Islam   97

4. Armed Resistance and Islamic Tradition   125

5. Military Action and Political Authority   155

6. Muslim Argument and the War on Terror   198

Notes   227
Acknowledgments   251
Index   255

INTRODUCTION

On June 18, 2005, President George W. Bush addressed military personnel stationed at Fort Bragg, North Carolina, and also, by way of television, the nation and the world. Although the announced topic of the speech was policy in Iraq, during his address the president asserted that the conflict there is part of something much larger. The United States and its allies, he declared, are fighting a global war, one between democratic nation-states, dedicated to the protection and spread of liberty, and movements determined to resist those efforts. The war thus has an ideological dimension. Although the antidemocratic forces had taken aim at the United States and its allies much earlier, that war came home to the United States on September 11, 2001, along with the message that there are people who hate the United States and the values it espouses. They are not only determined to resist the spread of those values; they are also committed to attacks against the power and interests of the United States. In June 2005 the president stated that Iraq had become the epicenter of this struggle, and then quoted Osama bin Laden: "This third world war is raging in Iraq. The whole world is watching, and the struggle will end in victory and glory or in misery and humiliation."[1]

President Bush depicted the fighting in Iraq, along with the global struggle against those who practice "murder and destruction," in ideological terms, although he did not name the "hateful ideology" of the enemies of democracy and freedom until August 2006, when he spoke about "Islamic fascists."[2] The set of notions articulated by Osama bin Laden and like-minded persons has been called by many names: "bin Ladenism," "Islamofascism," "Talibanism," "jihadism," and, most commonly, "fundamentalist," "radical," or "militant" Islam.[3] Whatever else it may involve, the ideology of those associated with attacks on U.S. embassies in Kenya and Tanzania (1998), on the USS *Cole* and on U.S. forces stationed at Khobar in Saudi Arabia (2000), on the World Trade Center and the Pentagon (September 11, 2001), on coalition forces stationed in Iraq (since March 2003), and on public transportation facilities in Madrid (March 11, 2004) and London (July 7, 2005) is associated with appeals to Islam. Those carrying out the attacks were and are Muslims. More importantly, in the context of the president's speech and of this book, when these people give reasons for their actions, they cite Islamic sources and speak in Islamic terms. Noting this fact, many Americans and Europeans argue that the global war of which the president spoke is not well described as ideological. It is better construed as religious.

Many of the president's most ardent supporters speak in this way. Evangelical Christians, in particular, describe such events as encounters between Christian and Islamic civilizations. They portray the conflict as one between the children of light and the children of darkness, between the truth of God and the deception of the devil.

Following 9/11, when the president proclaimed that "Islam means peace" and asserted that those carrying out the attacks had "hijacked" Islam, prominent evangelicals like Franklin Graham, Charles Coulson, Jerry Falwell, and Jerry Vines declared him wrong. For these men and their followers, Islam is a false religion, inevitably associated with wickedness, especially in the form of indiscriminate violence. Other, less theologically minded commentators speak more in terms of a conflict of civilizations, but the view of Islam is much the same. Most of these people have seized on statements by Osama bin Laden and his associates to make the point that the attacks of 9/11 were not an aberration in the tradition of Islam. Rather, those who carried out the attacks were true followers of Muhammad, while those attempting to disassociate Islam from the policies of al-Qaʿida were said to be "ostensible" Muslims, lacking in conviction, untrustworthy, or unrepresentative of the faith.[4]

One of the purposes of this book is to provide a systematic description of the religious perspective of al-Qaʿida and other militant groups.[5] Those who wish to argue that Islam has nothing to do with the attacks of 9/11 or with the tactics of Iraqi "insurgents" will find no comfort here. The facts are plain. Osama bin Laden, Ayman al-Zawahiri, and other militants lay claim to some of the central practices and themes of Islamic tradition. In fact, statements by al-Qaʿida leaders are best understood as attempts to legitimate or justify a course of action in the terms associated with Islamic jurisprudence, or what I shall call Shariʿa reasoning. Invocations of the Shariʿa speak to notions that are very basic in Islam. Ultimately, *al-shariʿa* signifies the faith that there is a right way to live, a way that leads to happiness in this world and the next. According to Islamic tradition, not all ways of ordering life are morally equivalent. As creatures who come from, and ultimately will return to, God, human beings must live within divinely ordered limits.

The close relation between militants and Islamic tradition is not the whole story, however. Those trying to drive a wedge between "true Islam" and the declarations of al-Qaʿida have good reasons for doing so. The point of such an observation is *not* simply that there are some "moderate" Muslims who want to be good citizens of the United States, the United Kingdom, and other European countries. Nor is it that there are numerous Islamic texts that suggest a view different from that of bin Laden and his comrades—Qurʾan 5:32, for example, which indicates that anyone who kills another without cause symbolically kills the entire world. However beautiful the thought, the citation of such a text does not provide an adequate response or an alternative to the statements of militant Muslims. The latter present arguments in order to legitimate particular ways of acting, and these arguments display a determined intention to engage the full range of sources approved in the practice of Shariʿa reasoning. To counter them, one must develop arguments that suggest a similar intention.

The fact is that Muslims today are involved in a serious argument about political ethics. This argument is framed in terms of practices that are central to Islamic tradition. Post-9/11, leading Christian evangelicals, conservative commentators, and others claim that Islam is intimately or even intrinsically bound up with indiscriminate violence. Muslim apologists and those committed to cultural diversity assert that Islam has nothing to do with violence of this type. The truth, as in most cases, is more complicated. Islam is a *living* tradition, in which men and women attempt to forge links between the wisdom of previous generations and the challenges posed by contemporary life, in hopes of acting in ways consistent with the guidance of God. Shariʿa reasoning is one of the modes, if not the primary mode, in which contemporary Muslims make this attempt.

The overarching purpose of this book is to describe the practice of Shariʿa reasoning among contemporary Muslims, particularly with respect to the debate over armed force and political ethics inspired by the arguments of militant activists. The form of argument associated with Shariʿa reasoning involves appeals to tradition. Arguments are evaluated as better or worse, persuasive or not, in terms of the ways in which advocates of various positions make use of historical precedents. Differences between the political ideas advanced by militants and those advanced by other Muslims are not settled by way of appeals to broad or abstract principles like equality or respect for the autonomy of persons. Rather, those engaged in Shariʿa reasoning cite texts, which are interpreted in connection with particular instances in the story Muslims tell about the beginnings and subsequent development of their tradition. Respect for tradition manifests itself in the ways in which people interpret, for example, the Prophet Muhammad's orders to Muslim soldiers or the military response of Abu Bakr, the first *khalifa*, or leader, of the Muslims following the death of the Prophet in 632, to the "turning" or "apostasy" of certain Arab tribes.

An understanding of Muslim arguments about the just war thus requires a good deal of knowledge about the ways Muslims tell the story of the emergence and development of their community. Some of the most basic aspects of this story are outlined in Chapter 1, in response to the question "What is Islam?" The various answers provide the historical and religious context in which Muslim arguments about war and political ethics make sense.

Chapters 2 and 3 extend this historical discussion. Chapter 2 explains how Muslims came to a consensus regarding the range of sources appropriate for those engaged in Shariʿa reasoning, as well as the rules governing the interpretation of approved texts. In this development, the growth of a class of specialists, al-ʿulama (literally, "the learned," sometimes referred to as "Muslim clerics"), was critical. Chapter 3 outlines the most important political and military judgments advanced by members of this class between 750 and 1400 C.E.[6] Most of the *ahkam al-jihad*, or judgments pertaining to armed struggle, emanate from this period, when Muslim political power was at its height. These opinions provide a set of standard references or "consensual precedents" by which contemporary Muslims try to measure the rights and wrongs of specific proposals regarding the political uses of military force.

Chapters 4 and 5 discuss contemporary arguments and their consequences. Chapter 4 details the ways in which today's militants may be understood as the most recent exponents of an argument advanced by numerous Muslims over the last two centuries. At its simplest, this is an argument about how Muslims should conduct themselves when they are *not* in a position of power. In its details, the argument deals with questions about the justification and conduct of armed resistance. It proceeds by way of an attempt to "stretch" the consensual precedents associated with the premodern *ahkam al-jihad* to the new situations created by European colonialism and, more recently, by the geopolitical predominance of the United States. The resistance argument is controversial, to say the least. The important questions are *"How* is it controversial?" and "What does the controversy say about contemporary Muslim political discourse?" Chapter 5 demonstrates that the controversy over militant justifications of armed resistance indicates a crisis of legitimacy in Muslim thought. Arguments on all sides in this controversy reflect the lack of Muslim consensus regarding the identification of legitimate or right authority in affairs of state. They may also be interpreted as reflecting a crisis in the practice of Shari'a reasoning itself. The question *Who* has the right to make decisions about matters of politics, including those related to the use of military force, is intimately related to another: *Who* has the right argument, with respect to the kind of political order required by the Shari'a? Militants set their program of armed resistance in the context of a particular vision of political order. In doing so, they lay claim to the mantle of historical precedent, that is, to the mantle of the Shari'a. Other Muslims, articulating a different vision, point to sources of Shari'a reasoning that underwrite democratic political forms.

Given such competing visions, is it possible to say which side is correct, or who is likely to win? Chapter 6 concludes that much depends on the ways in which groups of Muslims perceive their political context, and that this perception varies, depending on whether one is speaking about the United States, the European Union, or the historical heartland of Islam. Not least important, in thinking about the prospects for success of the arguments made by Muslim advocates of democratic government, are the perceptions Muslims have regarding the conduct of the United States and its allies in connection with the war on terror.

CHAPTER ONE
SOURCES

Islam is peace.
—President George W. Bush, September 17, 2001

[Islam] is a very evil and a very wicked religion.
—Franklin Graham, December 20, 2002

[Islam] is the religion of Jihad in the way of Allah so that Allah's
Word and religion reign supreme.
—Osama bin Laden, November 24, 2002

The disparate statements above demonstrate clearly that Islam is a contested notion. Since September 11, 2001, "Islam," "Muslim," *jihad, fatwa,* and related terms have featured regularly on television and radio talk shows. Politicians, evangelical preachers, talk-show hosts, and ordinary people use them with apparent ease. But their use is reflexive: their use shows more about where the speaker stands in the spectrum of political debate than about the historical and current meanings of the words. Even the statement by bin Laden is reflexive; for the arguments of contemporary Muslim politicians, preachers, talk-show hosts, and ordinary people also reveal a wide range of interpretations of the meaning of Islam. It seems that in this context at least, language, ostensibly an instrument of communication, can become an obstacle to it.

It is possible to bring some order to this confusion by identifying some standard sources of Muslim political argument. The story of Muhammad and the early Muslims, the theological perspective mediated by the Qur'an and the sayings of the Prophet, the institutional and legal arrangements developed as Islam came to prominence as a civilization—when contemporary Muslims talk about politics, each and all of these are cited as precedents indicative of what it means to practice Islam. Islam is a living tradition, in which people attempt to discern links between historical patterns construed as exemplary and the facts of current political life. To exert oneself, to expend one's resources in this attempt, demonstrates one's responsibility toward God and one's fellow humans. As Muslims carry out this task, they call upon foundational narratives, beliefs about God and the world; they cite examples from the past in order to present reasons for current or future action. They demonstrate their connections with a transgenerational community and invite others to evaluate and respond to their claims about God's will.

Basic Terms

Let us first examine lexical meanings. *Al-islam* literally means "the submission."[1] In standard Arabic references, where the term indicates the importance of the submission of human beings to God, *islam* refers to the attempt to order life in ways that acknowledge God as the "Lord of the worlds," the one "from whom you come, and to whom you will return." *Muslim* refers to "one who submits," that is, to someone engaged in the attempt to order life in ways that acknowledge the lordship of God.[2]

"Islam" thus signifies a way of life undertaken with the intention of serving God. In this context, President Bush's assertion that "Islam means peace" has some legitimacy. The Arabic *al-islam* is derived from the same root as *al-salam,* and the latter does in fact mean "peace." In taking up the service of God and in submitting themselves to his will, humans acknowledge who and what they are; they act according to their nature, which is to seek peace in this world and the next. Happiness and peace, on both personal and social levels, follow. This notion of Islam, which amounts to a promise to those who believe and do good works, today attracts more than a billion believers in every nation on Earth. In the United States alone, the number of Muslims is estimated at 4 million, roughly equivalent to the number of Episcopalians.[3]

Now, what is the substance of this submission to the will of God? To put it another way, what is Islam? Of the many possible answers, I shall focus on three. Islam, the submission to the will of God, may be defined as (1) a religious movement that begins with the life and work of the man Muhammad, in the Arabian Peninsula in the seventh century C.E.; (2) the natural religion of humanity; and (3) the driving force behind a great world civilization. We may think of (1) as focused on the story of Muhammad and his followers; of (2) in terms of Islamic theology, particularly in terms of notions of the nature and destiny of human beings as creatures of God; and of (3) as expressing the cultural and political significance of Islam as the dominant religion in a region stretching from North Africa to China and from south-central Europe to the Indian subcontinent, Indonesia, and beyond.

The Story of Muhammad

According to tradition, Muhammad, son of 'Abdullah, was born in the Year of the Elephant. In the standard scholarly estimation, this would be equivalent to 569 or 570 C.E. The terminology of Muslim biographers makes it clear that we are dealing with "holy history." Such biographers relate the story of Muhammad in ways familiar in the history of religion. Like the founding narratives of Judaism, Christianity, and other long-standing religious traditions, the available sources are not crafted in the framework of the "scientific history" practiced in academic departments since the mid-nineteenth century. Rather, they are "proclamatory biographies," the purpose of which is to build faith. There is no reason to doubt the broad outlines of the stories associated with Muhammad and the early Muslims, even as there is no reason to doubt the historical basis of the broad outlines of the gospel narrative concerning Jesus of Nazareth, or of reports concerning sayings of the rabbis of the Talmud. But in all these cases we ought not to push the details. When Muslim writers related the stories of Muhammad and his companions, they meant to provide an account of the work of God in the world—and such an enterprise is always, in some sense, a matter of reaching beyond scientific history. The point of holy history is to answer religious questions: not simply or even primarily "How did these events transpire?" but "Why did they occur?"

With respect to the story of Muhammad, the answer of Muslim biographers is clear: Muhammad, son of ʿAbdullah, was born in order to fulfill the plan of God for humanity. Just as that plan included the birth and career of Moses, prophet to the "tribe of Israel," and Jesus, son of Mary, prophet to the "followers of the messiah," so it was to be that, at the end of days, God would send a prophet to the Arabic-speaking tribes living in Hijaz (the Arabian Peninsula, including the area we know as Saudi Arabia, Yemen, and the other Gulf states). This prophet would call the tribes, and with them all humanity, to faith, even as Moses and Jesus had done in other places and times.

Thus the oldest extant biography of Muhammad begins with a genealogy by which we learn that the Arabic-speaking prophet was descended from Abraham, and hence ultimately from Adam, the first human being. There follows a narrative of kings and prophets, centered on relations between Mecca, city of Muhammad's birth, and Yemen, site of a powerful kingdom in the fifth and sixth centuries.

We learn that the rulers of Yemen eventually came under the sway of Abyssinia (Ethiopia), and that the allied kingdoms repeatedly tried to extend their dominance to Mecca. In every case, however, they were foiled because of God's protection of the (eventual) birthplace of the Prophet. In fact, they were warned to leave Mecca alone:

> . . . lo from Qurayza came
> A rabbi wise, among the Jews respected.
> "Stand back from a city preserved," said he,
> "For Mecca's prophet of Quraysh true-guided."[4]

Muhammad, we are told, was born in the Year of the Elephant. This nomenclature derives from a story in which the tribes of the Arabian Peninsula repelled an Abyssinian/Yemeni invasion. The invaders made use of an elephant or elephants, which the Arabs perceived as providing an overwhelming advantage.[5] The Arabs' only hope was that God, the "defender of the *Ka'ba*" (the "Cube," a building in Mecca), might intervene. And indeed, this is what happened: the elephant refused to march in the direction of Mecca, and a flock of stone-throwing birds executed an aerial bombardment, causing the invaders to retreat.

This episode yields some valuable information about the context of early Islam—the political, social, and religious life of Arab tribes in the sixth and early seventh centuries. First, it is clear that at this time the Arabian Peninsula was a political backwater. Prominent Jewish tribes had established a small imperial state in Yemen in the late fourth and early fifth centuries, but by 550 any power it retained depended on the maintenance of good relations with the Abyssinian ruler in East Africa. The Abyssinian ruler combined religious and political power. He bore a staff resembling a bishop's crosier, signifying his status as the head of a very ancient Christian church. At the same time he ruled over an empire, which was from time to time a player in the great-power rivalry between the Byzantines and the

Sassanids. That rivalry provides at least a partial explanation for the Abyssinian involvement in south and central Arabia. Byzantine and Sassanid rulers fought over and dominated the heartland of the Middle East, which the Arabs called *al-shams*—Syro-Palestine, the region in which late Hellenistic kings like Antiochus Epiphanes reigned supreme after the death of Alexander the Great. The Romans added the area to their vast holdings by the late first century B.C.E. By the Year of the Elephant, the great cities of Damascus and Jerusalem were solidly under Byzantine (and thus Christian) control, although the Sassanids, based in Iran and organized around Zoroastrianism, maintained enough strength in Iraq to threaten these Byzantine holdings.

In late antiquity as today, trade was a major interest of great powers. This interest brought the Byzantines and Sassanians into frequent conflict, particularly with respect to the travel of merchant caravans between Damascus, Jerusalem, and the shoreline of the Arabian Sea, where several ports provided access to ships traveling to and from India. Most of the conflicts between the great powers played out north of the vast deserts of the Arabian Peninsula; no ruler wanted to send fighting forces there. But by the early to mid-sixth century the great powers began hiring the "uncivilized" tribes living in the Peninsula to raid rival caravans and thus disrupt trade. As the activities of these mercenaries affected merchant traffic through the desert, reducing the flow of people with goods and money to the southern ports in Yemen, and thereby threatening Abyssinia's revenues from Middle Eastern trade, Abyssinian interest in the region increased.

The Arabian Peninsula of the sixth and early seventh centuries was a bit player in the drama of great-power politics, and social organization there was based on a tribal order. The sources are filled with names like Banu Qurayza (tribe of Qurayz), Banu Hasaniyyah, and, above all, Banu Quraysh. In each case, the name is tied to a clan ancestor, an indication that the tribes were understood as extended family units. Arab tribes divided themselves along the lines of "settled" and "plain," the former referring to those whose ancestral traditions established them as living in one place, the latter to the more stereotypical nomads (Bedouins, *al-badu*). Tribal units provided Arabs with a notion of territorial and social boundaries. Members of the Banu Quraysh, for example, were immediately associated with "settled" Arabs whose habitual territory included the city of Mecca and its environs. "City" is really an exaggeration; during the sixth and seventh centuries, Mecca was a kind of outpost with a few buildings and a well, which served as a way-station for merchant caravans. One of the buildings—the *Ka'ba,* or "Cube"—and the well, which in the stories is identified as Zamzam, the well from which Hagar and Ishmael drank, loom large in the story of the Abyssinian/Yemeni invasion. As Ibn Ishaq has it, 'Abd al-Muttalib, the grandfather of the Prophet, tried to dissuade the invading forces from attacking Mecca. When asked why he did not rather appeal to them to avoid harm to the Ka'ba, which the invaders identified as a holy site, 'Abd al-Muttalib replied that the shrine had its own protector (that is, God), who might fight for it if he wished. This account reveals not only a strong sense of tribal identity and vocation, but also the eminence of the Quraysh, and within it, the family of the Prophet, among the Arab tribes.

Most of the sources indicate that the tribes were fiercely devoted to living out patterns identified with their clan ancestors. As the Islamic narrative has it (with some support in the historical record), the tribal order might also be viewed as a loose confederation, in which groups speaking mutually recognizable dialects shared enough in the way of culture and religion that they could be rallied against a common enemy. In the story of the Year of the Elephant, leaders among the Quraysh apparently developed policies intended to foster unity among the tribes by describing the Ka'ba as a "house of prayer for all Arabs" and by referring to Mecca as a cultural center for all

Arab tribes. The various tribes were encouraged to observe a tradition of pilgrimage to the Ka'ba during months set apart for this purpose. During these months Mecca was considered a zone of peace, with no fighting allowed. The various tribes were encouraged to bring along, and to place within the Ka'ba, symbols of their patron deities. Observances included ceremonies of animal sacrifice, circumambulation of the Ka'ba, and ritual feasting, the last accompanied by songs celebrating the *muruwwa,* or manliness, of the great tribal ancestors.

From these reports, we learn much about the religious and moral aspects of Arab tribal culture. Thus, the stories recounting that each tribe was to set a talisman of its favorite deity in the Ka'ba point to a kind of polytheism. Each tribe had its favorite or patron deity, but all were part of a pantheon of gods and goddesses, and the special powers of some apparently made them attractive across tribal lines. For example, *al-lat* (the goddess) had her sphere of influence in the field of fertility; *al-uzza* (the mighty) had power over health; and *al-manat,* whose name may be translated as "fate" or even "death," controlled the time and means of that reality. These three are depicted as special intermediaries between human beings and the powerful, distant Creator, known simply as *al-lah* (the god).

The central moral value of the tribes seems to have been *muruwwa.* The remnants of tribal poetry cited by biographers of Muhammad suggest that we should think of *muruwwa* in terms of the set of virtues associated with a tribal chief. Thus, the notion includes bravery in battle, for the chief leads his tribe into battle. It includes wealth and generosity, for the chief holds large numbers of livestock, and is thus able and willing to put on great feasts for the members of his tribe, who are best construed as "clients" under the patronage of the "big man." Along with his holdings in livestock and other goods, the *muruwwa* of the chief appears in the number of women (wives and concubines) and children he maintains.[6]

Such virtue is worthy of remembrance, in the sense that those whose lives show them as great men are celebrated in songs. Our sources suggest that the tribes did not dwell much on life after death. For them, the goal was to live life to the fullest, and the greatest tragedy occurred when it might be said that someone died "too soon," that is, before taking a proper measure of the goods associated with manliness.

Finally, Arab tribal culture placed great importance on the *sunna* (literally, "beaten path"), or way of the ancestors. Indeed, acknowledgment of tribal deities, the bravery and generosity associated with manliness, and the hope that one might be remembered come together in connection with this *sunna*. The stories of attempts by the Quraysh to foster connections among the tribes by means of the symbol of the Ka'ba point to such a cultural system, as do songs like the following:

> But for three things, that are the joy of a young fellow,
> I assure you I wouldn't care when my deathbed visitors
>   arrive.
> First, to forestall my charming critics with a good swig
> Of crimson wine that foams when the water is mingled in;
> Second, to wheel at the call of the beleaguered a curved-
>   shanked steed
> Streaking like the wolf of the thicket you've startled lapping
>   the water;
> And third, to curtail the day of showers, such an admirable
>   season,
> Dallying with a ripe wench under the pole-propped tent,
> Her anklets and her bracelets seemingly hung on the
>   boughs of a pliant, unriven gum-tree or a castor-shrub.
> So permit me to drench my head while there's still life in it,
> For I tremble at the thought of the scant draught I'll get
>   when I'm dead.

I'm a generous fellow, one that soaks himself in his
　lifetime;
You'll know tomorrow, when we're dead, which of us is the
　thirsty one.[7]

As the Muslims would have it, the culture of the tribes provided
an illustration of *al-jahiliyya*, a term variously translated as "heedlessness" or "ignorance." Islam stood in opposition to this system at
every point, replacing the pantheon of deities with the claim that
there is no god but *al-lah*; the virtue of manliness with the notion of
al-taqwa, meaning "piety" or "godly fear"; the ideal of remembrance
with pictures of a Final Judgment and an afterlife filled with rewards
and punishments; and the beaten path of the ancestors with a call
to judge by "that which God has sent down," that is, by revelation.
This constitutes the challenge of Muhammad to Arab tribal culture;
as our sources have it, just before his death in 632 Muhammad
would claim that "Arabia is now solidly for Islam." Thus the foundational narrative of Islam is one in which Muhammad and his companions participate in a kind of cultural revolution, by which the
tribes of the Arabian Peninsula are transformed into the *umma*, or
community of faith.[8]

The story of Muhammad and the early Muslims thus begins in the
context of Arab tribal culture, and ends in a claim that this culture has been transformed by the movement of Islam. The Muslim
proclamatory biographies presume God's preparation of the Peninsula for the coming of the Arab Prophet. The invasion in the Year of
the Elephant, the moves by the Quraysh to emphasize the Ka'ba as a
house of prayer for all Arabs—these are not random developments.
Rather, they occur within the plan of God. And thus, the birth of
Muhammad comes "in the fullness of time." Grandson of 'Abd al-
Muttalib, son of 'Abdullah, Muhammad comes into the world accompanied by signs. According to Ibn Ishaq,

It is alleged in popular stories (and only God knows the truth) that Amina d. Wahb, the mother of God's messenger, used to say when she was pregnant with God's messenger that a voice said to her, "You are pregnant with the lord of this people and when he is born say, 'I put him in the care of the One from the evil of every envier; then call him Muhammad.'" As she was pregnant with him she saw a light come forth from her by which she could see the castles of Busra in Syria.[9]

Such signs would be a continuing part of the life of the Prophet. The biographies tell us that, in his teens, Muhammad accompanied a caravan to Damascus. On the way, the experienced drivers were startled when Bahira, a well-known Christian monk, stopped them on the road and invited them to his hermitage for a meal. The drivers had passed by many times; until that day, Bahira, unwilling to interrupt his devotion of prayer and fasting, had not acknowledged their presence. On this day, however, he brought the caravan into his hermitage, provided the travelers with food, and examined Muhammad carefully. As the story goes, Bahira identified Muhammad as the one whose appearance and life story matched the descriptions "in the Christian books." He then directed Abu Talib, Muhammad's uncle and guardian: "Take your nephew back to his country and guard him carefully against Jews, for by God, if they see him and know about him what I know, they will do him evil; a great future lies before this nephew of yours, so take him home quickly."[10]

Such interactions with a Christian or warnings about Jews are at this point simply a means of affirming the role of God's providence. As we learn from other reports, there were other, more immediate challenges for Muhammad to deal with. The deaths of his father (before Muhammad's birth), his mother (shortly after), and his grandfather (before he turned eight) left the boy an orphan. Abu Talib became his guardian. As with everything else in the story, the protection of Abu Talib came as a gift of God:

> By the morning brightness and by the night when it grows
> still,
> Your Lord has not forsaken you, nor does He hate you.
> The future will be better for you than the past.
> Your Lord will give you so much that you will be well
> satisfied.
> Did He not find you an orphan and shelter you? Did he
> not find you lost and guide you?
> Did He not find you in need and make you self-sufficient?
> So do not be harsh with the orphan and do not chide the
> one who asks for help.
> Talk about the blessings of your Lord.   (Qur'an 93)[11]

Indeed, as Ibn Ishaq has it,

> The Prophet grew up, God protecting him and keeping him
> from the vileness of heathenism [that is, the religiosity of
> the tribes] because he wished to honor him with the role of
> prophet, until he grew up to be the finest of his people in
> manliness, the best in character, most noble in lineage, the
> best neighbor, the most kind, truthful, reliable, the furthest
> removed from filthiness and corrupt morals, through lofti-
> ness and nobility, so that he was known among his people as
> "the trustworthy" because of the good qualities which God
> had implanted in him.[12]

The way was thus well prepared, and Muhammad with it. Once he married Khadija, a somewhat older woman of means, Muhammad began to engage in retreats, perhaps in imitation of the hermetic practices of monks like Bahira.[13] It was during one of these retreats that Muhammad heard the call to prophesy. The story is worth quoting at length:

Every year during [the month of Ramadan] the prophet would pray in seclusion and give food to the poor that came to him. And when he completed the month and returned from his seclusion, first of all before entering his house he would go to the Ka'ba and walk round it seven times or as often as it pleased God; then he would go back to his house until in the year when God sent him, in the month of Ramadan in which God willed concerning him what He willed of His grace, the prophet set forth to Hira as was his wont, and his family with him. When it was the night on which God honored him with his mission and showed mercy on His servants thereby, Gabriel brought him the command of God. "He came to me," said the prophet of God, "while I was asleep, with a coverlet of brocade whereon was some writing, and said, 'Read!' I said, 'What shall I read?' He pressed me with it so tightly that I thought it was death; then he let me go and said, 'Read!' I said, 'What shall I read?' He pressed me with it again so that I thought it was death; then he let me go and said 'Read!' I said, 'What shall I read?' He pressed me with it the third time so that I thought it was death and said 'Read!' I said, 'What then shall I read?'—and this I said only to deliver myself from him, lest he should do the same to me again. He said:

Read in the name of your Lord who created,
Who created the human creature from a clot of blood.
Read! Your Lord is the most beneficent.
He taught by the pen.
Taught humanity that which it did not know."
    (Qur'an 96:1–5)[14]

The report continues, indicating Muhammad's confusion, even despair, with respect to comprehension of what had happened, until the angel Gabriel returned to confirm that this was a call to prophesy. Khadija encouraged Muhammad, as did her cousin, Waraqa. In keeping with the notion that Muhammad's mission fulfilled a prior plan of God, we learn that Waraqa "had become a Christian and read the scriptures and learned from those that follow the Torah and the Gospel." Waraqa also indicated that Muhammad would find the way of prophecy difficult: "You will be called a liar, and they will use you despitefully and cast you out and fight against you."[15]

From this point, the story of Muhammad may be described as a dialectic between struggle and hope. By tradition, the date of the encounter with Gabriel is 610. Over the next twenty-two years, until his death in 632, Muhammad received periodic visitations by the divine spirit, and with these, revelations that make up the Qur'an. Many of these revelations are, by tradition, correlated with specific challenges posed by the residents of Mecca, that is, the Quraysh. Leading men of the tribe perceived a challenge in Muhammad's preaching. And, as any impartial reader would admit, in this perception they were not mistaken.

We should now return to the tribal structure of Arab society. Here, our sources indicate that many who heard Muhammad preach understood him to accuse their ancestors, the great men whose deeds constituted a legacy for and identity of particular tribes, of error. Thus, Ibn Ishaq relates that the great men of the Quraysh tribe in Mecca said to Muhammad's uncle: "O Abu Talib, your nephew has cursed our gods, insulted our religion, mocked our way of life and accused our forefathers of error. Either you must stop him or you must let us get at him." Or again, Muhammad is one who "brought a message by which he separates a man from his father, or from his brother, or from his wife, or from his family."[16]

Such characterizations are common in the history of religions.

New religious movements constitute an attack on established life-ways, which in some sense have their own sacred legitimacy. At the heart of Muhammad's preaching was a call for his kin to renounce the ties of ancestry and to constitute a new community. This community would be defined by its worship of one god, *al-lah,* the Creator and Lord of all.

> Say to the ingrates: I do not worship what you worship,
>   and you do not worship what I worship. I will never
>   worship what you worship, and you will never worship
>   what I worship. You have your religion, and I have mine.
>   (Qur'an 109)

The story Muslims tell reflects a steady effort on the part of the Prophet, with small numbers of converts at first. The community of Muslims meets with resistance; its members must endure the opprobrium of their Arab kin. At times the resistance breaks out in acts of violence; for some period, some of the leading men of the Quraysh sustain a boycott of the families of the Muslims. Throughout the early years of the Prophet's ministry, Muhammad counseled his followers to endure and to preach, but never to fight. They were to bear witness to the "clear evidence" of the Qur'an regarding the judgment of God:

> When the sky is ripped apart, in rightful obedience to its
>   Lord's command;
> When the earth is leveled out, casts out its contents, and
>   becomes empty, in rightful obedience to its Lord's
>   command;
> You humans, toiling laboriously towards your Lord, will
>   meet Him.
> Whoever is given his record in his right hand will have an
>   easy reckoning and return to his people well pleased.

Whoever is given his record from behind his back will cry
out for destruction, and will burn in the blazing fire.
(84:1–12)

In later years, the Qur'an would remind the Muslims of the "grace"
by which God called them into a new community and gave them a
mission: to command the right and forbid the wrong.[17] In this early
stage, though, their ability to carry out the mission was limited. Not
only were they few in number; when persecuted, they were not allowed to fight back. That stance would change in 622 C.E.—in Islamic terms, the year 1—when Muhammad moved his followers to a
new location. The migration to Medina, *al-hijra*, constitutes a defining moment in the story. For the time being, the community would
carry out its mission not only by means of preaching and worship,
but by means of fighting and other political activity. From this point,
Muhammad is to be regarded as both prophet, in the sense of one
who proclaims a religious message, and statesman, in the sense of
one who exercises leadership in connection with the aims of a community competing for power.

Traditional biographies symbolize this shift, first, by giving an account of agreements between Muhammad and the tribes living in
Medina. We are told that certain of the great men of these tribes
came to Mecca and entered into negotiations with Muhammad. The
ostensible reason for this was their need to arbitrate an intertribal
conflict in Medina, and their hope that the "Arab prophet" might
provide assistance. The negotiations took place over several years,
and by time of the migration, a few of Muhammad's companions
were already living in Medina, acquainting its residents with Islam.
When the move finally took place, representatives of the Medinan
tribes took an oath that bound them to Muhammad. They were to
support him, respect his orders, and, above all, to fight with him
against the Meccans. Why the stress on fighting? As the biographers

have it, God gave the order, specifically by revealing the verses re-
corded in Qur'an 22:39–40:

> Those who have been attacked are permitted to take up
> arms because they have been wronged.
> God has the power to help them; those who have been
> driven unjustly from their homes only for saying, "Our
> Lord is God."
> If God did not repel some people by means of others,
> many monasteries, churches, synagogues, and mosques,
> where God's name is much invoked, would have been
> destroyed.

Fighting is thus justified, in the sense of permitted, in order to resist
injustice. And the accounts of the agreements between Muhammad
and the Medinan tribes suggest that the Prophet understood this
permission to fight as requiring preparation for the coming campaign.[18]

Thus Muslim biographies present a second signification of Muhammad's move toward politics, by way of accounts of his approach
to intertribal relations in Medina. Of these, the most significant
had to do with relations between the followers of Muhammad and
Medinan Jews. Although we do not know much about the practice
of Judaism (or, for that matter, of Christianity) in Medina, Muslim
biographers provide names of Jewish leaders who interacted with
the Prophet. These are typically listed along with some indication of
tribal affiliation; from this evidence, it appears there was a Jewish presence in a number of the Medinan tribes, with particular
strength in three or four. The account of Muhammad's relations
with these begins with presentations of the agreement Muslims call
the Medinan Constitution, which is striking in its stipulations of
parity between Muslims and Jews. According to the document, each
community maintained its independence; each was to fight along-

side the other, to bear its own costs and keep its own war prizes; each
was to observe its own customs and patterns of worship.

Such parity did not last long, however. The account of the constitution leads into a tale of the steady degeneration of relationships
between Muslims and Jews. Ibn Ishaq, for example, moves quickly to
stories of Jewish criticism of the Prophet, followed by a long account
of the revelation of *surat al-baqara,* chapter 2 of the Qur'an, in
which the recalcitrance of the Jews of Medina is interpreted as consistent with the ways the people of Israel treated Moses. Christians,
too, are criticized for their errors with respect to the religion of Jesus.
Both Moses and Jesus, we are told, practiced the religion of Abraham, and that is *al-islam.*

> They say, "Become Jews or Christians, and you will be
>   rightly guided."
> Say: "No, ours is the religion of Abraham, the upright, who
>   did not worship any god besides God."
> Say: "We believe in God and in what was sent down to us
>   and what was sent down to Abraham, Ishmael, Isaac,
>   Jacob, and the Tribes, and what was given to Moses,
>   Jesus, and all the prophets by their Lord. We make no
>   distinction between any of them, and we devote
>   ourselves to God."   (Qur'an 2:135–136)[19]

Hereafter the story is all downhill with respect to Muslim-Jewish
relations, to the point where the Jewish tribes were accused of violating their agreement with Muhammad by providing assistance to the
Meccans. Those tribes with particularly large concentrations of Jews
were either banished or, in one memorable episode, treated as a conquered foe, with all adult males executed, and women and children
taken by the Muslims as slaves.[20]

The charge that Medinan Jews provided assistance to the Meccans
leads to the third and most prominent way by which traditional bi-

ographers signified the Prophet's political authority: the campaign against the Meccans. Here the major accounts focus on battles between the Muslims, their Medinan allies, and the Meccans. Those who fight under Muhammad's command are praised as true Muslims who obey God and God's Prophet. These make sacrifices, for which they will receive rewards:

> Do not think of those who have been killed in God's way as dead.
> They are alive with their Lord, well provided for, happy with what God has given them of his favor;
> Rejoicing that for those they have left behind who have yet to join them there is no fear, nor will they grieve;
> Rejoicing in God's blessing and favor, and that God will not let the reward of the believers be lost.   (Qur'an 3:169–171)

Others, who are reluctant to fight, are encouraged to do so:

> Why should you not fight in God's cause and for those oppressed men, women, and children who cry out, "Lord, rescue us from this town whose people are oppressors! By your grace, give us a protector and helper!"?   (Qur'an 4:75)

Those who fail to answer the call or who (as in the case of the Meccans) actively resist are variously described as hypocrites, ingrates, or idolaters.

The story of the Prophet's campaign against the Meccans is not only military. Diplomacy plays a part, as the stories depict Muhammad cultivating and solidifying relations with tribes throughout the region by means of treaties of mutual protection and, in a number of cases, marriage. In the end, the Meccans are isolated and defeated, and the Prophet concludes his life with the pronouncement: "Arabia is now solidly for Islam." In the place of tribal loyalties, the stories tell us, there is now a community of those who submit to God. In the place of the pantheon of patron deities, there is the worship of *al-lah*, the Creator and Lord of all. In the place of manliness and associated virtues, there are piety and obedience to God and God's Prophet. In the place of fame, there is the promise of resurrection and judgment. And finally, in the place of the *sunna* of the ancestors, there are the Qur'an and the example of the Prophet.

The Natural Religion of Humanity

In one sense, the story of Muhammad is self-contained. The narrative by which Muslims speak of the Prophet's call and his struggles with the Meccans is one that needs no additional data. If one asks the question "Why this story?" or "What justified Muhammad in this campaign to bring the Arabian Peninsula under the influence of Islam?" one has only to look at the reports of the Prophet's call. His was a divine mandate, and from the standpoint of the faithful, that fact is sufficient.

In another sense, though, the story reaches beyond the career of Muhammad. We have already seen how traditional biographers stressed the role of providence in preparing the way for the Arab Prophet. We have also seen how accounts of his relations with Medinan Jews correlate with Qur'anic texts that stress the continuity of Muhammad's mission with those of Moses, Jesus, and, behind them both, Abraham. This is, indeed, one of the more striking features of the story of Muhammad: from the Muslim point of view, his is the latest, and perhaps the last, great chapter in the story of God's dealings with human beings.

To put this in the language of theologians, we might say that the mission of Muhammad rests on the fact that he is proclaiming the "natural" religion of humanity. Muslims say that every child is born

a Muslim, and that the child's parents then make him or her into a
Jew, a Christian, a Zoroastrian—or a member of the *umma* of the
Prophet.[21] For an explanation of this claim, we may turn to the
Qur'an, beginning with the chapter called "Heights" (7:172–173):

> When your Lord took out the offspring from the loins of
>   the Children of Adam and made them bear witness
>   about themselves,
> He said, "Am I not your Lord?"
> And they replied, "Yes, we bear witness."
> So, you cannot say on the Day of Resurrection, "We were
>   not aware of this,"
> Or, "It was our forefathers who, before us, ascribed
>   partners to God, and we are only the descendants who
>   came after them: Will you destroy us because of
>   falsehoods they invented?"

On first reading, these verses relate something very strange, and
Muslim commentaries devote many pages to explaining the process
by which God "took out the offspring from the loins of the Children
of Adam." Nevertheless, the import is clear. These verses proclaim
that all human beings are responsible to worship the one God—that
is, to practice Islam. They cannot escape this responsibility, nor can
they cite their inherited traditions as an excuse for failure to fulfill it.
One might speak of the verses as depicting a kind of primordial covenant between God and humanity. Thus, to speak of God as taking
the offspring from the loins of the children of Adam is to suggest
that all generations, all peoples, and all individuals are rightly called
to bear witness to the God from whom they come, and to whom
they will return.

To elaborate further, we may turn to other verses in the Qur'an.
The claim is that *al-islam,* submission to the will of God, is natural to humanity. Submission describes the proper disposition of

creatures whose life and capacities have their source in the power and will of a divine other. Thus, in Qur'an 30:30, God exhorts the Prophet to "stand firm" in devotion to *al-din* ("the religion," meaning Islam). This, the verse continues, "is the natural disposition God instilled in humankind." Or again, at 33:72, a verse reminiscent of 7:172–173, we read that God offered *al-amana,* or the trust, to the heavens, the earth, and the mountains, but they refused to undertake it. Only human beings were bold enough to do so. As Muslim commentators suggest, this verse points to a notion of humankind as the "vice-regent" of God.[22] Acceptance of the trust involves a responsibility of stewardship, in accord with which God will call each human being to account. The world, and with it humankind, was not created "for play. If We had wished for a pastime, We had it in Us." Rather, God created the world, and set humankind within it, as a demonstration of God's glory, and to that end "We hurl the truth against falsehood, and truth obliterates it . . . Everyone in the heavens and the earth belongs to God, and those that are with God are never too proud to worship God, nor do they grow weary; they glorify God tirelessly, night and day" (21:16–20).

The notion of Islam as natural to humanity has as its corollary the claim that human beings are capable of acknowledging God. Here, the Qur'an insists that the capacity to "reflect" or to engage in dialectical reasoning provides access to the divine. In particular, human beings are able to reflect on a variety of "signs" by which creation points to its maker.

> One of God's signs is that He created you from dust and—
> lo and behold!—you became human and scattered far
> and wide.
> Another of God's signs is that He created spouses from
> among yourselves for you to live with in tranquility: He
> ordained love and kindness between you.

There truly are signs in this for those who reflect.
Another of God's signs is that He created the heavens and
the earth, the diversity of your languages and colors.
There truly are signs in this for those who know.
Among His signs are your sleep, by night and by day, and
your seeking God's bounty. There truly are signs in this
for those who can hear.
Among His signs, too, are that God shows you the
lightning that terrifies and inspires hope; that God sends
water down from the sky to restore the earth to life after
death.
There truly are signs in this for those who use their reason.
Among God's signs, too, is the fact that the heavens and
the earth stand firm by His command.
In the end, you will all emerge when He calls you from the
earth.
Everyone in the heavens and earth belongs to Him, and all
are obedient to Him. He is the One who originates
creation and will do it again—this is even easier for
Him.
God is above all comparison in the heavens and the earth;
God is the Almighty, the all wise.   (Qur'an 30:20–27)[23]

The power and scope of the capacity for reflection is shown, above
all, in the story of Abraham, to which the Qur'an recurs sixty-nine
times, in twenty-five chapters; these constitute almost one-fourth of
the chapters of the Qur'an. In chapter 2, Abraham proves his faithfulness by obeying God's commandments (122–124). He and his
son, Ishmael, build the Ka'ba as a sanctuary dedicated to worship of
Allah (125–129). Such exemplary behavior lends itself to the rhetorical question of 130–132:

Who but a fool would forsake the religion of Abraham?
We have chosen him in this world and he will rank among
    the righteous in the Hereafter. His Lord said to him,
    "Devote yourself to me."
Abraham replied, "I devote myself to the Lord of the
    universe," and commanded his sons to do the same.

But what is the religion of Abraham, and how did he come to practice it? At 3:65–67, Jews and Christians listening to the Qur'an are challenged: "Why do you argue about Abraham when the Torah and the Gospels were not revealed until after his time? . . . Abraham was neither a Jew nor a Christian. He was upright, in a condition of submission [*hanifan musliman*]." That Abraham's submission is to God is indicated by what immediately follows: "and he was not with the idolaters." That the submission is not mediated by Jewish or Christian sources is important, as is the obvious fact that Abraham's religion is also not mediated by the Qur'an. All these texts come after Abraham's discovery of true faith, which provides the paradigmatic example of the religious potential of human reflection.

At 6:74–82 we read a brief account of what might be called Abraham's religious quest. The account begins at night, when Abraham sees a star and says, "This is my Lord." When the star sets, however, he is not satisfied with it as an object of devotion. The moon rises and soon replaces the star in Abraham's estimation: "This is my Lord." It also sets, of course, and is then replaced by the sun. Only now does the seeker exclaim: "My people, I disown all that you worship besides God. I have turned my face as a true believer towards Him who created the heavens and the earth." As the Qur'an has it, "In this way We showed Abraham a mighty dominion over the heavens and the earth, so that he might be a firm believer." God, in other words, is guiding the process. But Abraham's understanding comes through the exercise of his capacity to reflect. He does not hear a prophet; he does not read or recite a sacred text. His quest exemplifies the natural capacity of human beings to interpret the evidence of creation as requiring the acknowledgment of that One which is the true source of all. That One, *al-lah,* exercises dominion over the creation. Whereas the creation is contingent, that One is eternal. Whereas the creation is finite, that One is infinite.

The natural state of human beings, as of all creation, with respect to God is submission. But the Qur'an indicates that most humans do not realize this. While Abraham exemplifies the human potential, most do not reflect, and thus do not acknowledge the right of their Lord. As the Qur'an states at 30:30, although submission is the "natural disposition" of humankind, "most people do not realize it." More typically, the Qur'an indicates that human beings "do not reflect"; that is, they fail to exercise the capacity by which their religious potential becomes active. The reason for this failure? "Rivalry in worldly increase distracts you," says the Qur'an at 102:1. Human beings seek security. To that end, they strive for goods that enable them to negotiate the realities of the natural, and especially the social, world. Such striving yields some success. But "some success" is never "enough"; someone else always has more, and this state of affairs means that no one is ever really secure. And, in the end, the quest for security must be futile, because all human beings must die.

The quest for security inhibits reflection and, with it, the kind of awareness of God associated with submission. Given this circumstance, it seems that human beings are doomed. Created in order to serve God, placed in a world conceived as a theater for God's glory, the this-worldly existence of humanity is best construed as a test, at the end of which comes the Day of Judgment. The Qur'an holds that on that day each and all will stand before God, who will distribute rewards and punishments according to what each has done.

The crashing blow!
What is the crashing blow?
What will explain to you what the crashing blow is?
On a Day when people will be like scattered moths, and the
    mountains like tufts of wool,
The one whose good deeds are heavy on the scales
Will have a pleasant life.
But the one whose good deeds are light will have the
    bottomless pit for a home.
What will explain to you what that is?
Blazing fire.   (Qur'an 101:1–11)

Humankind, it seems, is in a troublesome situation. Created to serve God, and thus responsible for their deeds, they are nonetheless blinded by their striving for worldly security. For most, the kind of God-consciousness advocated by the Qur'an involves a radical departure from the activities they experience as normal. Most suffer from a "sickness of heart." Is there a cure?

To this question, the Qur'an poses an answer: God sends prophets as an act of divine mercy. God is not required to provide assistance with the human plight. Nevertheless, God does so, and this fact is one of the reasons for the persistent Qur'anic description of God as "the merciful, the compassionate." Prophets come in order to remind human beings of their situation. In accord with the emphasis on submission as the religious disposition natural to humanity, they do not reveal anything new. Rather, the point of prophecy is to state that which is obvious upon reflection. The uniqueness of prophets consists in the clarity and power by which they convey this truth.

Prophecy is thus a matter of restating that religion which is natural to humankind. And God, in his mercy, sends prophets to every nation. Each brings the message of submission to a particular people, proclaiming it in their language. Thus any list of prophets is theoretically quite extensive. The Qur'an is most interested, however, in recalling the names of those familiar to its audience: heroes from biblical tradition and others (such as Thamud) whose preaching formed part of Arab lore. The message of all prophets is the same: human beings come from God and will return to God. God is one, unique, not to be confused with any creature. Human beings are created to serve God and will be held accountable for what they have done. God, responsibility, and judgment—these constitute the three-fold theme of the natural religion. One might put it this way: the history of humanity is the history of God's attempts to remind human beings of their true nature, and to warn them of the consequences flowing from a lack of attention.

We can sharpen the Qur'anic notion of prophecy if we attend to its most characteristic formulations of the mission of Muhammad. He is the prophet who speaks Arabic; the Qur'an is an "Arabic scripture." Muhammad's vocation is to perform for his people the same task performed, for other communities, by Moses and Jesus. Moses brought the Torah to the people of Israel. Later, Jesus brought the *Injil,* or Gospel, to this same people; their rejection of his mission led to the division between the people of Israel and the people of the messiah. Even so, Muhammad brings the Qur'an to the Arabs.

We must go further, however. When Moses brought the Torah to the people of Israel, he did not found a religion called Judaism. Moses proclaimed *al-islam,* that submission which is the natural or appropriate condition of God's creatures. Judaism is an add-on, created by later generations who inherited the preaching of Moses, and then added to or took away from the Torah. Similarly, Jesus brought the Gospel to the people of the messiah, but he did not found Christianity. That term refers to the practice of followers of Jesus, some of whom were faithful, while others interpreted the Gospel in ways that mixed error with the truth that Jesus proclaimed—that is, the truth of submission. Thus, when Muhammad brings the Qur'an to the

Arabs, he also provides a fresh statement of the natural religion. Muhammad calls Jews and Christians, as well as Arab idolaters, to practice submission. The Qur'an presents itself as a "criterion" (25 and elsewhere) by which differences between previous religions may be adjudicated. And the followers of Muhammad have, as their mission, the continuing task of reminding Jews, Christians, and others of the truth of Islam. Faced with error, or more particularly with the kind of stubborn resistance to truth illustrated in the behavior of the Jews of Medina, the *umma* of Muhammad is called to command right and forbid wrong by appropriate means; as an old and prominent tradition has it, to correct error by the hand (signifying political and, if necessary, military action), the tongue (preaching and instruction), and the heart (disapproval).[24]

The Driving Force behind a World Civilization

Muhammad died in 632. Still flush with the surrender of Mecca, it seems the Muslim community was at first confused. Should the movement continue? If so, who would succeed the Prophet? And how should that person, or persons, direct the community?[25]

Traditions preserved by Muslims are fascinating in this regard, suggesting a considerable disagreement among those attached to Muhammad.[26] For our purposes, however, it is more important to describe the resolution than the range of disagreement. In brief, the answers were (1) yes, the movement should continue; (2) leadership, in the sense of *al-khilafat,* the succession or in some sense continuation of the Prophet's role, should fall to outstanding companions of Muhammad; and (3) the leadership, in the first instance assigned to Abu Bakr (d. 634) and 'Umar (d. 644), should direct the Muslim community in a sustained mission of commanding right and forbidding wrong, by the hand, tongue, and heart. As Abu Bakr puts it in a standard report: "O people, those who worshipped Muhammad [must know that] Muhammad is dead; those who worshipped God [must know that] God is alive [and] immortal." The statement continues, with Abu Bakr quoting Qur'an 3:144:

> Muhammad is only a messenger; and many a messenger
>   has gone before him.
> So if he dies or is killed, will you turn back on your heels?
> He who turns back on his heels will do no harm to God;
>   and God will reward the grateful.[27]

Practically speaking, this statement meant two things. First, Abu Bakr made sure that Muhammad's consolidation of Arab tribes held. In the most famous instance, the new leader ordered military action designed to compel the payment of taxes used to fund the Muslim mission.[28] When several of the tribes indicated they considered their duty to pay, and thus to provide material support for the Muslim mission, null and void, Abu Bakr declared that their agreement was not simply with the man Muhammad, but with God. In that sense, failure to pay constituted a special mix of religious and political wrongdoing, which was termed al-ridda. Usually translated as "apostasy," the term is in fact more suggestive of renegade behavior, by which one harms the ability of a community to fulfill legitimate goals, while at the same time violating a contract with God. Al-ridda, in other words, is neither a simple matter of treason nor a matter of changing one's mind about matters of religious belief. Abu Bakr's campaign constitutes an important precedent, pointing to a special relationship between religion and politics—in Arabic, between al-din (religion, law, custom, that to which one is obligated, and which connects one to others) and al-dunya (the affairs of this world, including economics, ordinary political activity, and the like).

Having secured the religious solidarity of Arabia, Abu Bakr and 'Umar turned to spreading Islam to the rest of the world. The speed and expanse of the Muslim "conquest" are well known. By the time of 'Umar's death, Muslim forces dominated Egypt, Syro-Palestine, and most of Iraq. Under two subsequent leaders, 'Uthman (d. 656) and 'Ali (d. 661), the remainder of Iraq and much of Iran came under the sway of Islam.[29] In later centuries, northern Africa, the Indian subcontinent, Anatolia (or Turkey), and portions of southern and central Europe came under Islamic control; at the outer edges, Muslim influence stretched into sub-Saharan Africa, throughout the realm of Mongols and Turks (including portions of China), to Indonesia and the Philippines.[30] Such geographic scope prohibits generalizations about the influence of Islam on religious and political behavior. Nevertheless, certain ways of speaking about the expansion of Islam became common. We may speak of these as precedents, in that subsequent generations of Muslims would recur to them as modeling important—because legitimate—values.

One of the standard reports concerning Muhammad's last days has the Prophet dictating letters to the rulers of the great empires of his day—the Byzantine Caesar, the Sassanid great king, the Abyssinian negus—and summoning them to *al-islam*. It will be best, he writes, if these rulers accept Islam, and they may do so by bearing witness that there is no god but God, with Muhammad as God's prophet. In this way, they may avoid strife and bring blessings to their people.

If the rulers in question will not accept Islam, they should at least enter into a tributary relationship with the community of Muhammad. In this way they will acknowledge the supremacy of Islam, and in some sense point their people toward Islam as the true religion. Failing this, however, these rulers should understand that Muhammad is the recipient of a divine mission, which he will carry out using all necessary and appropriate measures. That mission is to call people to *al-islam;* for this purpose, God gave the Prophet the Book (that is, the Qur'an) and a sword.[31]

We may set aside questions about the historical accuracy of this report, in the sense of questions like "Did Muhammad really write such letters?" For our purposes, the important datum is that this report provided a precedent for subsequent generations of Muslims. For the vast majority of Muslims, the expansion of Islam was an act of divine providence. It established governments that acknowledged Islam as the true and natural religion of humanity and replaced regimes that, by reason of their religious and moral errors, could be described as tyrannical. The expansion of Islamic government thereby increased the chances for groups of human beings to live together in (relative) peace and to attain a degree of justice. Such expansion also provided an opening by which people liberated from tyranny might hear the message of Islam and accept it, should they wish to do so. Alternatively, the recipients of liberation might continue in their inherited religion, provided they accepted the protection of Islamic government and observed certain proprieties. In all, the way in which Muslims spoke about the territorial expansion of Islam suggests an intention one might describe as "beneficent paternalism." This perspective casts the expansion as a matter of "opening" territory to Islam, rather than of "conquest." Similarly, the Muslims did not consider that they were bringing something foreign or strange to other lands. Islam is natural to humankind. It is not a thing that one human being gives to another, but is the gift of God, to be acknowledged as such. Bringing human beings into a right relationship with their Creator is the purpose of God; it is the reason why God sends prophets. In this sense, then, Muslims came to speak of the early expansion as *al-jihad,* an aspect of the struggle "to make God's cause succeed" (Qur'an 8:39).

Islamic expansion thus involved a systematic program of regime change, in which *jihad* became the symbol for Muslim effort. Notions of honorable combat developed in connection with this, as did notions of martyrdom and sacrifice for the cause of God.

We shall return to these notions. More significant at this point is that the story Muslims tell about their community suggests that the Islamic notion of "regime change" involved replacing tyrannical governments with something better, that is, with Islamic government, or rule by *al-shari'a*. Usually translated as "Islamic law," *al-shari'a* is more appropriately rendered as "the path" or "the way." The term suggests that there is a right way to live, and that is the way associated with Islam, the natural religion. As we are using it here, *al-shari'a* indicates an Islamic version of the "rule of law," that is, of the notion that there is a standard by which rulers and ruled alike must be judged. Through centuries of Islamic expansion and dominance, rulers and ruled appealed to this notion as a way to debate questions of legitimacy. What are the obligations of a legitimate ruler? That person should possess many attributes—a good character, physical health and strength, a sound mind, proper ancestry.[32] Above all, however, a ruler is obligated to govern by the Shari'a. In essence, this is what is meant by speaking of government as *al-khilafat,* and the ruler as *al-khalifa.* Both terms imply succession. The system of government "succeeds" or "follows in the path of" the Prophet, as does the ruler or, in some cases, the ruling class or governing elite.

Rule by the Shari'a also speaks to the obligations of citizens in an Islamic state: they should pay taxes, participate in the *jihad* in an appropriate manner, honor the ruler in all legitimate claims. This constellation of duties gave rise to a large and continuing debate over the legitimacy of rebellion. Should citizens in an Islamic state depose a ruler who strays from the divine path? At the very least, it is clear that the duty of citizens to obey or honor the claims of the leader is limited to policies that are legitimate, that is, associated with the Shari'a.[33]

The phrase "obligations of citizens" applies, in the first place, to Muslims living under an Islamic government. Under the new regime of Islam, non-Muslims had obligations, too. The phrase "people of the Book," which applied primarily to Jews and Christians, but was eventually enlarged to include Hindus and others living in the territories that came under the sway of Islam, correlated with a standing signified by the term *ahl al-dhimma*, "protected people." Such people lived as recognized minority communities, with their own structures of authority, religious observances, and laws. Yet their status was set by, and Muslims recognized it in terms of, the overarching rule of Shari'a. According to this norm, the non-Muslim communities paid special taxes, were required to observe restrictions on public demonstrations of worship, experienced limits on their ability to build churches and synagogues, and in general were required to behave in ways deemed respectful of the priority of Islam. Thus, in one sense, the Shari'a did not apply to them—for example, in terms of laws of marriage and divorce. In another sense, it certainly did, for the terms of their protection were set according to the Shari'a standard.

Thus, if we were to highlight one feature of Islamic civilization as central, we could make a strong case for the notion of "governance by the Shari'a." But what was the Shari'a? And how is it ascertained?

That is the subject of the next chapter. Before turning to those questions, let us return briefly to the quotations at the beginning of this chapter. Who is right? Does Islam "mean peace"? Or is it a "very evil and very wicked religion"? Is it the religion of "Jihad in the way of Allah so that Allah's Word and religion reign supreme"?

If we attend to the story of the Prophet Muhammad, to claims about Islam as the natural religion of humanity, and to the development of Islamic civilization as built on the notion of deposing tyrants in the name of a kind of rule of law, then we must in some sense grant the first and last characterizations. Islam promises peace to those who follow the natural religion of humanity. It commands its followers to strive for peace. It does not, of course, understand peace as a simple matter of the absence of conflict. Rather, Islam is associated with the idea that peace requires justice, and that these terms signify a condition best served when human societies are ordered in ways that may be described as legitimate.

Similarly, Islam is the religion of *jihad*, in the sense of struggle. That is the premise of Islamic mission. Through the ministry of Muhammad and the proclamation of the Qur'an, God created a community dedicated to commanding right and forbidding wrong. The community fulfills this duty by spreading the blessings of legitimate government, and by calling humanity to return to the natural religion.

The claim that Islam is a "very evil and very wicked" religion emanates from a different kind of discussion, one that is not well adjudicated by historical or sociological description. Perhaps, though, we might change the question slightly, and instead ask whether Islam presents anything very different from other religions of the world. The evidence suggests that the answer is no, whether one is thinking about notions of deity or revelation or political order. Christians and Jews, at least, will find strongly familiar elements in the story of Muhammad, the claims of Islamic theology, and the motifs of Islamic civilization outlined here. The familiarity stems from the fact that Islam is built upon a set of ideas common throughout the ancient Near East. These traditions all taught, and still teach, that there is one God, Creator and Lord of the universe; that human beings are accountable to this God, who fills the earth with signs of his power and beneficence; that this accountability is to be measured by a divine standard, an "instruction" or "law." They teach that human beings should order their common life by that standard, and that they will be judged by its terms. To speak of such commonalities is not to deny important differences between faiths. For those who are Christians, for example, the identification of intimacy between God and Jesus the Christ suggested by the designation "son of God" is critical to understanding the relationship that obtains between God and humanity. Islam denies this identification, and indeed sees it as an error. For those who are Jews, participation in the continuing life of a particular people, with its special history of God's providence and election, is not to be denied. But Islam does deny this, at least in the sense of criticizing Judaism as fostering a kind of ethnic consciousness that runs contrary to the universality of God's judgment and mercy. Judaism, Christianity, and Islam are not the same religion. They are, however, close relations. To speak of Islam, in particular, as "very evil and very wicked" is to separate it from its obvious moorings in the history of the ancient Near East, and to deny facts that are obvious to any objective reader of the Qur'an or of the story of Muhammad. In assessing the value of Islam, we do well to defer judgment until we know more about the ways Muslims, as people involved in an attempt to ascertain and submit to God's will, have conducted themselves over time. Judaism, Christianity, and Islam all claim a special revelation that serves to orient the lives of believers. In this, they claim a kind of suprahuman status for certain notions about the world and about human responsibility. In working out the meaning of these notions, however, these three faiths are very much an affair of human beings, involved in an attempt to negotiate existence in diverse historical and political contexts.

CHAPTER TWO

SHARI'A REASONING

Historically, Muslims have dealt with questions about right and wrong in a variety of ways. Early on, Islamic civilization produced a number of exceptional philosophers. The great al-Farabi (d. 945) modeled his work *The Virtuous City* on Plato's dialogue *Laws*. Ibn Sina (d. 1045) wrote on medicine and politics. Ibn Rushd (d. 1145) composed a number of important and innovative commentaries on the works of Aristotle.[1]

Even more substantial is the literature Muslims call *adab*, letters, the reflections of cultivated and learned people on the manners and morals appropriate to particular issues and types of work. Thus, al-Jahiz (d. 839) compiled a formidable collection of tales about miserly behavior, the moral import of which was to demonstrate the problems stemming from a lack of generosity. Others wrote works reflecting on the professional ethics appropriate to the practice of medicine. Still others composed "mirrors for princes," reflecting on the problems of statecraft.[2]

Alongside these modes of reflection is another that stands out partly because of its endurance and partly because of its contemporary significance. This is the way of thinking I call Shari'a reasoning.

Al-shari'a is usually translated as Islamic "law."[3] But it is more than that. Literally, *al-shari'a* means "the path." In a more extended sense, it refers to the path that "leads to refreshment." With the advent of Islam, this extended sense lent itself to the notion of a path leading to "success," a way to paradise, a way associated with happiness in this world and the next. *Al-shari'a* is thus a metaphorical representation of a mode of behavior that leads to salvation. As the Qur'an has it, those who walk the "straight path" *(sirat al-mustaqim)* are "successful" with respect to the judgment of God (1:6–7).

More prosaically, *al-shari'a* stands for the notion that there is a right way to live. The good life is not a matter of behaving in whatever ways human beings may dream up. It is a matter of "walking" in the way approved by God; or, reflecting the notion of Islam as the natural religion, the good life involves behavior that is consistent with the status of human beings as creatures. As Muslim theologians had it, it is possible to imagine God creating other worlds, in which creatures unlike human beings might be judged according to a different standard.[4] Once God created the world in which we live, however, he did so in a way that distinguished right from wrong, good from evil. Further, God set these distinctions in the context of a world that ultimately moves toward judgment. On the great and singular day which the Qur'an speaks of in terms such as *al-akhira* (the hereafter) or *yawm al-din* (the Day of Judgment or of Justice), human beings will see clearly the rewards or punishments they have acquired by acting in certain ways.

Given such notions, it is hardly strange to find Muslims inquiring about right and wrong very early on. The Qur'an summoned its hearers to right behavior and exhorted believers to refer questions to God and God's Prophet. Indeed, the Qur'an indicates that submission is measured in terms of obedience to these two sources, which Muslim tradition came to associate with the Qur'an and with the *sunna*, or example of Muhammad, particularly as related in *ahadith*, or reports, of the Prophet's words and deeds, as witnessed by his companions.

From very early on, then, Muslim inquiry regarding right and wrong was associated with the interpretation of texts. Not surprisingly, a class of specialists emerged, trained in the reading and interpretation of the Qur'an and *ahadith*. The *'ulama*, or learned ones, became an important resource for a community devoted to inquiry regarding the Shari'a, particularly in contexts where literacy levels were low, and where the available means of book production made texts rare and expensive. More recently, however, groups of "lay" Muslims have asserted their right and duty to read and interpret, sometimes in conversation with the *'ulama*, and sometimes in opposition to them. As such groups have it, comprehension of the Shari'a is the duty of all Muslims, who must read and interpret the sacred texts to the best of their ability. As we move through the twentieth and into the twenty-first century, the participation of such groups must be viewed as one of the most important developments in the story of Shari'a reasoning.

Early Developments

When 'Umar, second leader after the Prophet, died in 644, the first wave of Muslim expansion was drawing to a close. According to standard tradition, 'Uthman, as third leader, inherited 'Umar's system of administering the newly established Muslim regimes. In this system, a centrally located group of officials, buttressed by a military presence, governed a prescribed territory. Income from taxes levied on land held by (pre-Islamic) residents of each territory provided both funding for local administration and revenues to the leader in Medina. The latter used these funds to support further expansion, in line with the mission of Islam.

In each territory, the establishment of a new administration bore witness to the hegemony of Islam; the priority of Islamic values provided legitimacy for political authority. Territorial governors, along with the fighters supporting them, conducted prayers after the pattern established in the Arabian Peninsula. Along with the prayers came religious instruction. In this connection, the foremost activity, requiring the specialized knowledge of teachers, was recitation of the Qur'an. Although it is difficult to evaluate the traditional report that credits 'Uthman with standardizing the written text of the Qur'an, it makes sense that systematization of the scriptural text would coincide with the expansion of Islam. When pre-Islamic residents of the territories converted to Islam—and certainly some did—the specialists trained in reciting the Qur'an acquired additional authority and importance.[5]

Given the report of 'Uthman's role in establishing the Qur'anic text, it is ironic that opposition to his rule developed around the charge that he failed to govern by the Book of God. In 656 a group of fighters dissatisfied with the administration of affairs in Egypt came to Medina, seeking 'Uthman's intervention. Seemingly satisfied with his response, the group began the return journey. Along the way, it seems they began to doubt the leader's intention to carry through as promised. Some returned to Medina and assassinated 'Uthman.[6]

By prior agreement, leadership passed to 'Ali ibn Abi Talib, the cousin of Muhammad and one of the earliest converts to the prophetic mission. 'Ali sought reconciliation with those responsible for 'Uthman's death. In doing so he offended the members of 'Uthman's family, in particular the territorial governor of Syria. Mu'awiya, arguing that 'Ali's failure to punish the rebels constituted a failure of

justice, brought his army to challenge the leader. As the opposing forces approached each other, ready for battle, Mu'awiya's men
placed copies of the Qur'an on their lance points and advanced,
chanting "Let the Qur'an decide!" 'Ali accepted the challenge,
thereby sending the dispute to arbitration. Conducted by those who
knew the Qur'an best, the judgment nevertheless failed to provide a
clear resolution. Even more, the process of arbitration led to further
divisions among the Muslims, so that a certain number seceded
from the ranks of 'Ali's supporters, declaring themselves bound only
by God and God's Book. These Kharijites (al-khawarij, those who
exited) constituted a kind of pious opposition. In the ensuing strife,
they declared themselves opposed to both sides. In the end, however,
their activities did more harm to 'Ali than to Mu'awiya. One of their
number assassinated the fourth leader in 661.

Thus began a period of great disorder, which in Islamic tradition
received the name "first fitna"—what one might call a civil war—as
various groups competed for power. Of these, Mu'awiya's was the
strongest, not least because the territory of Syria provided economic
resources superior to those elsewhere. When the Syrian forces, by
now commanded by Mu'awiya's son Yazid, destroyed the army of
'Ali's son Husayn at Karbala (in southern Iraq) in 680, the great conflict was, for all practical purposes, resolved. Rebel forces in Iraq and
in the holy cities of Arabia continued to mount an intermittent resistance, and in 692 'Abd al-Malik even attacked the Ka'ba to put
down a rebellion. Nevertheless, for the next sixty years (that is, until
the 740s) the political and military epicenter of Islam would be Damascus.

Polemics between the two most important divisions within Islam
take the events of this first fitna as a point of departure. The Shi'a, or
partisans of 'Ali, claim that the victory of Mu'awiya and his descendants constituted a rejection of right leadership, and thus a departure from the Prophet's (and God's) design for the Muslim commu-

nity. Sunni Muslims, or, as the traditional description has it, "the people of the prophetic example and the consensus (of the Muslims)" *(ahl al-sunna wa' l-jama'a),* also perceive these early struggles as critical, though typically they assign blame to all involved. Both labels, Sunni and Shi'i, cover a multitude of subgroupings, and their use with respect to Muslims in this very early period is not entirely appropriate. But the labels would emerge strongly as the different perspectives of these divisions became relevant to the development of Shari'a reasoning.

More interesting is the clear priority of the Qur'an in arguments about right and wrong, even in this very early period. The slogan "Let the Qur'an decide!" indicates that most Muslims recognized the relevance of the revealed text in ascertaining guidance. Similarly, the role of the mediators in the dispute provides a glimpse of the importance of a class of specialists whose role was to preserve and recite the Qur'anic text.

The importance of this class increased with the consolidation of power by Mu'awiya's descendants in Damascus. Sometimes known as the Marwanids, and more typically as the Umayyads, these constituted the first imperial rulers in Islam. As their critics put it, with the Umayyads, leadership changed from *al-khilafat,* or governance by one fit to be called the successor to Muhammad, to *al-mulk,* the kingship, meaning a system in which leadership is passed from father to son, without concern about qualities of character.

The Umayyads, of course, preferred to cast their regime as *al-khilafat,* and presented themselves as God's appointed rulers. In court poetry from the time, we read propaganda consistent with this claim:

> The earth is God's.
> He has entrusted it to his *khalifa.*
> The one who is head in it will not be overcome.[7]

Again,

> God has garlanded you [Umayyad rulers] with the *khilafa*
>   and guidance;
> For what God decrees, there is no change.[8]

Indeed, Umayyad rule is crucial to the maintenance of true religion:

> We [God] have found the sons of Marwan [Umayyads]
>   pillars of our religion,
> As the earth has mountains for its pillars.[9]

And again,

> Were it not for the caliph and the Qur'an he recites,
> The people had no judgments established for them and no
>   communal worship.[10]

Of course, recitation of the Qur'an was not confined to the caliph. The class of specialists responsible for it was to some extent sponsored by Umayyad rulers, as is suggested in this poetry. Nevertheless, some reciters apparently maintained an independent center of power.

One of the first of these independent scholars was al-Hasan al-Basri (d. 728). As the name indicates, al-Hasan's location was Basra, in the south of Iraq, the geographic center of resistance to the Umayyads. Al-Hasan's fame seems to exceed our actual information about him. Subsequent generations have claimed him as the inspiration for Sufism, that peculiar form of popular Islam that gained a massive following in later centuries. At the same time, various Sunni and Shi'i groups claim al-Hasan as one of the early advocates of their favorite doctrines.[11] His exploits are legendary, and sayings attributed to him often cryptic.

What does seem clear is that al-Hasan functioned as a critic of some Umayyad claims, and that he did so in a way that advanced the notion that learning itself constitutes a kind of authority. When asked about Umayyad claims to divine legitimacy, al-Hasan supposedly said: "There is no obedience owed to a creature in respect of a sin against the Creator," thus pointing to a limit on Umayyad (or other human) authority. That this claim follows from the Qur'anic text seems obvious; after all, there is no god but God.[12]

As noted, al-Hasan claimed authority on the basis of 'ilm, or knowledge, and specifically of knowledge of Islamic texts. By the 730s the phenomenon of authority based on learning was widespread, with particular centers in Damascus (or, more generally, Syria), Iraq, and the holy cities of Mecca and Medina.

We know only a little about the activities of scholars in Damascus. Local traditions focus on a figure called al-Awza'i, who is cited as the founder of a distinctive approach to Shari'a reasoning. No works of al-Awza'i are available to us, though some of his opinions are quoted by other scholars. We can surmise that there was a sustained conversation between Muslims and Christians (and perhaps Jews) in the region, not least because works by John of Damascus (d. 750), a prominent Christian theologian, are posed in terms of dialogues between scholars of these traditions concerning issues related to the attributes of God.[13] These dialogues (and, one assumes, the attendant discussions) would become important in the development of Shari'a reasoning somewhat later, in the ninth century.

The most notable learned figure in Mecca and Medina at this time was Malik ibn Anas (d. 795). Here again, information is not extensive. If we take Malik's great work, al-Muwatta (The Well-Trodden), as representative, it seems clear that some Muslim scholars were developing a way of thinking in which verses from the Qur'an were connected with, and thus interpreted through, reports of the practice of Muhammad, his companions, and the continuing tradition of practice of the Muslims in Mecca and Medina.[14]

By contrast with Damascus and with the holy cities, we have a great deal of information regarding Iraq. If we take al-Hasan al-Basri less as an individual, and more as a "type," representative of the behavior of a group of learned people in the first half of the eighth century, we begin to see the lines of a religious critique of Umayyad rule. Indeed, much of what we have from later generations of Muslims suggests that scholars located in Iraq in the 720s and 730s spent a great deal of time and energy discussing the grounds of such criticism and, beyond this, the proper mode of resistance to what they deemed illegitimate rule. One must use such reports with caution, of course, as later generations often read back into the eighth century something of their own concerns—such as the tendency of various groups to claim al-Hasan al-Basri as the source of their own movements. There is no reason to doubt, however, that numbers of religious specialists in Iraq constituted an intellectual wing of a growing "pious opposition" to Umayyad rule. Our information about these is connected to the success of the Abbasid revolt, which by the late 740s or early 750s attained a level of success sufficient for historians to speak of a relocation of power in the Islamic empire from Damascus to Baghdad, and from the Umayyad to the Abbasid clan.

Formative Developments

By the time the Abbasid clan established its *khilafat,* there was a growing class of religious specialists in Iraq, claiming the authority to distinguish right from wrong on the basis of religious knowledge. All of these connected authority with the text of the Qur'an, and the Abbasids took note of this fact. They promoted their cause by promising to establish "government by the Book of God." Having acknowledged the priority of the Qur'an, however, those claiming authority by reason of knowledge differed considerably in approach. Some, who came to be associated with the kind of the dialectical theology Muslims called *al-kalam,* literally "speech," but in this context "theological disputation," held that the import of the Qur'an was best extracted through a process of rigorous, systematic argument. The most influential of these, in the early years of Abbasid rule, came to be known as Mu'tazilites, separatists. Mu'tazilites focused on clarifying the system of doctrine outlined in the Qur'an. Their interpretations are not themselves an example of Shari'a reasoning, though they had clear political import and, through the ministrations of the Abbasid caliphs, would come to play a critical role in the development of the practice.

For late eighth-century examples of Shari'a reasoning, we must turn to a different circle of Iraqi scholars, of whom the most famous were Abu Hanifa (d. 767), Abu Yusuf (d. 798), and al-Shaybani (d. 804). Muslim sources assign credit to the first of these as the founder of the circle, which eventually came to bear his name. Abu Yusuf and al-Shaybani were the two greatest students of Abu Hanifa, and their works bear witness to the approach taken in his "school." Two such works are particularly important. Abu Yusuf's *Kitab al-kharaj* deals with the administration of territories in which an Islamic regime comes to power. It thus reflects a continuing discussion regarding governance of conquered or liberated areas.[15]

Al-Shaybani's *Kitab al-Siyar*, by contrast, deals with "movements" or "relations" between territories. Al-Shaybani was thus interested in international relations. Indeed, the modern historian of international relations Majid Khadduri once spoke of this early Iraqi scholar as the Hugo Grotius of Islam, implying that al-Shaybani stands to the development of an Islamic "public international law" as does Grotius to the development of the Western version of such norms.[16] Whether or not Khadduri's comparison is apt, it is true that al-Shaybani's work reflects judgments or opinions on a number of important political and military topics: the declaration and conduct of war, the status of treaties between rulers, grants of safe passage for persons traveling from one territory to another for purposes of diplomacy, trade, and the like are all at issue, as are matters of policy within Islamic territory—for example, the status of rebels, the collection of taxes, and the obligations of Jews, Christians, and other "protected" communities.[17]

In the works of Abu Yusuf and al-Shaybani, we see the emergence of a specific class of religious specialists, and also of a particular style of reasoning about matters of right and wrong. Al-Shaybani's work is especially instructive. The book is constructed in terms of a series of judgments, or more properly "opinions" (al-fatawa), issued by Abu Hanifa, Abu Yusuf, or al-Shaybani. At one point, for example, the text indicates a question directed to al-Shaybani: "Would a sudden attack at night be objectionable to you?," that is, as a tactic in war. The reply, "No harm in it," is to be taken as al-Shaybani's response, reflecting the consensus of the school on this point.[18]

We get a better sense of how these scholars worked by attending to a story related by Muslim historians. Here, Harun al-Rashid, the Abbasid ruler in Baghdad from 786 to 809, famous to all readers of the Thousand and One Nights, calls on several scholars to render an opinion on a vexing question. Faced with unrest in Iran, Harun sought peace by offering clemency and protection to a rebel leader. Having accepted Harun's offer, the leader returned to his province, where he promptly reorganized his forces and resumed his troublesome activities. Does this subsequent behavior render Harun's promise of clemency and protection moot?

The question is not to be taken lightly. Technically, Harun provided the rebel leader with al-aman, a trust or pledge of safe passage. On pragmatic grounds, it is not good policy for rulers to violate their word; further, the granting of such a pledge establishes a religious obligation. As the story proceeds, we find Abu Yusuf and al-Shaybani arguing that, having given the pledge, the Abbasid ruler is obligated to treat the rebel leader in a distinct fashion. He may entreat the leader to cease his troublesome activities, of course. And if rebel troops violate certain standards of conduct, the Abbasid fighters may act as a police force quelling a public disturbance. But Harun ought not to authorize his troops to capture the leader directly, nor, if the leader is captured in the course of a police action, is Harun permitted to authorize the summary execution of the man in question.

Abu Yusuf and al-Shaybani do not stand alone in this instance. Other scholars provide Harun with a different opinion. In this case, the argument is that the grant of *al-aman* presumed the rebel leader would behave in a certain way; since he did not, the trust is null and void. Harun is justified in authorizing his troops to capture the leader, and further in ordering his execution.

In this particular instance, the Abbasid ruler chose the second opinion. Nevertheless, both Abu Yusuf and al-Shaybani subsequently served in an official capacity, and Muslim historians remember their names—not the names of those scholars whose advice pleased Harun al-Rashid.[19]

The primary work of scholars like Abu Yusuf and al-Shaybani, of course, was teaching. The Hanafi school developed as men like these trained others. As we read their texts, we see them citing the Qur'an and reports of the practice of Muhammad and his companions. We also see them issuing opinions that do not directly invoke these sources, but rather appear to involve a claim that learned men, devoted to a life of study, can render trustworthy opinions on matters of right and wrong. Their authority thus rests on the notion that devotion to learning creates a disposition for justice, or a leaning toward virtue. Here, it is interesting that the Hanafi school spoke of *al-ra'y* (opinion) and of *al-istihsan* (good opinion) as legitimate grounds of judgment. The combination of learning and piety makes for wise people—not perfect or infallible, of course, but nevertheless "sound"—and for wise judgment.

We know more about the Hanafi school than about others, for the obvious reason that scholars like Abu Yusuf and al-Shaybani had dealings with the Abbasid court. The existence of the schools associated with al-Awza'i and Malik ibn Anas, as well as the existence of disagreement among scholars (as, for example, in the story about Harun and the rebel leader), suggested to some that the Hanafi approach, however exemplary, did not command universal assent. It is not strange, then, that we find scholars arguing for a synthesis that would take the best of the various schools and place Islamic practical reason—that is, Shari'a reasoning—on a firmer, more systematic theoretical ground. Of these, the most outstanding was and remains the great al-Shafi'i (d. 820). His works, in particular *al-Risala* (The Treatise), on the sources by which one comprehends the guidance of God, set forth proposals that transformed the practice of Shari'a reasoning.[20]

Standard histories of Islamic jurisprudence credit al-Shafi'i with establishing a full-blown theory of Islamic law. That claim is not quite accurate.[21] Al-Shafi'i's real contribution lies in his insistence that all local or regional traditions, as well as all scholarly opinions, must be judged with respect to two sources: the Qur'an, and the *sunna,* or exemplary practice of the Prophet. With respect to developments described thus far, this meant, for example, that the traditions associated with al-Awza'i, Malik, and Abu Hanifa and his students could not stand on their own. Even Malik's *Muwatta,* with its claim to represent a continuous tradition of practice going back to the earliest Muslims, must be subjected to review. One can be certain of God's guidance only by referring to a sound or well-documented report of the Prophet's words and/or deeds.

The import of this point becomes clear if we attend to the fullness of al-Shafi'i's argument. He begins with praise of and petition to God:

> Praise be to God who created the heavens and the earth, and made the darkness and the light . . . Praise be to God to whom gratitude for one of his favors cannot be paid save

through another favor from him, which necessitates that the giver of thanks for his past favors repay it by a new favor, which in turn makes obligatory upon him gratitude for it . . . I ask him for his guidance: the guidance whereby no one who takes refuge in it will ever be led astray.[22]

Al-Shafi'i's petition for guidance sets the tone for his argument, which is that God provided for this human need by sending the Prophet Muhammad with a "book sublime." With respect to this Book, God "made clear to [human beings] what He permitted . . . and what He prohibited, as He knows best what pertains to their felicity in this world and in the hereafter."[23] Al-Shafi'i stresses that the guidance offered in the Qur'an is comprehensive and sure: "No misfortune will ever descend upon any of the followers of God's religion for which there is no guidance in the Book of God to indicate the right way."[24]

According to al-Shafi'i, the general mode by which God provides guidance may be described as *al-bayan,* a declaration. There are, however, several categories of declaration, and some of these suggest the necessity of other sources accompanying or alongside the Qur'an. Thus, one may speak of declarations "explicit" in the Qur'an, as in commands that believers pray. One may also speak of declarations tied to specific Qur'anic texts, but for which the Prophet's words specify the proper form of obedience. An example is that prayer should be performed five times a day, and at specific times. Then, too, there are declarations from the Prophet, establishing duties even where there exists no specific Qur'anic text. Finally, there are declarations apprehended by human beings through the use of their capacity for reason, for example in locating the precise direction of prayer.[25]

This discussion of the various types of declaration by which God provides guidance serves to establish that the quest for the Shari'a, or path, involves reference to a set of sources, which must be con-

strued in relation to one another. Theoretically, the entire world constitutes a "sign," a source by which human beings may ascertain
God's guidance. More concretely those in search of guidance refer to
texts—to the Qur'an, which as God's speech constitutes a source
"about which there can be no doubt" (2:1); to reliable reports concerning the exemplary practice of the Prophet; and to "reasoning" in
the sense of interpreting and applying the signs provided by God in
the interests of obedience.

In each and all of these sources, God's declarations are clear. That
does not mean, however, that ascertaining them is simple. To begin,
al-Shafi'i says, the Qur'an and reports of the Prophet's practice are
in Arabic. This is not a language everyone knows; and those who do
know it are not equal in their comprehension of its rules. For some
(in effect, many) purposes, reading and interpreting these texts requires expertise, and there is thus an important role for experts—
that is, the "learned"—in ascertaining the guidance of God. Al-
Shafi'i reinforces this point with reference to a series of distinctions
designed to facilitate interpretation of revealed texts. Some have
"general" applicability, as in "God is the creator of everything, and
He is a guardian of everything" (Qur'an 39:63). Some have "particular" reference; that is, the declarations are directed toward particular
people or contexts, as in "The people have gathered against you, so
be afraid of them" (Qur'an 3:167). Of course, in some cases declarations with particular references may take on or contain a general
point.[26]

In some cases, the meaning is clarified with reference to the *sunna,*
or exemplary practice, of Muhammad. At this point, al-Shafi'i's unique contribution becomes clear. As he has it, the Qur'an contains
God's declaration that obedience to God requires obedience to the
Prophet. For

> God has placed His Apostle [in relation to] His religion, His
> commands, and His Book, in the position made clear by

Him as a distinguishing standard of His religion by impos-
ing the duty of obedience to him [the Prophet] as well as
prohibiting disobedience to him.[27]

For this reason, one who wishes to identify with Islam must pronounce the *shahada* (confession of faith), indicating faith in God
and in Muhammad as the messenger of God.

As al-Shafi'i has it, the authority of the Prophet is such that reports of his words and deeds confirm and explain the guidance contained in the Qur'an. They also extend it, in the sense that a sound
report of the Muhammad's words or deeds may itself establish a
duty in cases in which there is no Qur'anic text. We have, as it
were, two sets of texts with which Shari'a reasoning must work: the
Qur'an, as the Book of God; and *ahadith,* reports of the *sunna,* or
practice, of the Prophet. The latter may interpret the former but will
never contradict it; the former establishes the importance of the latter. To show this, al-Shafi'i embarks on a long discussion of "the ab-
rogating and the abrogated," by which we come to understand that
interpretation of the divine declarations sometimes involves understanding that a text revealed at one time may be abrogated or rendered null and void by a text revealed at a later point. For al-Shafi'i,
verses of the Qur'an may be abrogated only by other verses of the
Qur'an; while one report of the Prophet's practice may abrogate another report, it can never be the case that any report of the words
and deeds of Muhammad abrogates any verse of the Qur'an.[28] Of
course, such stress on *ahadith* makes it crucial that one have a way of
distinguishing "sound" reports—those in which one may have confidence that its text stems from the Prophet himself—from those
which are "weak," and thus not suitable for use in making judgments. And if some sound reports abrogate others, one must have a
way of relating specific sayings or deeds of the Prophet to particular
times in his career. Al-Shafi'i's treatise relates some of the basic rules

of what one might call "*hadith* criticism," particularly with respect to the problems of judging the "chain" *(al-isnad)* by which reports are transmitted. During the next century several other scholars would devote their skills to this issue, with the result that six major collections of *ahadith* came to be identified as useful in the context of Shariʿa reasoning.[29]

If all this sounds very complex, that is because it is so! Al-Shafiʿi's text promises that God provides guidance. The comprehension of guidance involves struggle, however, and in that struggle, not everyone is equal. In particular, those who understand the language and rules of interpretation pertaining to the signs provided by God serve as guardians of right and wrong, in the sense of rendering opinions on the duties incumbent on human beings.

The learned are not infallible, of course. Indeed, the system outlined by al-Shafiʿi is made to order for disagreement. After all, the meaning of God's declarations is not obvious. This much al-Shafiʿi has said, and he reinforces it again and again. As the argument continues, we learn of the variety of ways by which scholars attempt to extract guidance from the Qurʾan and from the practice of the Prophet. Some, by which al-Shafiʿi means the scholars of the Iraqi school, rest their opinions on *raʿy* or *istihsan*. Others trumpet the validity of other modes of reasoning. All are engaged in *ijtihad,* meaning that they exert "effort" in the attempt to ascertain the path of God. But the best form of such effort, says al-Shafiʿi, is one that stays as close as possible to God's declarations. This is called *al-qiyas,* a kind of reasoning by analogy, in which the texts of the Qurʾan and the *sunna* are treated as precedents from which one may draw wisdom. In this connection, the objective of interpretation is to establish a fit between precedent and current circumstance, by way of identifying a principle or ground that unites them. As an example, consider al-Shafiʿi's discussion of the duties pertaining to parents and children:

The Book of God and the sunna of the Prophet indicate that it is the duty of the father to see to it that his children are suckled and that they are supported as long as they are young. Since the child is an issue of the father, the father is under an obligation to provide for the child's support while the child is unable to do that for himself. So I hold by analogical deduction [that] when the father becomes incapable of providing for himself by his earnings, or from what he owns, then it is an obligation on his children to support him by paying for his expenses and clothing. Since the child is from the father, the child should not cause the father from whom he comes to lose anything, just as the child should not lose anything belonging to his children, because the child is from the father. So the forefathers, even if they are distant, and the children, even if they are remote descendants, fall into this category. Thus I hold that by analogy he who is retired and in need should be supported by him who is rich and still active.[30]

The duties of children to support their elderly parents, and even a more extended duty of those who are active to support those who are retired, are drawn by way of analogy from textual precedents requiring parents to care for children.

As al-Shafi'i's text shows, such judgments are not self-evident. Throughout, he engages the views of others from the learned class. In the end, effort is what is required; in effect, God requires a conscientious attempt at the comprehension of guidance. How does one distinguish one opinion from another? According to al-Shafi'i, one should look for consensus, a convergence of views. The more extensive the consensus, the more likely that a particular opinion is in fact correct. Even here, however, disagreement is possible, unless one finds an opinion on which the entire Muslim community agrees. In that case, the opinion must be correct, for the Prophet said: "My community will never agree on an error." Such agreement must have been a rare thing, however; al-Shafi'i provides no examples.[31]

The Classical Theory

Al-Shafi'i did not develop his system in a vacuum. That much is already clear, by way of the relation of his argument to the regional "schools" in which religious specialists developed their distinctive approaches to the problem of guidance. But we must fill out the picture with a brief account of the religious policies of the Abbasid caliphs.

The Abbasids came to power in the 740s. In doing so, they rode the wave of religious criticism of the Umayyads. Promising government by the Book of God, the new rulers appealed to many in the developing class of the learned, and through them to popular religious sentiment. In so doing, the Abbasids obtained a measure of legitimacy. They also pointed to a problematic that would persist throughout the centuries of their dominance.

The problem was as follows: a slogan like "Government by the Book of God" is appealing, in part, because it is simple. Followers of Iraqi scholars like Abu Hanifa understood it, as did everyone else in the 740s. Once in power, however, the Abbasids found such general appeals of limited use. What mattered, with respect to actual governance, was the ability of a ruler to command the loyalty of particular groups, each of which varied in important details. One might, of course, decide to rule by using a large measure of coercion. The Umayyads had shown that such a strategy could work, at least for a time. And, from another point of view, the true problems of governance in the far-flung realm now controlled by Muslims had to do with economic integration and reform, especially as these matters affected the competing interests of merchants and the landed class.

Abbasid rulers clearly spent a great deal of time on such matters, and they showed themselves willing to use coercive measures.

As Max Weber put it in his studies of political economy, however, rulers seek legitimacy, at least in part to avoid the costs of coercive governance. The goal is to rule with authority, meaning that the subjects of rule believe there are reasons to follow the ruler's directives other than those associated with fear.[32] The Abbasids understood this psychology, and they sought to ally themselves with various religious parties, searching for a message of broad appeal. Indeed, in some cases the search seems to have been not only a matter of political expediency. The caliph al-Ma'mun, for example, is reported as a man genuinely interested in the debates of the learned, responsible for (among other things) the institution of a major translation project by which works from antiquity were put into Arabic.[33]

Al-Ma'mun ruled from 813 to 833. His quest for religious allies led him, first, to break with precedent by appointing someone other than a family member as his successor. In 817 'Ali al-Rida, a man of piety revered by large segments of Muslim society, agreed to succeed al-Ma'mun as ruler. When al-Rida died the following year, this particular plan became moot.[34]

Al-Ma'mun possessed other resources, however. Thus he turned to some of the scholars associated with the Mu'tazila, which formed part of the general religious movement during the Abbasid revolt. Its members practiced a highly distinctive form of religious reasoning called al-kalam, a kind of dialectic argumentation focused on doctrinal concerns. By the time of al-Ma'mun, members were known for adherence to five principles: al-tawhid, or unity, stressing the uniqueness of God in relation to God's creatures; al-'adl, or justice, in the sense that God is the author of moral law, always does what is right or best for God's creatures, and requires that human beings use their freedom to follow in this path; "the promise and the threat," meaning that God will enforce the moral law by means of rewards and punishments, in this world and the next; "commanding right and forbidding wrong," in the sense that human beings have a duty to pursue justice; and "the intermediate position," indicating the distinctive way the group approached the religio-political disputes associated with the early conflicts between ʿAli and Muʿawiya.[35]

For our purposes, the Muʿtazili teaching on al-tawhid is the most important; for it was this principle that led to a highly distinctive and controversial judgment regarding the Qurʾan. When al-Maʿmun's alliance with members of the group led him to impose a mihna, or test, upon important members of the learned class, the resulting outcry had important consequences for the development of Shariʿa reasoning.

For the Muʿtazila, al-tawhid meant that God is "incapable of description" in human terms. In a certain sense, this is a notion shared by all Muslims. The Qurʾan declares:

He is God, the one;
God, the eternal, absolute;
He does not beget, nor is He begotten;
And there is none like Him.   (112)

At the same time, the Qurʾan speaks of God as "all-seeing," "all-knowing," "powerful," "wise"—in effect, attributing to God the kinds of abilities characteristic of human beings, albeit in superlative quantities. At 2:256 we read:

God! There is no god but God,
The Living, the self-subsisting, supporter of all.
No slumber can seize Him, nor sleep.
To him belong all things in the heavens and on earth.
Who can intercede with Him, except as He permits?
He knows that which is before, and after, and behind his
   creatures.

> They shall not comprehend any aspect of His knowledge,
> save as he wills.
> His Throne extends over the heavens and the earth, and He
> feels no fatigue in guarding and preserving them, for He
> is the Most High, the Supreme.

The image of God here is as a king—a superlative one, to be sure, but comparable to those familiar in human experience. The suggestion is that one trying to think about God should take human kingship to the maximum, and in doing so will begin to understand the awesome power of deity.

The Mu'tazila feared the possibility of misunderstanding presented by such anthropocentric language. Their interpretation of *al-tawhid* was designed to clarify the meaning of the Qur'an, specifically by means of a proposal about the relationship between human language and the deity of God. Mu'tazili thinkers insisted that *all* speech about God was metaphorical. This stricture applied not only to ordinary speech but even to the "divine speech" enshrined in the Qur'an. When the sacred text speaks of God's throne extending over the heavens and the earth, this is a kind of accommodation on God's part, employing a vivid image in order to suggest the sense of awe appropriate to creatures encountering the deity. The "throne verse," powerful as it is, does not reach to God's "essence," which ultimately must be described in negative terms: God is "not finite," "has no beginning and no end," "begets not, and is not begotten."[36]

The Mu'tazila spoke of the Qur'an as "God's *created* speech." They insisted that the Holy Book provided the best guide with respect to human attempts to acknowledge and respond to the maker of heaven and earth. Yet they thought it important to signify that even this book, "within which there is no doubt," and which provides "guidance for the pious," did not constitute a mode of direct address by God to humanity.[37]

There were several reasons for this Mu'tazili version of *al-tawhid*. Not least was their worry that popular modes of interpretation might elide the distinctions between Islamic and Christian representations of deity. As Muslims understood it, the practice by which Christians referred to Jesus of Nazareth as "son of God" confused the creature with the Creator. If popular piety presented God as sitting on an actual, albeit heavenly, throne, or as actually seeing (by means of some superlative capacity of vision), how much difference would remain between Muslims and their Christian subjects?[38] And there is in fact evidence that Muslims did speak in ways that suggested the kind of embodied God who might be able to sit on a throne, watch over humanity, and so on. Popular creeds promised that the blessed would "behold the face of God" in paradise. In doing so, the creeds rested on the notion that the Qur'an, as God's speech, is God's self-description. For many reciting the creeds, the pages of the Qur'an might be created, as were the ink and the voice of the reader. But the speech is God's speech. One who hears the Qur'an recited or reads with comprehension does not simply encounter notions of deity. Such a person is in the presence of nothing less than the living God.

Under Mu'tazili tutelage, al-Ma'mun determined to institute a test by which the learned would testify to their adherence to the doctrine of God's created speech. According to standard accounts, the test focused on well-known scholars in and around the capital. The same accounts insist that most of those subjected to the test swore their allegiance to the Mu'tazili doctrine of the Qur'an. It seemed that al-Ma'mun was well on his way to ensuring a uniform notion of orthodox practice, which would certainly serve well in the Abbasid quest to secure religious support.

The main (and, in some accounts, the sole) holdout among the learned was Ahmad ibn Hanbal (d. 855).[39] Ahmad was a scholar of *ahadith;* that is, he specialized in collecting reports about Muhammad's words and deeds, and in searching these out so as to ascertain those that were sound.[40] The connection between Ahmad's scholarship and the work of al-Shafi'i is striking. Not that they agreed on all points; however, Ahmad shared with al-Shafi'i the idea that the divine path was best comprehended by a faithful reading of the precedents established in the Qur'an and the *sunna*. It is significant that much of the substance of popular piety involved appeals to the Prophet's words and deeds. Thus, the notion that the blessed will see God's face rests not on the Qur'an, but on reports from the Prophet. Similarly, stories of God shaping the human creature out of clay and breathing life into it are prophetic extensions or elaborations of verses in the Qur'an. Perhaps most important, sayings attributed to the Prophet tie the Qur'an and other scriptural texts to a heavenly book, specifically characterizing the Qur'an as an Arabic version of the divine speech enshrined in this "mother of books."

Accounts of the *mihna* thus present Ahmad ibn Hanbal as the champion of the kind of popular piety associated with *ahadith*. He was an adherent of the *sunna* of the Prophet who did not substitute his own theory of religious language for the Prophet's characterization of the Holy Book. And, true to this image, Ahmad did not swear allegiance to Mu'tazili doctrine. Rather, he insisted that he would not answer, because the caliph lacked competence to put the question.

It is important to note the technical and reserved way in which Ahmad ibn Hanbal resisted the *mihna*. Traditional accounts do suggest that his differences with al-Ma'mun and thus with the Mu'tazila were substantive. For Ahmad, faithfulness required staying within the language of revealed texts. One might qualify the throne verse by saying something to the effect that God's throne is unlike any present to ordinary experience. One would not, however, speak of the depiction as metaphorical; the verse is God's self-description. Nevertheless, Ahmad's resistance to the test was technical. Claiming that the authority of the caliph rested on adherence to the Shari'a, he noted that there was no text in the Qur'an or in sound reports of the prophetic *sunna* on which to base the claim that the Qur'an was "created" speech. Where there was no text, there could be no binding judgment; where there was no binding judgment, there could be no obligation; where there was no obligation, there was no right or duty of the ruler to demand obedience. With respect to the question at hand, the caliph had no right to restrict the conscience of a Muslim. Al-Ma'mun had overstepped his bounds.

Answering the caliph's summons, Ahmad appeared at court. By this time, al-Mu'tasim (833–847) held the office, al-Ma'mun having died. Having been flogged and imprisoned by order of the ruler, Ahmad presented a careful justification for resistance. A Muslim, he said, is obligated to honor the ruler, and to obey all lawful orders. Faced with an unjust command, the same Muslim is obligated to refuse obedience. According to Ahmad, such refusal ought not to be confused with a right to revolt. Ahmad seems to have been one of those scholars who held that revolution is never (or almost never) justified. Rather, the refusal of an unjust command should be construed as "omitting to obey." Ahmad's resistance to the *mihna* thus provides a fascinating instance of political behavior. On the basis of the stories of the *mihna* and of Ahmad's continuing refusal of association with the Abbasids, even after the caliph al-Mutawakkil (847–861) succeeded to power and reversed al-Ma'mun's order, Michael Cook speaks of Ahmad's "apolitical politics."[41] By this, Cook means to capture the political relevance of a life devoted to religious testimony, inclusive of a refusal of any and all direct associations with governing institutions.

One could say more about this episode in Islamic history. However, the point with respect to our interests has to do with Ahmad ibn Hanbal as an exemplar of developing trends in the practice of Shari'a reasoning. Devotion to the Prophet and, with it, the interest of the learned in identifying sound reports of the prophetic *sunna* had tremendous implications for the development of Shariʿa reasoning. Al-Shafiʿi and Ahmad ibn Hanbal are two of the most important figures in this development. Indeed, Ahmad would be remembered as much for his collection of prophetic reports as for his various responses to questions, even as al-Shafiʿi would be remembered for his systematic statement defining the Qurʾan and the prophetic *sunna* as primary sources for comprehending the Shariʿa.

By the eleventh and twelfth centuries, the system toward which al-Shafiʿi and Ahmad ibn Hanbal pointed was firmly in place, with scholars like al-Mawardi (d. 1058), al-Sarakhsi (d. 1096 or 1101), Ibn ʿAqil (d. 1119), and Ibn Rushd (d. 1198) as exemplary practitioners. Their goal, via Shariʿa reasoning, was comprehension of the divine path. To this end, they worked with *usul al-fiqh*, the sources of comprehension, meaning a system of agreed-upon texts and rules of interpretation by which the learned might craft *al-fatawa*, opinions or responses to questions raised by the faithful, and thus facilitate the Muslim community's fulfillment of its mission, namely, commanding right and forbidding wrong, for the good of all humankind.

As an example, consider the brief account given in Ibn Rushd's prefatory remarks to *Bidayat al-Mujtahid*, a book intended to aid in the training of the special class of the learned trained in *al-fiqh*, or comprehension, of the Shariʿa.[42] Ibn Rushd's work is a compilation of the opinions of the learned on a variety of questions. The opinions gathered on these questions show the ways in which the learned work with texts (the Qurʾan and the *sunna*) in order to judge cases. In some cases, judgments are based on explicit texts. There may nevertheless be important issues of interpretation, such as those related to whether a given prescription is general or particular. Thus, when the Qurʾan (at 9:103) orders the Prophet to "take *zakat* [alms] of their [believers'] *mal* [wealth], wherewith you may purify them and may make them grow," it is important to know that the word *mal* applies only to certain kinds of holdings. Or again, when Qur'an 17:23 orders "Do not say 'fie' unto them nor repulse them, but speak to them a gracious word," it is important to understand that the prohibition is not only of one specific kind of act, but of all sorts of rude or antisocial behavior: "beating, abuse, and whatever is more grievous."[43]

Similarly, it is important to know the type of prescription or prohibition implied by a particular text. Some judgments indicate that a particular act is "obligatory," as in the order to establish right worship by praying five times daily. Others are recommended, as in acts of worship above and beyond such required prayers. Still others are forbidden, as in the command against eating carrion. Others are "reprehensible," in that they make it easier for one to perform forbidden acts. Finally, some judgments indicate that a particular act is "permissible"; that is, there is choice with respect to its commission or omission. In each case, it is critical to know not only how to classify an act, but also how it applies to particular agents. Thus, some acts are "communal" obligations; that is, so long as some perform them, others may be excused. Others, by contrast, are "individual" obligations, which no one can perform for anyone else. Fighting in war, at least in most circumstances, provides an example of a communal obligation. Praying five times a day provides an example of individual duty.

In ascertaining the type of judgment enshrined in the Qur'an and the *sunna*, some opinions are clear, in the sense that there is no dispute about them, while others must be described as "probable." The latter are within a range of acceptable interpretations, and thus reasonable or conscientious disagreement is tolerated.

There are cases, however, for which there is no clear text. With respect to these, a scholar must exert his reason. The preferred mode for such effort is *al-qiyas,* or analogy, already mentioned in our discussion of al-Shafi'i's work. As Ibn Rushd puts it, legitimate "analogy is the assigning of the obligatory judgment for a thing to another thing, about which the Shari'a is silent, [because of] its resemblance to the thing for which the Shari'a has obligated the judgment or [because of] a common underlying cause between them."[44] In some cases, the analogy between a judgment enshrined in the Qur'an and the *sunna* is established through a kind of similitude *(al-shabah)* of cases; in others, by an appeal to a common principle *(al-'illa)* that joins them. As Ibn Rushd has it, the differences between these are subtle, and they often lead to disagreement. With respect to such differences, one may often be instructed by the consensual judgment of the learned, which suggests that a given judgment (attained by reasoning) is "considered definitive [because of] predominant probability."[45] But the fact that such consensus *(al-'ijma)* rests on interpretations of the Qur'an and the *sunna* always leaves open the possibility that a specific judgment might be overturned or overridden as a result of new information, difference of circumstance, and the like. Thus Ibn Rushd establishes the notion that independent judgment—that is, the promulgation of a learned opinion that overturns a precedent established in the judgment of earlier generations of scholars—always remains a possibility.

Wael Hallaq characterizes the work of Ibn Rushd and other *'ulama* of the eleventh and twelfth centuries as a kind of "golden age" of Shari'a reasoning among Sunni Muslims. The terminology of Sunni and Shi'i is not particularly useful for the very early period of Islamic history. It is relevant at this point, however, and thus it is useful to think of a comparable golden age among Shi'i scholars, either in connection with the work of noteworthies like al-Mufid (d. 1023) and his students Sharif al-Murtada (d. 1044) and Muhammad ibn al-Hasan al-Tusi (d. 1068) in eleventh-century Baghdad, or in connection with the school of al-Hilla, a town located between Kufa and Baghdad, in the thirteenth and fourteenth centuries.[46] As the locations suggest, a distinctively Shi'i approach to Shari'a reasoning grew up in the southern and eastern portions of Iraq; Iran also became an important center. Both Baghdad and Hilla scholars may be associated with the *Ithna ash'ari,* or Twelver, version of Shi'ism, meaning that they accepted the notion that after the death of Muhammad, leadership of the *umma* passed to 'Ali as his designated successor, and then to a series of others, up to the twelfth imam, Muhammad, son of Hasan al-Askari.[47] As the Shi'a had it, the infant Muhammad was taken into hiding by the will and purpose of God in 873/874, where he will remain until the day of God's decision. At that point the hidden imam will appear as al-Mahdi, the rightly guided one, who will lead the faithful in establishing the reign of justice and equity, and will rule over humanity for a thousand years.

From the Shi'i point of view, the events of the first *fitna* thus constituted a rejection of the Prophet's plan for his community, and further created a context in which the majority of Muslims were prevented from following the straight path associated with *al-shari'a.* This rejection, confirmed in the subsequent careers of 'Ali's sons and their successors, meant that important parts of the enterprise of Shari'a reasoning were to be viewed with suspicion. In particular, the use of reports of the Prophet's *sunna* needed critical scrutiny, so as to ascertain when and where persons involved in the rejection of 'Ali's leadership might have altered or even fabricated these important texts.

The work of Shi'i *'ulama* thus presupposed an alternative to the great collections of *ahadith* utilized by Sunni scholars. In this regard, the Shi'a drew on tenth-century works by collectors like al-Kulayni (d. 941/942) and Ibn Babuya (d. 991), each of whom focused on the *isnad,* or chain, of transmitters attached to a specific report. Reports were judged "sound," and thus useful for the normative purposes of Shari'a reasoning, only in cases in which the chain was secured through the inclusion of the name of one of the designated imams or leaders, or of the names of people whose trustworthiness was established by the leaders' testimony.[48]

Interestingly, certain of the reports approved in Shi'i collections testify to the authority of "reason" *(al-'aql)* in the affairs of humanity. These reports correlate with the general tendency of Twelver *'ulama* to affirm *al-'aql* as one of the sources of Shari'a reasoning. The precise import of this affirmation—that is, in what way it serves to distinguish Shi'i from Sunni versions of the practice of Shari'a reasoning—is a matter of some debate. We might note the way in which Shi'i scholarship and piety delighted in stories whereby the learned find consensus on a certain matter, only to have one dissenter rise and prove the consensus wrong—in which case "consensus" is the error of the majority, and "right reason" the mode by which the dissenter makes the case. Such stories fostered a culture in which the learned considered themselves more independent, and thus more willing to revise precedent than in the Sunni case.[49] At the same time, the development of the Shi'i approach to Shari'a reasoning indicates that the Twelver *'ulama* were not always clear about the extent to which reason should be viewed as an independent source of judgment. In the sixteenth- and seventeenth-century debates between *usulis,* advocates of reason, and *akhbari,* advocates of textual precedent, Twelver *'ulama* engaged in complicated disputes regarding this question. While all parties asserted that, in principle, a sound judgment is in accord with right reason, it was not—some would say, still is not—clear just how this claim works in relation to specific cases.[50]

The Modern Setting

The eleventh and twelfth centuries saw the emergence of a large number of brilliant practitioners of Shari'a reasoning. For both Sunni and Shi'i Muslims, the work of these scholars helped to define the framework of Shari'a reasoning for subsequent generations, so that *'ulama* thought of themselves as participating in a transgenerational conversation about the rights and wrongs of human behavior. In this conversation, the methods of interpreting and applying the Qur'an and the *sunna* developed by the learned during the formative period and golden age of Shari'a reasoning provided a framework by which subsequent practitioners shaped their own arguments. Further, the judgments scholars in these periods reached about specific questions—for example, "When may the ruler of the Muslims authorize military force?" or "What tactics are acceptable in the conduct of war?"—served as precedents to which subsequent generations of scholars would recur.

In either case—that is, whether one is speaking about the framework of Shari'a reasoning or about judgments pertaining to specific questions of right and wrong—the practice of Shari'a reasoning involved a balance between continuity and creativity. With respect to continuity, the accomplishments of earlier generations demanded respect. A scholar working in the fourteenth century, as did Ibn Taymiyya (d. 1328), styled himself a follower of Ahmad ibn Hanbal and his disciples, referred to his predecessors as guides and teachers, and clearly thought that in some sense they were his betters. Similarly, al-Wansharisi (d. 1508) expressed his particular debt to Malik ibn Anas and his followers, and in his opinions showed particular deference to their approaches and judgments. In this emphasis on continuity with the past, Ibn Taymiyya and al-Wansharisi were typical. Scholars learned the craft of Shari'a reasoning at one or another center of Islamic learning—Damascus, Baghdad, Cairo, the holy cities—in terms of the practice of one of several *madahib*, schools, or, perhaps more accurately, trajectories of interpretation. Having mastered a set curriculum, a scholar received a certificate signifying qualification to advise believers regarding the Shari'a in a manner appropriate to his level of attainment. For most, this meant practicing *al-taqlid,* or imitation, meaning a qualification to repeat the consensual judgment of scholars associated with a particular trajectory of interpretation. For others, it meant practicing *al-taqlid* with a wider range; these were qualified to repeat the consensual judgments of each of the four standard schools, and to engage in comparison and contrast so that those seeking advice might select the judgment that seemed best, or most advantageous.

For a few, however—scholars like Ibn Taymiyya and al-Wansharisi—training in Shariʿa reasoning provided a platform by which to engage in independent judgment. Here, the ability to create might rest on fresh insight into the sources and framework of Shariʿa reasoning. As noted in the discussion of Ibn Rushd's summary of the theory of sources, analogical reasoning could be the source of much disagreement. Ibn Taymiyya understood this, and he argued that many of his predecessors leaned on this overmuch in their attempts to distinguish right from wrong. Appealing to the example of Ahmad ibn Hanbal, Ibn Taymiyya held that a direct appeal to *al-maslaha,* "that which is salutary with respect to public interest," in many cases constituted a more honest and better approach, not least because it did not attempt to force connections between textual precedents and contemporary judgment.

At other times, the ability to create rested on an understanding that distinctive circumstances call for new judgments. Thus, when al-Wansharisi dealt with the question "Are Muslims living under a non-Islamic government required to emigrate to the realm of Islam?" he argued that the proper answer would be yes, despite the fact that the consensual precedent of several generations suggested the opposite. In doing so, al-Wansharisi appealed to the special circumstances created by the Spanish *reconquista,* and argued that these constituted a renewed threat, not only to the security of Muslims living in this formerly Islamic territory but to the rest of Islamic civilization.[51] Muslims who continued to reside in Spain constituted a security risk, in the sense that their lives and property might be seized by the new regime and utilized to extort territorial or other concessions from the Muslim ruler.

Thus, new times or new insights might yield new approaches or judgments. Nevertheless, Shari'a reasoning is properly characterized as a conservative practice, in the sense that it requires that most participants follow the line of precedent. True creativity, in the sense of establishing new or further precedent, is reserved for the few. When those few claim the right of independent judgment, their claims are likely to be controversial. It is not surprising, then, that the history of Shari'a reasoning is a history of conflict, in which argument is often connected with violence. That Ibn Taymiyya spent much of his life, and wrote most of his books, in the prison of the Mamluk ruler in Cairo, is instructive.

Similarly instructive are the careers of several figures who stand out as early respondents to the great changes that began to affect Muslim societies in the mid to late eighteenth centuries. The first, Shah Wali Allah of Delhi (1703–1762), was the most eminent member of the learned class working during the closing decades of Mughal rule.[52] Beginning in the sixteenth century with Babur (d. 1530), the Mughal rulers asserted Islamic dominance in India. By the time of Wali Allah's birth, the power of the Muslims was fading, and Aurangzeb (d. 1707) was the last great Mughal ruler in the Indian subcontinent. Muslim scholars like Wali Allah hoped to revivify Islamic power through renewed attention to the practice of Shari'a reasoning. To that end, he established a new center for the training of young scholars, whose job it would be to call the Muslims of India to fulfill their vocation of exercising leadership by commanding right and forbidding wrong.

The project would prove difficult, however, not least because of the gradual yet seemingly irresistible growth of British power. One of the sons of Wali Allah would deem it necessary to declare in 1820 that India should no longer be regarded as Islamic territory. In part, 'Abd al-'Aziz's *fatwa*, or opinion, reflected intra-Muslim polemics. In solidifying their power, the British turned first to Shi'i Muslims, who were concentrated in the north; 'Abd al-'Aziz and other Sunni 'ulama regarded this recognition of the Shi'a as an establishment of heresy.

At the same time, the 1820 ruling reflected a more basic reality: whether working through the Shi'a or through the Hindus, the British were not dedicated to the Shari'a. From 'Abd al-'Aziz's perspective, British rule meant a non-Islamic establishment, in which the ability of the Muslim community to carry out its historical mission would necessarily be limited. For Islam to flourish, there should be a political entity dedicated to rule by the Shari'a. A Muslim ruler or a group of Muslim rulers should plan and carry out policy, in consultation with the learned class. And in such a context, the flourishing of Islam would redound to the benefit of all those governed, and indeed of all humanity—even, or perhaps especially, those members of the protected Jewish and Christian—or, more importantly in India, Hindu and Parsee (Zoroastrian)—communities. While 'Abd al-'Aziz did not declare that the new situation required armed resistance, his opinion did suggest the need for struggle aimed at change. The participation of Muslims in the 1857 rebellion known as the Sepoy Mutiny summons echoes of the opinion of 'Abd al-'Aziz. And when a number of the learned responded to this failed rebellion by founding a new center of Islamic Studies in Deoband in 1867, the spiritual and physical descendants of Wali Allah and 'Abd al-'Aziz were important participants.[53] Today their influence is most clearly felt in the activities of two quite distinctive groups: the Tablighi Jama'at, which aims at revival of Islamic influence through the cultivation of spirituality among Muslims; and the Taliban, best known for their brief but noteworthy period of governance in Afghanistan between 1990 and 2001.[54]

A second figure illustrating the early modern course of Shari'a reasoning is Muhammad ibn 'abd al-Wahhab (1703–1791), the founder of the Wahhabi movement.[55] 'Abd al-Wahhab's legacy in Saudi

Arabia and, through Saudi missions, throughout the world is perva-
sive. His career began in relative modesty, however. In the eighteenth
century, the Arabian Peninsula was regarded as a backwater by the
rulers of the Ottoman state. Perhaps, though, the very distance between economic and cultural centers like Istanbul, Damascus, and
Baghdad provided space for a reformer like 'Abd al-Wahhab. In any
event, he and his colleagues began to issue Shari'a opinions con-
demning much of the religious practice of those living in the historical land of Muhammad. In 1746 the group of scholars formed an alliance with the family of al-Sa'ud, adding political and military force
to their campaign against *jahiliyya*. As the Wahhabi-Saudi leadership
understood it, the combination of "calling" Muslims to repentance
and punishing (fighting) anyone who refused the invitation was
consistent with the Shari'a vision of Muslim responsibility. Commanding right and forbidding wrong through the establishment of
an Islamic state was the key in carrying out the mission of Islam.

For a third set of developments in the early modern period, we
turn to Iran, where Shi'i scholars found it neccssary to issue opinions urging the Qajar rulers to use military force in order to resist
Russian incursions into Iranian territory. In doing so, the Twelver
ulama presented themselves as guardians of the Shi'i (and thus,
from their point of view, the Islamic) character of the Iranian state.
While not without precedent in the premodern practice of Shi'i
scholars, such judgments did move the *ulama* in the direction of an
activism that would enhance their authority as leaders of a resistance intended to safeguard the territory of Islam against foreign in-
truders.[56]

Shari'a reasoning is best regarded as an open practice, in that
readings of its sources with a view toward discerning divine guidance in particular contexts can yield disagreement. So it is not surprising that the course of Shari'a reasoning from the 1700s to the
present is characterized by vigorous (and not always irenic) argu-

ment. Thus, even as some of those inheriting Wali Allah's mantle took Shariʿa precedents to suggest a duty of armed resistance to British rule in India, others suggested that the new context led in a different direction. Similarly, even as the Wahhabi scholars allied themselves with the Saudi clan in a movement that would issue in the founding of a new state, or as the Shiʿi ʿulama urged resistance to foreign influence in Iran, their judgments were subjected to criticism. For now, let us focus on India, where the scholars of Deoband could support the pietistic revival of the Tablighi Jamaʿat, as well as the political and military campaign of the Taliban. Even more distinct was the program of educational reform advocated by Sayyid Ahmad Khan. Declaring that armed struggle cannot be required in the face of superior force, Sayyid Ahmad cited Qurʾan 13:11 (God "never changes the condition of a people until they change themselves") in support of a program of modern scientific and technical as well as traditional learning. By this means, he argued, the historical stature of the Muslim community might be restored, for those who control scientific and technical knowledge hold the keys to political influence. And political influence, in turn, would create a space for Muslims to command right and forbid wrong.[57]

Sayyid Ahmad's program of reform provided the inspiration for a new center of learning, Aligarh Muslim University, which came to represent a kind of "modernist" or "reformist" approach to the new situation of Muslims. Whereas Deoband maintained a more or less traditional approach, particularly with respect to the training of religious specialists, Aligarh Muslim University sought to train a new type of Muslim leader: a "lay" person, literate in the sources of Shariʿa reasoning, but also trained in the kinds of scientific and technical learning that Sayyid Ahmad saw as the root of British power. But although both institutions could be described as "Shariʿa minded," in the sense of advocating a particular role for the Muslim community, connected with its historical mission of religious and moral leadership, Sayyid Ahmad's university came under serious criticism from those who thought they discerned in its program an overly cooperative, even conciliatory, approach to British rule. In particular, Jamal al-Din, known as al-Afghani (1839–1897), mounted a vigorous critique of Sayyid Ahmad, arguing that the first task before the Muslims was to free themselves from British dominance. Only afterward would it make sense for Muslims to determine the course of reform most appropriate for carrying out their mission in the modern world.

Al-Afghani advocated extensive reform.[58] From his perspective, the traditionalism represented by Deoband was inadequate to the condition of Muslims in the nineteenth century. Muslims must first comprehend the nature and scope of the change affecting the Indian subcontinent, and indeed the whole of the realm of Islam. Al-Afghani thought the change could be described only as a catastrophe. Moving from India to Turkey to Egypt to Iran, this mysterious and charismatic personality carried a message of reform based on a return to authentic Islamic sources. For al-Afghani, however, such return could not simply be a matter of reading and rereading precedents set in other generations. To cope with their loss of power, Muslims needed to recover a sense of the openness of the Shari'a vision, particularly with respect to scientific and technical learning. Quoting the Prophet, "Seek knowledge, wherever you may find it," al-Afghani argued that true religion—true Islam—supports scientific inquiry, and that a community practicing true religion—again, true Islam—would find itself, as a matter of course, fostering scientific and technical expertise. Noting that Christian scriptures are filled with such otherworldly sentiments as Jesus' or Paul's suggestions that poverty or celibacy might be of greater value than the creation of wealth or the building and maintenance of families represented in marriage, al-Afghani argued that Europeans had obtained scientific and technical prowess only by the abandonment of faith represented by the Enlightenment. By contrast, Muslims lost such prowess as a result of their lack of piety, and recovery of piety would go hand in glove with recovery of scientific power.

The first order of the day, however, should be the reassertion of the political vision associated with Shari'a reasoning. Given that Muslims were called to lead humanity, al-Afghani argued, how could they accept the dominance of Great Britain, of France, or of Russia, particularly in the territories historically associated with Islamic rule?

Al-Afghani's legacy transcended a career marked by recurrent failures. His encounter with Ahmad Khan occurred during a sojourn in India in 1879 after time spent in Afghanistan, Turkey, and Egypt. In every case, his personal charisma proved sufficient to secure him access to circles of power, seemingly with great ease. But his outspokenness proved equally sufficient to ensure that no circle of power could long abide al-Afghani's presence. By the early 1880s he was living in Paris, where he wrote several influential works, in particular a response to Ernst Renan's portrayal of an inevitable rivalry between science and religion. In the early 1890s al-Afghani reemerged as a player in the Iranian resistance to British rule, even traveling to Russia in order to explore the possibilities of support from that quarter. There he found allies among the Shi'i 'ulama, who increasingly viewed the Qajar rulers as ready to sacrifice the Islamic identity of the state for monetary gain. The Tobacco Revolt of 1890–91 saw these scholars joining with al-Afghani and others who sought to reverse the shah's sale of Iran's tobacco industry to Great Britain, on the grounds that this transaction (which would have required Iranian tobacco producers to sell their crop to the British, and Iranian tobacco users to buy from British suppliers) reduced the independence necessary to the maintenance of a viable state. When, in 1906, a coalition of Shi'i 'ulama and political activists moved to define and delimit the authority of the Qajar shah through the establishment of a written constitution, it was not difficult to perceive the influence of al-Afghani.

Throughout these travels, al-Afghani's most consistent intellectual partnership was with the Egyptian Muhammad 'Abduh (1849–1905), and it is through 'Abduh that one may see his most enduring legacy. 'Abduh, who would become the leading member of the 'ulama in Egypt, tried to walk a careful line by which political independence and religious reform might be combined. Egypt, and by extension other territories historically associated with Islam, needed to move toward political independence, and to that end, European dominance must not become a permanent fact of life. At the same time, Muslims must be ready to govern themselves and to carry out their mission in a new situation. To that end, a broad reform of education, both at the elite level of the training of members of the learned class, and at the level of educating lay experts in scientific and technical matters, would be necessary. In obtaining both goals, the one thing to be avoided at all costs was a premature standoff between Muslim activists and European military and economic might.[59]

As grand mufti, 'Abduh issued numerous opinions in the style characteristic of Shari'a reasoning. His enormous contributions are worthy of a separate study in themselves. Of chief importance for our purposes, however, he prepared the way for the crisis in the relationship between Shari'a reasoning and political vision that would occupy Muslims in the 1920s.

The First World War posed a major crisis for European civilization. It led to a loss of faith, to an unsatisfactory settlement in the Treaty of Versailles, and ultimately to the rise of National Socialism in Germany and the renewal of European conflict in 1939.

The war also posed a crisis for Islam.[60] The regional crises created by the expansion of British rule in the Indian subcontinent, the comparable struggles to which al-Afghani contributed in Egypt and

Iran, and the continuing Wahhabi-Saudi campaigns in the Arabian Peninsula all reflected the passing of great and long-standing political arrangements. By 1914 only the Ottoman empire remained as a symbol of the old territory of Islam and its universal *khilafat*. In 1921 the great powers of Europe had divided the heartland of that empire as spoils of war, with the French taking Syria and Lebanon and the British adding Palestine, Transjordan, Iraq, and the Arabian Peninsula to their already established hegemony in Egypt and India.

The Ottoman empire now consisted of one state, Turkey. However, that was changing as well. Already in 1914, a group of young military officers recognized the weakness of the old regime. By 1918 these "young Turks" were effectively in control of state administration. And by 1921 and 1922 Mustafa Kemal, better known as Ataturk, and his colleagues were on the road to declaring that the identity of Turkey would be recast as a secular republic rather than an Islamic state. By 1924 the new Turkish republic would announce that it could no longer support the Ottoman ruler. If others wished to do so, they could find a home and financial means to support the institution associated with the historical *khilafat*.

The abolition of Ottoman rule posed a crisis of legitimation in the realm of Islam. Interestingly, the greatest outcry came from India, which had never been under Ottoman rule. The real value of the Ottoman ruler, as the poet/philosopher Muhammad Iqbal (d. 1932) put it, was as a symbol of Islamic unity.[61] The Muslims of India, as elsewhere, were at a crucial point in their struggle with European power. The Ottoman *khilafat*, whatever its problems, constituted a focal point around which Muslims might rally. The *khilafat* movement, as a plea to the Turks to maintain the Ottoman ruler, formed a part of the landscape of the Indian campaign for independence in the mid-1920s.

The Turks deemed the call of Iqbal and other Indians as too little, too late. Turkey would attend to its own issues. Nevertheless, to Iqbal it seemed clear that the immediate future of Islamic renewal would involve the various regional communities focusing on their own struggles. Perhaps one day these communities would reemerge, strong enough to unite and once again play a world-historical role.

Egyptian and other Arab Muslim scholars interpreted the abolition of the Ottoman court variously, differing on the type of rule represented by the Ottomans. Clearly, these were sultans—an old word, quite literally associated with military power. And the rule of sultans had not been all bad. Insofar as the Ottomans acknowledged the priority of the Shari'a, consulted with the learned, and maintained the proper relationship between Muslims and the protected peoples, they approached the ideals of an Islamic state. But the 'ulama concluded that the Ottoman rulers did not really deserve the title "caliph"; if nothing else, their lack of connection with the Arabian Peninsula constituted a point against them.

The demise of the Ottomans thus represented an opportunity. Could Muslims reestablish khilafat, in its full and proper sense? As interest in this topic grew, so did consciousness of the importance of a settlement. The needs of Indian Muslims were one thing; the needs of Arab Muslims in Palestine were another. Agreement on the meaning of khilafat would give a unified focus to Arab resistance to expanded emigration and settlement by European Jews. The issue needed care, since it focused on the Shari'a and its sources. But it also needed resolve, given the crisis of Arab Islam.

As a matter of Shari'a judgment, discussion of the issue fell largely to the scholars of al-Azhar, the ancient seat of Islamic learning in Cairo. Discussion began in 1925, with a listing of the traditional qualifications for one who might hold the title khalifa: physically capable, from the tribe of Quraysh, knowledgeable in the sources of Shari'a, and so on. The scholars clearly sought a classical form of governance: a single ruler, legitimate by reason of acknowledgment of the Shari'a, governing in consultation with members of the learned class, establishing Islamic religion.

Early in the discussion, a challenge emerged. 'Ali 'Abd al-Raziq, a younger scholar of considerable promise, published a treatise on Islamic government. Colleagues viewed the argument as revolutionary, or—to put the matter in more strictly Islamic terms—as an "innovation." The term was, and remains, negative.[62]

In one sense, al-Raziq's thesis was simple. The sources of Islam indicate the importance of just government. Indeed, they support the view that the establishment of just government is an obligation, and that all human beings are required to work toward this goal. Some texts indicate that this obligation flows from reason; others, that it is a matter of revelation. In any case, no one should argue with the judgment that Muslims are obligated to exert themselves in the service of establishing just and wise governance.

That said (so al-Raziq argued), neither the Qur'an nor the *sunna* of the Prophet establishes a particular pattern of governance. True, the sources indicate that Muhammad exercised leadership in politics as well as religion, at least after the migration to Medina in 622. But his political leadership rested on a very different basis from his authority in religion. As Prophet, Muhammad was the recipient of divine revelation, by which God (through Muhammad) called people to faith and provided a discipline for the believers, establishing patterns of worship and ritual observance. As political leader, Muhammad derived his authority from his contemporaries' recognition of his trustworthiness and skill in managing affairs of state. Not least important in these considerations was his skill as a diplomat and a military leader. It was in view of these abilities that Muhammad's followers, as well as some non-Muslims, pledged loyalty to him in political and military affairs. And those who followed or succeeded him, holding the title of *khalifa*, attained that position on the basis of a similar set of worldly skills.

It is true (al-Raziq continued) that the rightly guided caliphs, meaning the first four successors to Muhammad, also commanded a certain respect in matters of religion. This authority, however, did not derive from a sense that they were somehow Muhammad's successors in the office of Prophet. Rather, the religious authority of Abu Bakr, 'Umar ibn al-Khattab, 'Uthman, and 'Ali ibn Abi Talib stemmed from their recognized status as significant companions of the Prophet, and thus from their familiarity with his *sunna*. Those who followed these early leaders and claimed the title *khalifa* were a diverse group. They did both some harm and some good, which is what one should expect from human beings attempting to fulfill their obligations. The community's acknowledgment of their leadership rested on recognition of their political and military skills. No one, al-Raziq asserted, should confuse authority in religion and authority in politics; they are distinct. The Muslim community should recognize this fact, and understand that restoration of the Ottoman caliphate, or of any other particular pattern of governance, is not a requirement of religion.

In one sense, al-Raziq's argument was not new. We have already seen that many Muslims regarded the Umayyads as "kings" rather than "caliphs." The practice of hereditary rule, by which the eldest son of the ruling clan assumed his father's duties, in itself mitigates the claim that Muslims should be ruled by the best of each generation. In addition, for most purposes the authority of the learned and the authority of rulers did involve a de facto division of labor, and some of the latter regarded a certain distance between their craft and the practice of ruling as required *de jure* as well.

Nevertheless, a firestorm of criticism greeted al-Raziq's treatise. In 1931 al-Azhar declared it a forbidden book. Al-Raziq never advanced professionally; when he died in 1966 he still held a position equivalent to that of a graduate student instructor.

Why this reaction?

One part of the explanation seems to be that al-Raziq's exploration of the sources went further than the al-Azhar scholars were prepared to go. It was one thing to criticize specific rulers like Mu'awiya,

Yazid, al-Ma'mun, and others for shortcomings in politics or religion. It was another thing entirely to suggest that Muhammad's political leadership was not intrinsically connected with his authority as Prophet, or to suggest that the rightly guided caliphs' recognition as particularly outstanding associates or companions of the Prophet was important only with respect to their religious, and not their political, role. Al-Raziq himself was at great pains in his treatise to note that his argument went further than others', and that his thesis regarding the distinction between religious and political authority ran counter to the historical consensus of the 'ulama. Nevertheless, al-Raziq was convinced that he was right, and said forcefully that the Muslim community would be better off if it followed his line rather than that of received tradition.

A second reason for the vigorous reaction to al-Raziq's treatise is closely related. The thesis that religion and politics are distinct, and that the Muslim community will do better to keep them so, was articulated at a time of great political ferment throughout the historical territory of Islam. As a scholar, al-Raziq made his points with great care. The argument is largely negative: Having examined the sources, he says, I think it highly probable that the consensus point of view is wrong. Others, more activist in nature, are busy putting the point into practice. If Muslims are not bound by the politics of the past, they are free to act on the notion that changing circumstances require new political arrangements. Precedents established by earlier generations do not bind the Muslim conscience. The point is to approximate justice in our own time, a goal that can (with all due respect to our predecessors) lead in new directions.

The reforms in Turkey, by which the post-Ottoman state was recast as a secular republic, present one example of this activist trend. In Egypt, the ferment surrounding the Wafd (Delegation) of Sa'ad Zaghlul Pasha and the struggle for independence from British domination present another. Those who viewed these developments as positive noted that the scholars of classical Islam took the best wisdom of their day and gave it an Islamic twist, and argued that Muslims thinking about political life in the 1920s should do the same. As reformers saw it, the forms of government associated with political success in the modern world were an admixture of monarchic and nonmonarchic forms; some countries had written constitutions, others did not. All converged on one point, however: they capitalized on the gifts of all their citizens and built institutions designed to encourage full participation, insofar as possible. It is possible to speak of this as democracy, or as a matter of republican virtue. In any case, the implication (for the Muslim reformers) was that one must avoid models of governance that restricted power to the one or to the few. A modern state needed the contributions of all its population if it was to flourish.

'Abd al-Raziq's treatise thus coincided with the program of activists who suggested that Egypt, and by extension other historically Muslim states, should view the descriptive "Islamic" less as a matter of formal institutions, and more as a matter of the implementation of values of justice and equity. Such activists did not necessarily believe that modern politics required the kind of radical separation of religious and political institutions characteristic of the new Turkish republic. Some argued, for example, that states with Muslim majorities should recognize some sort of Islamic religious establishment, along the lines of England's recognition of the Anglican Church. And most supposed that the policies of a state in which Muslims constitute a majority would bear an Islamic stamp. The reformists' vision of the precise nature of Muslim influence differed. The one thing on which they agreed was that a state ought not to restrict or foreclose participation or debate by any of its citizens. Nor should any instantiation of the sentiments of a Muslim majority arbitrarily restrict the participation of non-Muslims. A modern state needed the contributions of each and all.

With these details, it is perhaps clearer why al-Raziq's thesis was startling. In one fell swoop, a scholar of al-Azhar, steeped in the sources of Shari'a reasoning, mitigated or did away with the priority of the classical model of political order. There need be no *khilafat;* no ruler dedicated to governance by the Shari'a; no consultation between a religious establishment and political leaders; and no priority for Muslims as the first citizens of an Islamic state. The logic of al-Raziq's model can be taken further, so that the sense of mission that permeates the classical notion of order is altered. The Islamic community now exists as one among others, dedicated to the formation of individual conscience through education and persuasion, but drastically reduced with respect to the making of policy.

Al-Raziq's interpretation of the relevant sources did not develop in a vacuum. Muhammad 'Abduh had set the stage for much of the debate over the *khilafat,* and some of 'Abduh's *fatawa* lent themselves to the view that a modern state could not afford to forgo the contributions of any of its citizens. In Egypt, this meant that Coptic Christians, in particular, should receive rights and opportunities adequate to their participation as citizens. 'Abduh had also called for a reopening of some old theological debates, particularly with respect to the question "Does reason, apart from special revelation, give sound knowledge with respect to the basic precepts of social morality?" Although 'Abduh's discussion was circumspect, it seemed clear to many that his answer was yes, and that the many reservations classical theology associated with this question should be withdrawn or overridden. In the end, 'Abduh was willing to sacrifice much of the classical vision of order for the sake of *al-maslaha,* or public good.

On the opposite side, among those repudiating the reformer's treatise, one of the foremost critics was the venerable Rashid Rida, 'Abduh's student and close associate.[63] Rida did not deny al-Raziq's central claim, that the sources of Shari'a did not establish a detailed plan of government. He did, however, deny that religion and politics could be distinguished as sharply as al-Raziq suggested. Arguing that politics required a moral grounding more extensive than the vague phrase "basic precepts of social morality," Rida held that humanity was still in need of the superintendence of the Muslim community. Political order depended on a shared and secure sense of public morality; in turn, an adequate public morality depended on an establishment of true religion. And thus, Copts or Jews or other citizens of Egypt could benefit from the state's public acknowledgement of Islam.

Rida agreed that a modern state needs the contributions of all its citizens. But such an acknowledgment did not preclude the notion that those citizens have different contributions to make. Muslims, or at least those most knowledgeable in the sources and tradition of Shari'a reasoning, should provide leadership. Others, whose knowledge of religion and morality was less secure, should submit to the government of the best.

That said, Rida argued for a kind of consultative or even a parliamentary *khilafat,* in which representatives of the people would deliberate about the course of policy. He was not entirely clear on the makeup of such a representative or consultative assembly. One might, for example, imagine an assembly in which a certain number of seats were assigned to Muslims, another number to Christians, and so on. Or one might imagine an assembly in which some members were elected to represent particular districts or interest groups, while others were members of the religious class, chosen by their peers at al-Azhar or other institutions of learning. Rida also thought for a time that the Muslim community could benefit from the establishment of a universal *khilafat,* which would serve in ways analogous to the Vatican; that is, it would control the holy cities of Mecca and Medina, oversee the pilgrimage, and, on occasion, intervene as a kind of *primus inter pares* authority in Shari'a debates. It would not, however, possess the kind of imperial political control wielded by the Abbasids or Ottoman or Mughal rulers. That kind of authority would be left to the more regional communities that Europeans and North Americans call nations.

In the end, Rida's arguments carried the al-Azhar debate. They did not translate into political reality, however. As Egypt struggled toward independence, the combination of a declining monarchy and a nascent, almost anarchic parliamentary democracy could not bring order quickly enough. Beginning in 1948, the military began to take control. When, in 1952, Gamal 'abd al-Nasr led an officers' revolt, the pattern followed ever since emerged: rule by a strongman, ready to recognize, limit, and/or dissolve parliament whenever he deems fit; a recognition of Islam as the official religion and the sources of Shari'a as primary for legislation, but with its role effectively circumscribed to deal with questions of marriage and divorce; official recognition of Coptic Christians and other minorities as equal under the law, but in practice laboring under more or less severe restrictions on religious practice and social opportunities; and finally, a way of regulating Islamic practice, including Shari'a debate, that ensures that its most vital expression takes place in private associations, outside the officially sanctioned public centers of learning.

This last is signified, most importantly, by the movement known as *ikhwan al-muslimin,* the Muslim Brothers, whose founder, Hasan al-Banna, established the movement almost at the very moment 'Ali 'abd al-Raziq published his controversial thesis.[64] In 1928, as the learned at al-Azhar began their critique of al-Raziq, a high school instructor in an outlying town (Americans would call it "the boondocks") began his program of renewal. Members of the learned class would view Hasan al-Banna and his successors as ignorant and unreliable in the art of Shari'a reasoning. The appeal of the movement, however, lay at least in part in its reiteration of an old theme in Islamic tradition: the equality of Muslims with respect to the duty to seek God's guidance, and the correlative right to do so by consulting the Qur'an and the example of the Prophet.

Hasan al-Banna spoke of his movement as combining the virtues of every populist approach in the history of Islam: a *shari'a madhab*, a Sufi way, a school of *kalam*, or theology, and so on. He gave talks, and issued opinions, on the subject of *jihad*, on women's roles, and on the right form of Islamic government. With respect to the last, Hasan held that an Islamic state is by definition a Shari'a state. Otherwise, it would be illegitimate. And the Shari'a should, by dint of textual precedent, be discerned through a process of consultation among the Muslims. In this process, Hasan and his followers were prepared to listen to members of the learned class. But they reserved the right to judge for themselves which, if any, of the learned articulated the right opinion.

With the Brothers, we actually see something new in the history of Shari'a reasoning. The deference to the learned class as experts in religion is shown as a historical accident; for it rested largely on certain social facts: most Muslims could not read, or if they could, they could not obtain access to the texts necessary for the practice of reasoning about the Shari'a. By the 1920s, however, the growth of a professional class, able to read and discuss matters of religion, combined with the increased availability of books made possible by developments in print technology, meant that deference would no longer be the rule. With Hasan al-Banna, the movement toward a serious Islamist movement had begun.

Hasan's political vision might be viewed as a crudely expressed form of the ideas presented by Rashid Rida. Islamic government, in the sense of government by the Shari'a, is critical for the Muslim community to carry out its mission. In turn, that mission is critical, if humanity is to flourish. The human creature is, by dint of the plan of God, a social being. Men and women bear the imprint of the primordial covenant outlined in Qur'an 7:171–172. They are thereby able to ascertain the fact of their responsibility. They may even be able to discern the broad outlines of their obligations to God and to one another. Yet in their quest for security, and given the truncated witness of other prophetically founded communities, human beings need a clear and forceful articulation of moral precepts, if they are to have a hope of living in a just social order. Islam provides this, by means of the sources and practice of Shari'a reasoning. And the Muslim community provides an outlet for the dissemination of principles of justice.

In the hands of an obviously charismatic figure like Hasan al-Banna, this message swept over Egypt, and by 1948 the Brothers constituted a strong force in Egyptian politics. Hasan's assassination the following year proved less a defeat for the movement, and more a confirmation that Egyptian elites were not yet ready to listen to the message of Islam. When Nasr came to power in 1952, he called on the Brothers to mobilize support. When he turned on the Brothers in 1954, jailing their leaders on charges of sedition, Nasr recognized their power in another way. A lay movement, formed around the symbol of Shari'a and prepared to engage in Shari'a reasoning, had found its way to prominence. If it lacked the direct power associated with the established institutions of government, it nevertheless proved able to exercise considerable indirect power by means of its standing as a popular embodiment of the classical Shari'a vision.

Hasan al-Banna's vision, and the movement developed around it, was and remains the best-known example of a broad and popular trend in twentieth-century Islam. Abu'l a'la Mawdudi and the Jama'at-i Islami represent a south Asian equivalent.[65] Mawdudi, a journalist by trade, began writing in the 1930s, arguing for the importance of India as a Muslim state. When Muslim desire for a state independent of Hindu influence gained momentum, Mawdudi took an opposing view. Once Pakistan attained independence in 1947, however, Mawdudi moved to the new country and began a campaign to ensure that Pakistan would truly be a Muslim state. One of the first tests of his influence came in the 1954 debates over the constitution, particularly with respect to the import of describing Pakistan as an Islamic state, in which the Shari'a would be recognized as the law of the land. The crux of the issue, for Mawdudi, had to do with the status of the movement known as Ahmadiyyat. Formed around the revisionist teachings of Mirza Ghulam Ahmad (d. 1908), the movement stressed that Islam should be a missionary religion, devoted to the preaching of the word of God delivered through Muhammad. While that notion was not, in itself, controversial, the Ahmadiyyat surrounded it with arguments for freedom of conscience, including freedom of religion, speech, and association. The formal position of the group tied these arguments to the text of the Qur'an, and used that text as a means of criticizing a number of Shari'a precedents in which the learned relied on reports of the prophetic *sunna* for guidance. Among these, laws governing apostasy, blasphemy, and the status of non-Muslims were especially prominent.

On Mawdudi's view, Ahmadiyyat's platform challenged important features of the Shari'a vision of political order. In a tract discussing the finality of the prophecy of Muhammad, he argued that any community must set boundaries, lest its role in identity formation become a dead letter. The Muslim community through the centuries accomplished this in part by way of its insistence that Muhammad is the "seal" of the Prophets, meaning the final moment in God's call to humanity to follow the natural religion of submission. Mirza Ghulam Ahmad's preaching rendered this point moot by opening the truth to endless debate. According to Mawdudi, both reason and revelation make necessary the judgment that Ahmadiyyat is not an Islamic movement, and that its followers are not true Muslims. They may live in Pakistan, or in any other Islamic state, but only according to Shari'a provisions for the protected peoples. Their preaching and practice thereby contained, they will pose less of a threat to themselves and to others.

Here, Mawdudi reiterated aspects of the classical Shari'a vision of order. At the same time, he established himself and his movement as legitimate participants in debates about God's guidance, despite his lack of formal standing among the learned. Indeed, when the 1956 Constitution declared Ahmadiyyat a non-Islamic movement, Mawdudi's Jama'at became an important player in Pakistani politics, a role it has maintained ever since.

For our purposes, the most important aspect of movements like the Muslim Brothers and the Jama'at-i Islami is the impetus provided for a kind of "democratization" of Shari'a reasoning. In its early stages, the social practice of Shari'a reasoning developed in tandem with the rise of an elite class. The learned were those dedicated to and entrusted with the task of preserving and interpreting the sources provided by God as signs. Their task was to render sound opinions regarding the import of these sources for particular cases.

By the mid-twentieth century, however, the habitual deference of ordinary Muslims to the opinions of the learned was fading. The one great exception to this trend was among the Shi'a, particularly in connection with their increasing prominence in Iran. The crisis over the abolition of the Ottoman caliphate did not have the same resonance for the Shi'a as it did for Sunni Muslims. In Iran, the promulgation of the Constitution of 1906 and, with it, of a *majlis,* or consultative assembly, provided material for Shari'a debate. While many, perhaps even most, of the Twelver *'ulama* supported the constitution, others argued that the establishment of an assembly suggested that laws would be made by human beings, rather than according to the sources and methods of Shari'a reasoning. After the First World War, the weakness of the Qajar rulers made the constitutional question moot. Religious authorities were more interested in maintaining the independence of the Shi'i state from European control. Reza Pahlavi's seizure of power in 1921 and his elevation to the throne in 1926 provided a partial resolution, though the debate over relations with foreign powers would continue, reemerging in particular with the development of Iran's capacity to produce oil and, after the Second World War, the development of Cold War politics. Particularly in connection with the pro-American policies of Shah Reza Pahlavi (ruled 1953–1978), one sees an enhanced role for the Shiʿi ʿulama. The speeches of the Ayatollah Khomeini provide a good example of the way that Shiʿi authorities during this period maintained their historical suspicion that doing business with foreign powers needed careful review, lest the independence of Iran be undermined. At the same time, Khomeini's various pronouncements provide a good illustration of the sense of vocation among the Shiʿi ʿulama, by which the learned are "guardians" not only of the religious tradition, but of the Shiʿi identity of Iran. While it is true that opposition to the Shah was widespread, and that lay persons like the sociologist/activist professor ʿAli Shariʿati and the literary figure Jalal Al-e Ahmad played a very important role in the public debate over the political definition of Iran, the role of the ʿulama in defining Iran after the revolution of 1978–79 makes attention to their historical place in Iranian society and in the practice of Shariʿa reasoning extremely important.[66]

It is not, of course, that the institutions associated with Sunni learning were passing, or that the Sunni ʿulama were without influence. The movements centered around Hasan al-Banna and Mawlana Mawdudi admired the learning of the scholarly class, and were happy to seek and to listen to their opinions.

However, these same movements reserved the right to judge for themselves which of the learned to follow; to put it another way, they effectively reserved judgment on matters of practice for themselves. And why not? As they saw it, God calls individuals to reflect on the signs that point toward divine guidance. Islam knows no priesthood; the learned are not be confused with a class set apart to handle the mysteries of God. Further, it is clear that the learned throughout the centuries argued among themselves, so that a distinction between "good" and "bad" or "better" and "worse" opinion has always been an aspect of the practice of Shariʿa reasoning. What is required is the ability to read texts, preferably in Arabic, and the willingness to engage in argument. Given the increased availability of books and higher levels of literacy common to historically Islamic as well as other modern societies, why should the merchants and schoolteachers, soldiers and government officials associated with the Muslim Brothers or Jamaʿat-i Islami wait for the scholars of al-Azhar or other institutions to render opinions? If the Qurʾan indicates that God changes the condition of a people only when they change themselves, then perhaps the call of the present time is to action on the part of each and all the Muslims. That, at any rate, would seem to be the heritage of Hasan al-Banna and Abuʾl aʿla Mawdudi.

And so began a new chapter in the history of Shariʿa reasoning. This chapter is still unfolding. We see sections of it in the career of the Egyptian writer, martyr for the cause of the Muslim Brothers, Sayyid Qutb.[67] We see further sections in the arguments advanced by members of the Islamic Group, connected with the assassination of Egyptian President Anwar Sadat in 1981, and in the activity of the "Afghani Arabs" whose consciousness formed in connection with the teaching of Abdullah Azam during the fight to repel Soviet forces during the 1980s.[68] And, in that connection, we see the continuation of this chapter in the history of Shariʿa reasoning in the career of one of the Afghani Arabs, Osama bin Laden, whose various statements are the most important example currently before us. The precise nature of his contribution, and those of other militants, is yet to be determined.

CHAPTER THREE

POLITICS, ETHICS, AND WAR IN PREMODERN ISLAM

Given the history of Shari'a reasoning, it is not surprising that we should turn to Iraq for an early example of the ways Muslim scholars dealt with questions of war. The Qur'an, of course, contains passages justifying military force, as do standard accounts of the Prophet's life and work. In the context of struggle between the early Muslims and their Qurayshi opponents, these sources suggest a developing sense that fighting is an appropriate means by which Muslims should seek to secure the right to order life according to divine directives. The notion of a just war is therefore an aspect of the foundational narrative of Islam.[1]

Similarly, we know that questions about the justice of fighting emerged in the context of the early conquests or campaigns to "open" neighboring territories to Islamic governance. The notion of the Prophet's letter to the rulers of Byzantium and other empires of late antiquity is instructive in this regard, as are the stories of arguments between 'Ali and others regarding the proper mode of response to Mu'awiya, the Kharijites, and other perpetrators of civil strife. Many of the texts cited as precedents in the developing discourse associated with Shari'a reasoning are in fact reports of actions taken, or of arguments confirmed or denied, in relation to the justification and conduct of war in this early period of Muslim expansion and self-definition. The brief chapter on *jihad* in the *Muwatta* of Malik ibn Anas is instructive.[2] It contains a collection of reports regarding the example set by the Prophet and his companions. Topics range from the advisability of taking copies of the Qur'an into enemy territory, to the distribution of war prizes and the proper care of horses. Overall, the point is to suggest the importance of participation in fighting under those conditions and according to those norms consistent with the notion of submission to the will of God. Thus we find Muhammad saying: "The man who fights in the cause of the Lord may be compared to one who fasts and prays and is not weary of prayer or fasting, until he returns from the fighting."[3] Endurance or persistence in the task one is given, whether fighting or fasting and praying—that is the key, for one who gives his or her life to the Lord of the worlds. Or again, we find Muhammad in conversation, as follows:

> The Prophet of God said: "One who spends his wealth in the cause of the Lord will be called on at the gate of heaven—'O servant of God, this is bliss!' The man of prayer will be admitted from the prayer gate, the man of fighting will be admitted from the fighting gate, and the man of fasting from the gate of fasting." Abu Bakr al-Siddiq said: "Prophet of God, for a man who is called from one gate, there would be no trouble, but would there be one who is called from all the gates?" The Prophet of God said: "Yes, and I would hope you would be among them."[4]

Such texts provided the material for the more developed treatises of the Iraqi school. Of these, Abu Yusuf's "Book on the Land Tax," which deals with questions arising from the administration of conquered territories, seems to be the earliest. For our purposes, al-Shaybani's "Book of the Foundations," and within that work, the chapters on *al-siyar*, are more interesting and worthy of sustained analysis.[5]

From the outset it is clear that al-Shaybani's text approaches the question of war in connection with broader issues of political ethics. The term *siyar*, for example, means "movements." The movements in question are those between and within two broadly defined political-territorial associations, namely the "territory of Islam" and the "territory of war." The first of these terms indicates the area within which Islam is the dominant political reality. The second is a generic term for political-territorial associations not governed by Islam. In the territory of Islam, the ruler is a Muslim, the system of government is organized to serve the expansion of Islam, and the people within the territory are identified according to their participation in various groups, each of these defined by its relation to Islam. The primary group is Muslims, but there are also "protected people" (*ahl al-dhimma*, mainly Christians and Jews, though other groups could come under this category), "rebels" (*bughat*, indicating groups of Muslims dissenting from the policy of the established leadership), "apostates" (*al-murtadd*, meaning those who were once Muslims but have in some way disassociated themselves from the true faith), and "brigands" (*muharibun*, indicating criminals who prey off ordinary people and live as "highwaymen"). In the territory of war, the overarching category is *harbi* (roughly, "war person"). Subcategories, for example women, children, the elderly, or, in some cases, Muslims residing in the territory of war, are referred to in discussions of the means of war, especially with respect to the protection of noncombatants. Al-Shaybani and his colleagues are thus concerned with the justification and conduct of war in the context of the kind of political-territorial arrangement outlined in previous chapters. Their judgments are developed in response to questions like "What is the proper behavior for Muslim fighters who cross into the territory of war?" or "What is the appropriate way to respond to Muslim rebels?"

War is a means to a political end, which is the establishment and governance of a political-territorial association governed by Islam. We may take this further: the establishment of an Islamic state is itself a means by which the Muslim community can carry out its divinely mandated mission of calling humanity to the relationship with God signified by submission, *al-islam*. In this connection, war is a means to a political end (establishing an Islamic state), which is itself a means to an overarching religious goal (calling humanity to Islam). This approach suggests that there is nothing particularly good or bad about war in itself. It is a means to an end, and should be viewed as such. Resort to war is thus a matter of estimating its probable effectiveness in attaining certain goals. Notions of just conduct in war are similarly suggested by the desire to gain particular objectives.

Perhaps the simplest way to illustrate this way of thinking is to cite a report with which al-Shaybani's text begins. Here the Prophet Muhammad is depicted as giving directions to Muslim fighting forces—first, to those in command, and through them, to all members of the army. The text establishes precedents to which everyone subsequently engaged in the practice of Shari'a reasoning about war will recur.

> Whenever God's Messenger sent forth an army or a detachment, he charged its commander personally to fear God, the Most High, and he enjoined the Muslims who were with him to do good.
> He said:
> Fight in the name of God and in the path of God. Fight

the *mukaffirun* [ingrates, unbelievers]. Do not cheat or commit treachery, and do not mutilate anyone or kill children. Whenever you meet the *mushrikun* [idolaters], invite them to accept Islam. If they do, accept it and let them alone. You should then invite them to move from their territory to the territory of the émigrés. If they do so, accept it and leave them alone. Otherwise, they should be informed that they will be in the same condition as the Muslim nomads in that they are subject to God's orders as Muslims, but will receive no share of the spoil of war. If they refuse, then call upon them to pay tribute. If they do, accept it and leave them alone. If you besiege the inhabitants of a fortress or a town and they try to get you to let them surrender on the basis of God's judgment, do not do so, since you do not know what God's judgment is, but make them surrender to your judgment and then decide their case according to your own views. But if the besieged inhabitants of a fortress or a town ask you to give them a pledge in God's name or in the name of God's Messenger, you should not do so, but give the pledge in your names or the names of your fathers. For if you should ever break it, it would be an easier matter if it were in the names of you or your fathers.[6]

There is much to learn from this text, which is basic to all Shari'a reasoning on the topic of war. In it, for example, al-Shaybani and others found precedent for limiting the right of war to the head of state. Muhammad, as W. M. Watt's biographical study suggests, was both prophet and statesman.[7] Scholars in the Shari'a tradition saw in this report an example of his statesmanship, which was to be followed by those who succeeded him in the office of *khalifa*.

Resort to war requires an order from a legitimate authority. It also requires a just cause and righteous intention. So scholars in the

Shariʿa tradition understood, as the words attributed to the Prophet echoed in their minds: "Fight in the name of God and in the path of God. Fight the *mukaffirun*." The purpose of war is the establishment and governance of an Islamic state. That state, in turn, finds its purpose in connection with the Muslim community's mission of calling human beings to Islam. A just war must be tied to these purposes. And those authorizing it show that their intention is consistent in this regard by carrying out a specific protocol, namely, the issuing of an invitation to the enemy.

One might well ask how the "enemy" is identified. The Prophet's statements seem to characterize them as *mukaffirun*, which literally means "ingrates" and is typically translated "unbelievers." Staying strictly with the terms of this report, we may say that such people are identified by their response to the invitation proffered by Muslim fighters. The mention of *mushrikun* a few sentences later provides further specification. Signifying "idolaters" or perhaps more literally "associationists," the term often bears the meaning of "polytheists." That would constitute a considerable limitation regarding resort to war, since the category specifically does not include Jews and Christians. For al-Shaybani and his colleagues, however, Jews and Christians are clearly among those to whom an invitation should be issued, unless and until they pay tribute and thus come under the sway of Islam as protected people. Thus practitioners of Shariʿa reasoning would find just cause for war in the fact that a given people refused the invitation of the Muslims to accept Islam or to pay tribute and come under the protection of the Islamic state.

The procedures outlined in this report establish a notion of war as a means of pursuing goals considered legitimate. The nature of the invitation makes it clear that war is not the first or primary means recommended for pursuing these goals. Fighting is prescribed only when other means have failed. Although this formula is not a precise equivalent of the Western just-war criterion of "last resort," it is nevertheless an indication that resort to war must follow an attempt to pursue legitimate goals by nonlethal means. Thus the tradition of Shari'a reasoning already provides an equivalent to the just-war criteria of legitimate authority, just cause, righteous intention, and (at least) "timely" resort.[8] We might also see in the overarching purpose of establishing and maintaining an Islamic state something equivalent to the just-war criterion of "aim of peace." Proportionality and reasonable hope of success, by which just-war tradition instructed those deliberating about resort to war to make a good-faith effort to estimate the overall costs and benefits of fighting in particular cases, do not show up, at least in this report.

The preoccupation of the report is of course with those who are not already under the protection of the Islamic state. As we read al-Shaybani's text, we come to understand that fighting against residents of the territory of Islam is also possible, though justified with somewhat different reasons. Governance of the non-Muslim "protected" peoples, for example, is set in terms of obligations established by treaties. If the protected peoples violate their obligations, for example by initiating fighting against the armies of the Muslim state, then the ruler of the Muslims is justified in disciplining them.[9] Again, if rebels rise up against the state, fighting can be justified.[10] In either case, the overarching purpose of fighting is to restore peace, order, and justice to the territory of Islam. Protected peoples are to be returned to their rightful status. The notion that rebels are to be reconciled implies that war not only is a means of discipline, but is to be conducted in such a way that any legitimate grievances of the rebels have may be redressed. In the somewhat different case of apostates, the point is to return those who have deserted it to the way of Islam or, failing success in the matter, to prevent injustice by killing them.[11] Similarly, in the case of highwaymen the objective is the security of the territory of Islam and its residents, and the ruler is justified in undertaking those measures necessary to protect it.[12] In

an interesting demonstration of confidence, al-Shaybani and his colleagues do not address the question of fighting in response to an enemy invasion.

Right authority, just cause, and other criteria already mentioned
are not the only measures of justice in war, of course. It is noteworthy that the prophetic dicta also include matters related to law-
fulness in the conduct of war. In particular, the saying of the Prophet
includes prohibitions on cheating, treachery, mutilation, and the
killing of children. This saying, along with other reports of the
Prophet's practice, gave rise to more extensive restrictions on targeting that should be seen as analogous to the just-war tradition's concern for "discrimination" or the "immunity of noncombatants" from
direct and intentional attack. Other considerations have to do with
fair dealing in the distribution of booty and with prudence in making agreements. As mediated by al-Shaybani and his colleagues, the
report does not contain any references to weapons that may or may
not be used—the typical concern associated in the just-war tradition
with just-war proportionality.

Al-Shaybani and his colleagues built on this and other reports of
the practice of Muhammad and his companions, providing answers
to specific questions raised in their own day. In reading their collected judgments, it is important to remember their role as advisers
at the Abbasid court, which explains their preoccupation with matters of administration. The following account of an exchange between two of the early masters of al-Shaybani's school is typical:

> Abu Yusuf said: I asked Abu Hanifa concerning the food
> and fodder that may be found in the spoil and whether a
> warrior in need may take from that spoil any of the food for
> himself and fodder for his mount.
> Abu Hanifa replied: No harm in all that.[13]

Such questions have little to do with the concerns of modern military thinking. They are connected with the questions of the early

Hanafi jurists, however, because of their focus on movements between the territories of Islam and territories of war, and probably also because of movements in Muslim military organization in the direction of a professional army.[14] The question emerges in connection with the repeated consensus of the school that booty should be divided only after its return to the territory of Islam. Such judgments attempt to ensure a just distribution of the booty, and also to keep the troops focused on their military task.

In dealing with the conduct of Muslim fighters in enemy territory, however, al-Shaybani and others addressed several questions of direct relevance to our concerns. Thus we read the following:

> If the army attacks the territory of war and it is a territory that has received an invitation to accept Islam, it is commendable if the army renews the invitation, but if it fails to do so it is not wrong. The army may launch the attack by night or by day and it is permissible to burn fortifications with fire or to inundate them with water.[15]

The first sentence is reminiscent of the Prophet's directives to fighters. The requirement of an invitation is critical for establishing just cause and righteous intention. It also reveals much regarding the overarching religious and political purposes that war is supposed to serve, and places war within a hierarchy of means to be deployed in pursuit of those purposes. Here we are to envision a case in which hostilities have begun. An invitation having been given and refused, the enemy is tasting the steel of the Muslims. Should the Muslims now renew the invitation, giving the enemy a second chance to submit, or should fighting be carried to a conclusion—as al-Shaybani seems to assume, a conclusion that involves decisive victory for the Muslims? The judgment is in the nature of a recommendation: renewal of the invitation would be a good thing but is not required. Commanders in the field have discretion in this matter.

The second sentence, however, moves in a direction not covered by the Prophet's statements. Here scholars directly address the question of military means, and they do so in ways that give a great deal of latitude to the fighters. The army may fight by night or by day—the former likely involving a greater risk of injury or death to the Muslim fighters, as well as to certain people on the enemy side who fall into the category of noncombatants. Similarly, the army may utilize tactics that increase the potential for injury, specifically burning fortifications with fire or inundating them with water.

Throughout, the text reveals a strong inclination toward a position one might characterize as "military realism." Given that requirements associated with just war are satisfied, and Muslim troops are thus engaged in a legitimate war, al-Shaybani and his colleagues are willing to grant wide latitude to commanders in the determination of appropriate means. Such latitude is not total, of course. The Prophet's dicta are clear regarding cheating, treachery, mutilation, and the direct targeting of children. With respect to the last, in particular, al-Shaybani and his colleagues demonstrate respect for early Muslim practice in classifying a number of enemy persons as, in effect, immune from direct attack. In addition to children, slaves, women, old people, the lame, the blind, and the helpless insane are immune from direct attack.[16] In addition, the text indicates a concern regarding the presence, or even the possible presence, of Muslims in enemy territory—a condition that must have been ubiquitous along the border between their respective territories, where Muslim and Byzantine forces often took turns conquering and reconquering particular towns and regions.[17] Muslims in the midst of the enemy are also presumed "innocent," and thus immune from direct attack, for the lives and property of Muslims had been considered inviolable from the earliest times. Direct and intentional targeting of any of these categories of people violates an express directive of the Prophet, or a legitimate extension of that directive. It also involves dishonor to fighters, who win their reputation in direct engagement with other fighters. As the Qur'an has it (2:190):

> Fight in the path of God
> Those who are fighting you;
> But do not exceed the bounds.
> God does not approve the transgressors.

"Do not exceed the bounds"; even in the revealed text, the reference is to a warriors' code. Now al-Shaybani and his colleagues, guided by the example of the Prophet and his companions, must elaborate such a code for their day.

As they do so, their judgments indicate both their adherence to precedent and a disposition toward military realism. Thus we read the following series of questions and responses:

> I asked: Would it be permissible to inundate a city in the territory of war with water, to burn it with fire, or to attack with hurling machines even though there may be slaves, women, old men, and children in it?
>
> He replied: Yes, I would approve of doing all of that to them.
>
> I asked: Would the same be true if those people have among them Muslim prisoners of war or Muslim merchants?
>
> He replied: Yes, even if they had Muslims among them, there would be no harm to do all of that to them.
>
> I asked: Why?
>
> He replied: If the Muslims stopped attacking the inhabitants of the territory of war for any of the reasons that you have stated, they would be unable to go to war at all, for there is no city in the territory of war in which there is no one at all of these you have mentioned.[18]

One who fights should employ the means necessary to win—or so it would seem, given the final statement in this sequence of judgments.

That is not all there is to it, however. In just-war tradition, military policy can be highly realistic even while adhering faithfully to the guidelines indicated by the just-war criterion of discrimination or noncombatant immunity. As more than one interpreter suggests, the idea is that noncombatants are immune from attacks that are direct and intentional, but they cannot be immune from any harm whatsoever. An attack that is legitimate, in the sense that it is directly intended as a strike against the enemy's ability to fight, may result in the deaths of noncombatants. This outcome may be purely accidental, such as when a child happens to wander by a military target and is caught in the crossfire. It may also be foreseeable but unavoidable, as when an enemy's military resources are deployed in the midst of a civilian population. In this case the deaths of civilians are the indirect or secondary (in the sense of "unintended") consequence of the deployment of means necessary to accomplish a legitimate military purpose. Soldiers whose actions take place under such conditions are excused from the guilt associated with unjust killing. Alternatively, the actions undertaken may be described as justified, though with some regrettable (secondary) effects. This judgment of acceptability holds so long as the incidence of unintended, collateral damage is proportionate with the military objective.

Given this line of thinking, it is not surprising to read:

> I asked: If the Muslims besieged a city and its people positioned behind the walls shielded themselves with Muslim children, would it be permissible for the Muslim fighters to attack them with arrows and hurling machines?
>
> He replied: Yes, but the warriors should aim at the inhabitants of the territory of war and not the Muslim children.
>
> I asked: Would it be permissible for the Muslims to attack

them with swords and lances if the children were not intentionally aimed at?

He replied: Yes.

I asked: If the Muslim warriors attack with hurling ma-
chines and arrows, flood cities with water or burn them
with fire, thereby killing Muslim children or men, or enemy
women, old men, blind, crippled, or lunatic persons, would
the warriors be liable for blood money or acts of expiation?

He replied: They would be liable neither for blood money
nor for acts of expiation.[19]

The reasoning is quite reminiscent of Western just-war tradition and
its approach to collateral damage. One would be quite wrong, in the
case of just war or of Shari'a reasoning, to read such a passage as ne-
gating respect for the immunity of noncombatants. The point is that
the attacks are not directly and intentionally aimed at noncombatants. Without this overarching categorization, the military acts described would be unjust, and those engaging in them would need to
make restitution. As it is, al-Shaybani and his colleagues are best
read as trying to combine military realism with respect for rules that
measure just conduct in the midst of war. In so doing, they mean to
establish norms appropriate to the conduct of a professional army.

The judgments advanced by al-Shaybani became part of a historical deposit with which subsequent generations had to deal. Not
all later practitioners of Shari'a reasoning agreed with al-Shaybani.
Even the title of a text written by the great al-Tabari (d. 923), the
"Book of the Disagreement of the Practitioners of *Fiqh* on the *Jihad*
and the Tax [imposed on conquered peoples]" *(Kitab al-Ikhtilaf al-
Fuqaha fi al-jihad wa 'l-jizya'),* indicates the conversational nature of
the discipline. Shari'a reasoning about war constituted a lively discourse, in which there could be considerable disagreement about the
administrative matters so important to al-Shaybani and his col-

leagues. There could even be disagreement over whether soldiers who participated in an action in which noncombatants were unintentionally killed should perform acts of expiation, or over the precise categories of people who belonged to the class of noncombatants.[20]

In Shari'a reasoning, it is best to think of judgments like those of al-Shaybani as precedents. As recent debates in American constitutional law show, the status of precedent in legal reasoning can be contentious. That seems the case with Shari'a reasoning as well, with some opting for a stronger, some for a weaker notion of precedent. It is clear, however, that the notion of Shari'a reasoning requires a balance between respect for the judgments of one's predecessors and the need for independent judgment *(ijtihad)*, reflecting the idea that changing circumstances require fresh wisdom.

By the time of al-Mawardi (d. 1058), the preoccupation of Shari'a reasoning appears to have shifted from the details of administrative law to the superstructure of right authority. Consider, for example, the following:

> When the Caliph appoints a governor of a province or city, the latter's jurisdiction may be either general and unrestricted or special and restricted. General governorship is of two kinds: regular (by recruitment), in which appointment is made by the sovereign's free choice; and usurped, in which the appointment is made through coercion . . .
>
> Governorship by usurpation is coercion in the sense that its holder acquires by force certain districts over which the Caliph gives him a decree of appointment, assigning him their management and the maintenance of public order therein. By seizing power, the governor becomes an independent and exclusive controller of political matters and administration, while the Caliph, by his permission, becomes

the implementer of the dictates of religion, thus transform-
ing unlawfulness into legality, and the forbidden into the legitimate. Although by doing so he does not adhere closely to
the conventions of appointment in respect of conditions
and procedures, his action upholds the canon law and its
provisions in ways that are too important to be disregarded.
Thus, decisions that would normally be unacceptable in reg-
ular appointment based on choice are permissible under
usurpation and necessity, owing to the difference between
ability and incapacity.[21]

As al-Mawardi's text makes clear, he presumes that designation of
a ruler is a requirement of Shari'a; that the office must be singular
(that is, there cannot be two legitimate rulers, even if they reside in
different cities); and that the person holding leadership must have
certain qualifications, most notably descent from the Quraysh, the
clan into which the Prophet Muhammad was born. It is noteworthy,
given other trends in the Muslim community of his day, that al-
Mawardi does not require that the ruler be "of the Prophet's house-
hold" or "of the family of the Prophet (or of 'Ali)"; this was a position held by the various Shi'i groups. Al-Mawardi further stipulates
that the ruler may be either designated by his predecessor or chosen
by electors. The latter may be any of the number of Muslims who are
truthful, who possess knowledge of the required characteristics of
the ruler, and whose prudence and wisdom make it likely that they
will choose the right person. As a matter of custom, he writes, this
role usually falls to the leading citizens of the capital of the territory
of Islam.

Thus far, there is nothing controversial about al-Mawardi's argument. Indeed, it reflects the standard presentation of Abbasid imperial practice. Similarly, when al-Mawardi comments on "the ministry" (al-wizara), noting that appointment to this office is the right of

the sovereign ruler and that appointment may constitute the minister's authority as "delegated" or "executive," he seems to reflect the standing practice of the Abbasid court. No ruler is able to administer the day-to-day affairs of a far-flung empire; the Abbasid caliphs tended to assign many of these tasks to court advisers, the most authoritative of whom held positions as ministers. "Delegated" authority of a minister, al-Mawardi says, suggests greater independence; "executive" authority indicates that the ruler himself is setting policy and restricting ministerial practice to carrying out his orders.

It is in the comments on "governors" that al-Mawardi's reasoning becomes creative. Many, perhaps most, commentators read his notion of a governor "appointed" by coercion as a pure example of *realpolitik*.[22] It was in fact the case from about 935 on that no Abbasid ruler really exercised power in the style of the High Caliphate. Instead, power was concentrated in the provinces of the empire, whose governors commanded armies, collected taxes, and generally carried out the duties of statecraft. Among these, the more powerful carved out larger territorial units than Abbasid practice allowed. Powerless to remove such "usurpers," what was the caliph to do? By al-Mawardi's lights, the caliph should do his duty, namely, maintain the unity of the territory of Islam by authorizing such governors to rule as agents of the Abbasid court. However irregular such a strategy may seem, he writes, a caliph who acts in this way "upholds the Shari'a and its provisions in ways that are too important to be disregarded." In effect, the ruler "delegates" authority to the usurping governor. The latter thereby achieves legitimation, and the former hopes to preserve the unity of Islam, as is his charge. Governors must therefore "uphold the office of the sovereign [the caliph] as a vicar of prophecy and manager of religious affairs, in order to fulfill the legal requirement of ensuring its existence and preserving the rights arising therefrom."[23] Insofar as the usurper lacks formal qualifications, "it is up to the Caliph to sanction his appointment as a means of winning him over and putting an end to his disobedience and intransigence."[24] In certain conditions, the caliph may even appoint a minister to work with the usurper and to exercise executive power.

With respect to war, al-Mawardi's judgment legitimating governorship by usurpation is a crucial modification in the notion of right authority. "General" governorship, in particular, comes with full power to make war.[25] There is a sense in which one who seizes power becomes the caliph's designated minister for political and military affairs. After al-Mawardi's time (and even, to some extent, during his lifetime), leaders of the Seljuq Turks played such a role, holding positions as *wazir* (minister) or *al-sultan* (the power) in concert with the Abbasid caliphs' role as guardian of Islam.[26]

If general governorship comes with the full power to make war, it also imposes duties. Al-Mawardi's comments on this matter are a subject for study in themselves. As commander, the general governor sees to the formation, equipping, and morale of a fighting force. He manages fighting against "the idolaters in enemy territory," as well as against apostates, rebels, and brigands within the territory of Islam. In the first group, al-Mawardi designates two classes: "those who have received the call to Islam but rejected it and turned away from it" and "those whom the call to Islam has not reached."[27] The former are subject to attack or the threat of attack at any time, depending on the commander's sense of what is best. The latter, of whom there would be "very few today on account of the victory the Almighty has accorded His Prophet's mission, unless there be nations unknown to us beyond the Turks and Greeks we meet in eastern deserts and remote western areas," cannot be subjected to a surprise attack.[28] The Prophet stipulated that an invitation is required before fighting. For al-Mawardi, such an invitation includes the presentation of material intended to persuade the unbelievers of the truth of Islam: "making the Prophet's miracles known to them, and informing them of such arguments as would make them to respond favorably."[29] In a style indicative of the conversational nature of Shari'a reasoning, he notes that, should a commander (improperly) initiate fighting without making an attempt to persuade such an uninformed enemy about the truth of Islam, "he will owe them blood-money, which, according to the more correct view in the Shafi'i school, is equal to that due to Muslims, although it has been suggested that it should be the same as the various amounts of compensation paid to the heathens according to their different beliefs. Abu Hanifa has, on the other hand, said: 'There is no compensation for killing them, and their lives are to be taken freely.'"[30] One must cite precedents in Shari'a reasoning; one need not follow each and all.

"Killing women and children is not permitted in war or otherwise so long as they do not fight, owing to the Prophet's injunction against killing them . . . God's Prophet . . . has also forbidden the killing of servants and slaves."[31] Here al-Mawardi acknowledges the authority of the Prophet's directives delimiting the range of legitimate targets. He also moves toward the identification of a general principle that we might see as underlying the listing of groups that fighters are not supposed to target for direct attack. The point is not simply that the Prophet identified women, children, and others as protected groups. Rather, these persons are listed because, as a general matter, they "do not fight." Indeed, if women or children do take up arms, they "should be fought and killed," albeit in ways that maintain honor.[32] In some ways al-Mawardi's account of the limits placed on just killing is more stringent than that of al-Shaybani and his colleagues. Al-Mawardi argues that Muslim fighters faced with an enemy that shields itself with Muslims should stop killing; if the Muslim fighters find it impossible to continue without killing the Muslim shields, they should stop attacking. Should the enemy take advantage of this proscription, surrounding the Muslim army while still protecting itself with Muslim hostages, the Muslim fighters should defend themselves, trying all the while to avoid killing their co-religionists; if one of the hostages is killed, the killer must pay blood money and/or make expiation, depending on whether he knew the religious identity of the one killed.[33]

Al-Mawardi shows both the continuity and change characteristic of Shari'a reasoning about war. Subsequent writers provide further illustration. Shortly after al-Mawardi's death in 1058, for example, al-Sulami of Damascus (d. 1106) produced the *Kitab al-Jihad* (Book on Armed Struggle). Al-Sulami was not and is not widely known for his practice of Shari'a reasoning; he was evidently an instructor in Arabic language and letters at the Grand Mosque in his home city. Much of his book on *jihad* has to do with language intended to evoke action by Muslims, especially those in positions of authority, in response to incursions into the territory of Islam by *al-faranj,* the Franks—that is, the Crusader armies. Nevertheless, al-Sulami's mode of reasoning and above all his indication of the formal duty to fight indicates participation in the practice of Shari'a reasoning.[34]

For our interests, it is particularly striking that al-Sulami's preoccupation is with defensive or "imposed" war. Al-Shaybani and other early Hanafi jurists seem entirely unconcerned about fighting in a context defined by the success of an external, non-Muslim enemy in occupying Muslim territory. For al-Shaybani and his colleagues, the focus of war with non-Muslims had to do with the ways Muslim fighters should conduct themselves during an incursion into enemy territory. Similarly, al-Mawardi's preoccupation is with the rights and wrongs of war aimed at expanding the territory in which Islam is established. His brief mention of the right of a governor "with limited powers" whose province is located on the border between the territory of Islam and the territory of war to fight non-Muslims if they strike first, and without obtaining the caliph's authorization, is exceptional.[35]

With al-Sulami, we have a different idea, and a different context:

the Crusades. Specifically, he writes in response to the First Crusade, which by 1099 yielded Christian control of Jerusalem, as well as significant portions of greater Syria.[36] Al-Sulami argues that the duty to extend the territory of Islam, expressed at least through an annual expedition organized and led by the ruler, was established by the Prophet and the early caliphs. Subsequent rulers followed this custom, until a particular caliph (unnamed in the text) failed to carry through, either through simple neglect or for reasons of state. Thereafter others failed in the custom for similar reasons. The incursions of Franks into Islamic territory are a judgment of God, executed in response to this sin of omission. And now, al-Sulami says, Muslims find themselves in a distinctive situation, which affects how they construe the duty to struggle for justice. Citing al-Shafi'i, al-Sulami notes that the raising of an army for purposes of carrying out expeditions into enemy territory is the minimum obligation of the Muslim ruler, and that if sufficient forces are not raised, it becomes the duty of those "in the rear" to fulfill God's command. The duty of fighting (al-Sulami uses the term *ghazw,* raiding) is, in cases of necessity, incumbent upon all the members of the community. The current situation, in which enemy forces are making inroads into the territory of Islam, constitutes such a case. With further citations from al-Ghazali (d. 1111), the greatest scholar of his day, al-Sulami goes on to stipulate that if a town in, say, Syria is attacked by the Franks and cannot defend itself, all the other (Muslim) cities of the region are obligated to come to its aid. Supporting and extending his argument with additional Shari'a references, he concludes with the judgment that "the Book [the Qur'an], the example of the Prophet, and the consensus [of representative practitioners of Shari'a reasoning] with respect to the community's obligation to fight makes clear that in cases of necessity, this duty becomes one of the individual duties."[37] As the last reference makes clear, al-Sulami's judgment is that in the type of context he describes, the duty to fight is like the duty of fasting. Only those unable by reason of sickness or other incapacity may be excused from its performance.

It seems unlikely that al-Sulami was the first to argue in this way. However, the precedents he cites do not say precisely that fighting becomes an "individual duty." Rather, they suggest that those who are "distant" from the affected area are called to step forward and give aid. Just how much distance there is between this and al-Sulami's judgment that the incursions of the Franks make fighting an individual duty is a matter in need of further exploration.

In any case, by the time one gets to the work of Ibn Taymiyya (d. 1328), reference to fighting as an individual duty in circumstances of emergency seems to come easily. If, he writes, the enemy attacks the Muslims, then the duty to fight becomes a personal or individual duty for both "those against whom the attack was made and those not directly affected by it."[38] Citing the Qur'an and the example of the Prophet, this scholar, much of whose career was spent in the prisons of those ruling in Damascus and in Cairo, writes that every Muslim must provide assistance, even if he is not a professional soldier. In the battle of the Trench (627), when the Muslims in Medina came under siege, "God permitted none to abandon the jihad." Once the siege was broken, and fighting involved pursuit of the enemy, a different set of judgments prevailed. Ibn Taymiyya writes that the defense of Medina "was a war to defend the religion, the family honour and the lives [of community members]; an obligatory fighting . . . [Pursuit of the enemy following the siege] was voluntary fighting to increase the prestige of the religion and frighten the enemy."[39]

Different circumstances suggest distinctive judgments about the nature of the duty to fight. Do they suggest distinctive rules? The answer, it seems, is no. Those who "do not constitute a defensive or offensive power, like the women, the children, the monks, old people, the blind and the permanently disabled should not be fought."[40] This general rule is supported as the consensus of the Muslims, the example of the Prophet, and Qur'an 2:190: "fight in the way of God against those who fight against you, but do not commit aggression. Truly, God does not love those who commit aggression." Ibn Taymiyya comments that "we should only fight those who fight us, if we really want the Religion of Allah to be victorious."[41]

Ibn Taymiyya does suggest that noncombatants may forfeit their protected status if they "carry on a kind of fighting with words" or serve as spies, provide transport for munitions, or in other ways participate more directly in the enemy war effort. Earlier writers had typically stipulated that women, children, and others moved to combatant status if and when they took up arms. The principle, in either case, seems to be that those who do not, or may be presumed not to, participate in the enemy's war effort are not to be the target of direct attack by Muslim forces.[42]

This matter brings us to an emphasis that many commentators view as a special focus of Ibn Taymiyya's judgments about war. He writes that the "heaviest jihad should be directed against the unbelievers and those who refuse to abide by certain precepts, like the abstainers from paying zakat-alms and the Kharijites."[43] The case of the tax evaders has drawn attention from many students of Ibn Taymiyya's work.

Ibn Taymiyya's wording suggests the notion of fighting against apostates (al-murtadd) and rebels (al-bughat). Discussion of the rules governing fighting against these groups was an established practice of Shari'a reasoning. Al-Shaybani and his colleagues discussed the matter, as we have seen. Apostates were understood along the lines of the precedent attributed to Abu Bakr, discussed in Chapter 1. Having received a communication from a particular group regarding its intention to maintain faith in God and God's Prophet, but to forgo payment of al-zakat to the common treasury, Abu Bakr declared his intention to fight in order to compel obedience. Al-zakat, he said, was not optional for Muslims. Believers must contribute to the common treasury, administered by a legitimate authority. Those who refused to do so had "turned" (the literal meaning of *al-murtadd*) away from the faith, even if they continued to recite the basic creed and to perform obligatory prayers. Ibn Taymiyya is consistent with his predecessors on this matter, even in his discussion of "the preacher of heresy contrary to the teachings of the Book and the Sunna."[44] In either case, the wrong has to do with public departure from Islam, as established and protected by a legitimate authority. Such wrongs are connected with Qur'an 2:214 and other texts that stipulate that *fitna*, or civil strife, is more blameworthy than the shedding of blood.

Similarly with rebels. The Kharijites, whom Ibn Taymiyya mentions explicitly, were an early group understood as "secessionists" (the literal meaning of the name *al-khawarij*). According to traditions consistently cited by practitioners of Shari'a reasoning, the group seceded from the rightful leadership of 'Ali ibn Abi Talib (d. 661), the fourth successor to the Prophet. Their secession was motivated by an objection to 'Ali's approach to conflict with Mu'awiya, governor of Syria and an opponent of 'Ali. In justifying their actions, the Kharijites cited Qur'anic texts. They understood themselves as advocates for justice and saw others as moral slackers, in need of encouragement or, in some cases, of punishment. 'Ali responded with a mixture of persuasion and force, the goal being to limit the damage done by this group of "irregular fighters" while at the same time hoping for reconciliation. Over time the Kharijites became a standard reference for those who, while well-motivated, committed acts that did more harm than good. In justifying fighting against such persons, Ibn Taymiyya again was consistent with Shari'a precedent. It is the duty of a Muslim ruler to establish and protect the practice of Islam. Such a ruler does not use military force to make new converts. Rather, the ruler fights to extend or protect the hegemony of Islamic values in what one might call "geopolitical space." Even within that space, fighting is not authorized to force conversion. As

Ibn Taymiyya writes, the protected peoples *(ahl al-dhimma),* for example Jews and Christians living under Muslim rule, may be fought only if they violate the terms of their treaty with the Muslim ruler. Their difference in religion is not itself a justification for fighting.[45]

Force is authorized, however, to protect the establishment of Islam. So apostates and rebels are seen as a greater threat than those unbelievers who live outside the boundaries of the Islamic state. A legitimate ruler is authorized, even required, to use force to limit the ability of such groups to "spread corruption in the earth" (Qur'an 5:33).

Thus far Ibn Taymiyya seems consistent with his predecessors in the practice of Shari'a reasoning. He does write as one intent on purifying the practice of Islam; his treatise on the institution of *al-hisba,* or the public exhortation of Muslims to fulfill their duties, is indicative of this concern, as are numerous tracts and formal Shari'a opinions about the danger of practices that depart from true Islam.[46] For Ibn Taymiyya, any Muslim refusing to perform those duties or to observe those prohibitions established by Shari'a reasoning is subject to punishment. If such refusal is a matter of performance only, the miscreant may be considered an unbeliever, an apostate, or a "half Muslim"—this, Ibn Taymiyya writes, is a matter on which Shari'a authorities disagree. If refusal is accompanied by explicit statements to the effect that regulations established by Shari'a reasoning do not hold, the person is simply an unbeliever. In any case, however, punishment does not rise to the level of fighting unless departure from duty is accompanied by armed resistance. If such resistance is present, then punishment with fighting is necessary. Depending on the circumstance, participation in fighting to discipline those who have departed from their duties may be a matter for the standing army, or it may be an individual duty incumbent on each and every Muslim.[47]

Ibn Taymiyya's zeal for purity in Islamic practice may or may not involve an expansion of the typical concerns of Shari'a reasoning. Where he does seem a bit different from his predecessors is in his construal of the relations between rulers and subjects. For Ibn Taymiyya, these are reciprocal. Rulers owe it to their subjects to provide leadership, to govern wisely, to establish institutions that will ensure that subjects understand their duties and are encouraged to fulfill them.

Subjects owe obedience; this is a standard judgment of Shari'a reasoning. At some times and in some places subjects are compelled to "omit to obey," as when a ruler commands something contrary to the Qur'an and the example of the Prophet. This again is standard. Ibn Taymiyya takes this thinking further, however; he says that it is a duty of subjects to remind rulers of the demands of obedience to God's law. Indeed, Ibn Taymiyya presumes that "commanding right and forbidding wrong" is a task in which all Muslims have a part. Certainly, not all Muslims are public officials with rights and duties associated with enforcement of the Shari'a. But all Muslims do have a share in the task of commanding good and forbidding evil, and this notion may be understood in ways that expand the rights of subjects in relation to rulers. For rulers, as well as subjects, may be negligent in their duties. Rulers, as well as subjects, may depart from Islam in ways suggestive of apostasy, rebellion, or unbelief. When this situation holds, who has the duty, and with it the right, of punishing the ruler? The establishment of legitimate authority, Ibn Taymiyya holds, is a requirement of the Shari'a. Who will establish such authority if and when those who hold the reins of power are themselves corrupt?

It is difficult to see Ibn Taymiyya as a full-blown advocate of just revolution. He wrote in a time when the unified caliphate presumed by his predecessors no longer existed. With the invasion of the Mongols, the Abbasid caliphate proved unsustainable, even in the special role envisioned by al-Mawardi. The Muslim state was in a time of transition, with competition between various claimants to power. The Mamluk sultanate in Cairo was preeminent. The Mongols themselves were in transition; having conquered large portions of the territory of Islam, they appeared to be quintessential unbelievers. They were, however, in the process of converting to Islam, and by the time of Ibn Taymiyya they governed their portion of the territory of Islam by a kind of mixed legal regime. Judgments associated with the Shariʿa were set alongside those characteristic of the Mongol code of honor. In this context, Ibn Taymiyya's concerns for pure Islamic practice seem to suggest the necessity of fighting against the Mongols, and in certain opinions he appears to say that such fighting is a duty for Muslims. Such judgments are put forth with care, however; much depends on the trajectory of the Mongol state with respect to adherence to Shariʿa norms. Thus the transitional nature of authority in Ibn Taymiyya's time makes it difficult to read his judgments as constitutive of a theory of just revolution.[48]

Sunni and Shiʿi Perspectives

At this point it is worth pausing for a brief discussion of the differences between Sunni and Shiʿi approaches to matters of politics and war. As we have seen, the Shiʿi insistence that leadership rightly belongs to the designated leader or imam had implications for the practice of Shariʿa reasoning—specifically, for the idea that the authority of *ahadith* needed careful examination, since one could not trust that people who rejected ʿAli and his successors would faithfully transmit the *sunna* of the Prophet. Trustworthy or "sound" reports were those transmitted by, or on the authority of, one or more of the imams. Practically speaking, this meant that the biographies of those mentioned as transmitters should be scrutinized, since even the inclusion of the name of a designated imam rested on the witness of a subsequent reporter. Indeed, in the case of Twelver Shiʿism, a small group of community leaders, noted for learning and piety, came to serve as "deputies" of the Hidden Imam, and thus to function as authorities in his stead, albeit with certain restrictions tied to the fact that, despite their standing as the imam's representatives, "they" were not "he."

The role of the ʿulama as, in some sense, deputies of the Twelfth Imam is the topic of a wide-ranging study by Abdulaziz Sachedina, *The Just Ruler in Shiʿite Islam*.[49] Sachedina shows that the precise dimensions of the authority attached to this designation are controversial. Nevertheless, it is clear that the Shiʿi ʿulama perceived themselves as advisers to rulers. In that capacity, they issued opinions intended to "bind and loose," that is, to set limits upon and provide justifications for the exercise of political and military authority by those wielding power.

In connection with the Sunni precedents outlined in this chapter, the most important of these opinions have to do with limiting the ruler's authority to initiate military action to instances in which war is "imposed" by the action, or threatened action, of an enemy. The great work of al-Muhaqqiq al-Hilli (d. 1277), for example, begins with a description of the rules of engagement which is compatible with the judgments offered by al-Shaybani, al-Mawardi, and others described above. Al-Hilli then makes clear, however, that he is describing the justification and conduct of fighting ordered by the designated leader, who, as the imam of his age, is protected from the commission of serious sin, and thus knows when war is a proper means of statecraft. In the absence of the designated leader, his deputies are not authorized to carry out wars in which the intention is to expand Islamic territory. The deputies' authority is limited to situations in which the invasion or threat of invasion by a non-Muslim power provides a context for "defensive" war.

In such a context, the normal rules governing the conduct of Muslim forces hold. That is, those fighting in order to defend the territory of Islam are to avoid directly targeting noncombatants, and to use weapons and tactics that are proportionate to the task. If the progress of enemy forces raises the specter of an emergency, then the ruler, and with him the Shiʿi ʿulama, call for help from neighboring Muslim rulers.

The Shiʿi trajectory, like the Sunni, thus establishes a set of precedents for the justification and conduct of war. The distinctively Shiʿi emphasis on leadership has important implications for the notion of right authority, however. As in the case of Ibn Taymiyya's writings, the Shiʿi emphasis on leadership is critical for an understanding of contemporary militancy, not least in the writings of the late Ayatollah Khomeini. Indeed, the logic of contemporary Muslim argument makes clear the role of precedent in Shariʿa reasoning about politics and war. As a *living* tradition, Islamic judgments about the order of society and the uses of military force always respond to new situations. Yet both the shape of argument and the form of reasoning employed by militants and their critics alike rely upon interpreting and applying historical, textual precedents set by premodern scholars— or, even better, by the Qurʾanic and Prophetic precedents to which these scholars referred. Shariʿa reasoning is a system of argument about the fit that obtains between precedents and the facts of political life. And so Muslim arguments about war and politics in contemporary settings proceed just as they did in preceding centuries: by asking "What guidance has God provided for the conduct of life?" "What is the path that leads to refreshment" corresponding to the example of the Prophet and the true nature of human beings?[50]

CHAPTER FOUR

ARMED RESISTANCE AND ISLAMIC TRADITION

Shari'a reasoning involves argument about precedent. The process, however, involves more than simply the citation of texts; it involves a search for a fit between history and present circumstance, or between approved texts and new contexts. A practitioner who believes that he or she has discovered such a fit tries to persuade others. The proof that a particular opinion is correct cannot be reduced to one's ability to persuade one's fellows. Over time, however, the strongest opinions are those that command a consensus among believers.

Since the eighteenth century, Muslim societies have been under stress. In south Asia and northern Africa, in the Balkans and Afghanistan, in the heartland of Islamic civilization and in the Arabian Peninsula itself, Muslims have felt the influence of European and North American—that is to say, non-Muslim—power. They have responded in a variety of ways, many of which involve the practice of

Shari'a reasoning, with the question "What is God's guidance for the new situation?" The old, standard judgments about politics and war were articulated by 'ulama in the context of an Islamic, imperial state. Dedicated to rule by the Shari'a, this state required that Muslims rule or provide oversight to the non-Muslims living under their protection. Lively consultation between recognized scholars and political leaders served to delimit heresy, blasphemy, and other evils within the territory of Islam. Further, rulers and ruled alike understood their duty to include the spread of Islamic government, and thus of the benefits of rule by the law of God, to those living outside the boundaries of Islamic territory. Eventually the world would be coextensive with the blessed territory of Islam—or so Muslims hoped. And they did not believe that in this, they were seeking power for the sake of power. How could that be the case, when Islam was the natural religion of humanity?

The power of Europe, and eventually of the United States, challenged the assumption of Muslim hegemony. In this context, the practice of Shari'a reasoning involved a search for precedents able to provide guidance for a time of diminished power. The writings of Ibn Taymiyya would provide an important source, though of course not the only one. To this day, the texts of militants are filled with references to this "shaykh al-Islam," that is, this "first among equals" in the tradition of Shari'a reasoning. The World Islamic Front *Declaration on Armed Struggle against Jews and Crusaders* assigns this status to Ibn Taymiyya, then quotes from his book on the Shari'a approach to governance: "As for fighting to repel [that is, 'imposed' war], it is aimed at defending sanctity and religion, and is by consensus an obligation. Nothing is more sacred than belief except repulsing an enemy which is attacking religion and life."[1] Muhammad al-Faraj's *Al-Faridah al-Ghaibah*, or *The Neglected Duty*, described as the "testament" of those who assassinated Egyptian President Anwar Sadat, connects Ibn Taymiyya's analysis of the apostasy of the Mongols to

Sadat's administration, and argues that fighting such criminals is a duty that most Muslims are neglecting. The author describes this duty as "hidden," in that most Muslims do not "see" it, and announces that he and his colleagues must bring it to light. Similarly, the testament of Ayman al-Zawahiri, known as "bin Laden's physician," goes to great lengths in arguing that the circumstance of present Muslims is identical with that of Ibn Taymiyya and his contemporaries, as do the statements of al-Qaʿida spokesman Sulayman Abu Ghayth and of bin Laden himself. Clearly, Ibn Taymiyya has caught the imagination of many involved in contemporary resistance movements.[2]

And indeed Ibn Taymiyya's opinions anticipated many of the peculiar stresses that would attend Islamic political ethics beginning in the mid to late eighteenth century. The various campaigns inspired by the teachings of Muhammad ibn ʿabd al-Wahhab and his followers directly challenged the claim of the Ottoman rulers, who presented themselves as successors to the Abbasids, to embody the Islamic ideal of political justice, on the ground that the Ottomans failed to implement Shariʿa judgments. The Ottoman state should thus be regarded as fostering "unbelief" (*kufr*), a category that included hypocrisy, idolatry, and apostasy. In the absence of a just polity, the Wahhabiyya claimed the right of a rightly guided vanguard to engage in armed struggle against these manifestations of unbelief in order to establish an Islamic state.[3]

The example of Shah ʿAbd al-ʿAziz (d. 1824) in the Indian subcontinent is also instructive. As British dominance expanded in the subcontinent, Muslims understood that India would no longer be ruled by the Mughal elite, or by any other power dedicated to the establishment of Islamic values. ʿAbd al-ʿAziz, the scion of a family long recognized for its importance among the learned, issued a Shariʿa opinion declaring that India could no longer be regarded as *dar al-Islam;* that is, the existing mode of governance should not be viewed as an embodiment of traditional notions of political justice. ʿAbd al-ʿAziz's judgment was not clear regarding the appropriate Muslim response. Some, however, took him to authorize armed resistance, and the series of revolts culminating in the Sepoy Mutiny of 1857 is usually interpreted along these lines.[4] Here we must recall the force of Shariʿa precedents: the establishment of an order capable of sustaining justice is obligatory. If one presumes, in a manner consistent with most precedents, that "just order" and "state in which an Islamic establishment prevails" are synonymous, then it would seem to follow that the British are invaders, and that fighting against them is an obligation. Further, the nature of the fighting is such that one might consider it analogous to the historical notion of imposed war, so that the duty to fight is in some way an individual duty.

These two cases provide early examples of how Muslims living in the shadow of colonialism related justifications of armed resistance to the tradition of Shariʿa reasoning. In the Wahhabi-Saudi case, precedents were construed to justify fighting against those who claimed to be Muslims but who were somehow neglectful of their duty. Fighting was justified to bring them into compliance or to punish unbelief, with the overall purpose of restoring just public order. The major difficulty here involves the designation of right authority. All the precedents discussed thus far envision such fighting as the result of a decision made by public officials. For Muhammad ʿAbd al-Wahhab and, later, for a Wahhabi-Saudi coalition to claim the right to bypass or otherwise ignore the Ottomans would seem a violation of the consensus of the learned.

The Indian resistance to the British saw the development of precedents relative to imposed war. The logic is fairly straightforward: the British are non-Muslim invaders, and they exercise power in ways that render Islamic authorities impotent. The issue is whether Muslims can and should live under the protection of a regime that has no intention of maintaining an Islamic establishment. ʿAbd al-ʿAziz himself does not provide a clear answer to this question. His direct focus is on classification: Is British India to be regarded as an Islamic state (a just political order) or not? Those who organized popular resistance movements in response to ʿAbd al-ʿAziz's negative answer would seem analogous to the publicists who called on Muslims to fight against the Crusaders in Syro-Palestine, or to Salah al-Din (Saladin) as the leader of an active and armed resistance to al-faranj.[5] Again, however, the analogy is imperfect. Shariʿa precedents cast the duty to fight in an imposed war as an individual duty. That terminology does not appear to suggest a popular uprising, however. Despite the language, premodern authorities presume a resistance organized by publicly established authorities. The notion of a popular resistance seems to require additional justification.

Current discussions of armed resistance attempt to fill this gap. The various pronouncements of militant Islamic groups, including those with which the United States and its allies are engaged in the war on terror, are best seen as attempts to stretch the precedents set by important practitioners of Shariʿa reasoning in ways that address the "facts" of contemporary international politics. The "facts," of course, are presented in ways that are controversial. Similarly, the arguments advanced, and the actions justified in such pronouncements, are susceptible of criticism *on Shariʿa grounds*. We should understand the arguments made by Osama bin Laden and other militants as genuine attempts to find guidance by engaging longstanding Muslim tradition. At the same time, it is clear that the framework of Shariʿa reasoning is one in which disagreement is not only possible, but to be expected. Thus, even as we do well to analyze the texts produced by contemporary militants—advocates of the "new *jihad*," who style themselves inheritors of the mantle of Shariʿa reasoning—we also do well to raise questions about their arguments and, in particular, to note the kinds of criticisms made by other Muslims who are equally engaged by the notion of following divine guidance.

Three examples of militant argument are instructive: *The Ne-*

glected Duty (1981), the Charter of Hamas (1988), and the *Declaration on Armed Struggle against Jews and Crusaders* (1998). Each attempts to provide a Shariʿa justification for popular, armed resistance by Muslims. Each calls forth responses, also crafted in the style of Shariʿa reasoning. The analysis highlights the commitment of Muslims in the twentieth and twenty-first centuries to think about political responsibility in ways consonant with the practice of Shariʿa reasoning. It also highlights the "crisis" of this practice—a condition of danger and opportunity, in which one of the most important components is the movement of the practice of Shariʿa reasoning beyond the small circle of elite scholars bearing the authority of "the learned" to a larger circle, in which literate and professional Muslims consider themselves qualified to engage in arguments about the guidance of God.

Arguments for Resistance

The Neglected Duty, which appeared after the arrest and trial of activists accused of killing President Anwar Sadat, was immediately described as the "testament of Sadat's assassins." It became a standard reference in accounts of the rise of militant Islam. The treatise is an attempt to develop a justification of armed resistance by utilizing the sources and techniques of Shariʿa reasoning.[6]

The author alludes to "a well-established rule of Islamic Law that the punishment of an apostate will be heavier than the punishment of someone who is by origin an unbeliever."[7] The background of the text is twofold: the precedent set by premodern *ʿulama,* and the political situation posed by Sadat's policies. Of the latter, the most important concerns are with the recognition and establishment of formal relations between Egypt and the state of Israel. In November 1977 Sadat visited Israel and addressed the Knesset—a first for an Arab head of state. Motivated by a desire to improve relations with the United States, and thus to secure aid for Egypt's ailing economy, Sadat broke ranks with a generation of Arab leaders. His boldness achieved the desired end: in 1978, President Jimmy Carter brought Sadat to Camp David for meetings with Israeli Prime Minister Menachem Begin. The resulting treaty established formal links between Egypt and Israel, and came with promises of large increases in American aid. For his efforts, Sadat shared the Noble Peace Prize with Carter and Begin. He also ensured that militants would judge him an apostate.

The charge against Sadat was that the treaty with Israel violated Shari'a precedents by ceding Islamic territory to an enemy. This was not the sole offense. Sadat's policies toward Egyptian Christians and his readiness to open Egypt to foreign investment also suggested a willingness to compromise the Islamic character of Egyptian society. As to the "heavier penalty" assigned for apostasy, *The Neglected Duty* reasons that an apostate is in breach of a contract with God, and must repent (that is, return to compliance with the terms of the contract) or be killed. If one is speaking of the apostasy of a ruler, then this judgment (that is, that the apostate must return to compliance or be killed) translates into a justification of armed struggle.

The Neglected Duty continues: precedent teaches that any "group of people that rebels against any single precept of the clear and established judgments of Islam must be fought . . . even if the members of the group pronounce the Islamic Confession of Faith." Muhammad al-Faraj notes standard examples, such as the authorization of fighting by Abu Bakr (d. 634), the first caliph following the Prophet's death in 632. If anyone or any group refuses "to apply [established precedents] on matters of life and property, or merchandise and commodities of any kind," they must be fought.[8]

Who are the apostates spoken of in the text? Alongside the Egyptian president, "The Rulers of this age are in apostasy from Islam . . . They carry nothing from Islam but their names."[9] The crime of which established leaders are guilty is "innovation" *(bid'a)*: they are introducing legislation that is not founded in (not only not consistent with, but not derived from) recognized Shari'a sources. They govern by a "mixed regime" in which laws are derived from European codes and customary law, as well as from Shari'a sources. Leaders who do such things—for example, concluding peace treaties of the type negotiated by Sadat—no longer deserve respect. They must be fought. One who is guilty of innovation "no longer has the qualifications needed in a Leader. To obey such a person is no longer obligatory, and the Muslims have the duty to revolt against him and depose him, to put a just leader in his place when they are able to do so."[10]

The argument as conceived supports a right of the Muslims to revolt, in the name of fulfilling the obligation to establish a just political order. In terms of Shari'a precedents, this is a difficult judgment. We have already seen that there are numerous texts suggesting that in a context in which a ruler is impious or otherwise unjust, the duty of Muslims is to withhold obedience. But such withholding is a rather different mode of action from a popular uprising, particularly one construed in terms of enforcing Shari'a provisions for the punishment of a crime (in this case, apostasy). The author acknowledges that a judgment supportive of popular revolution is difficult, saying that it is wrong in almost every case. The one exception occurs when the ruler "suddenly becomes an unbeliever" through a "public display."[11] It is not certain that the author has adduced a proof that is convincing within the framework of Shari'a reasoning. Thus, in what might be considered the author's ultimate appeal, he fuses the argument about the punishment of apostates with language suggestive of fighting against an invading power, so as to suggest an emergency situation: the enemy now "lives right in the middle" of Islamic territory and "has got hold of the reins of power, for this enemy is the rulers who have seized the leadership of the Muslims." In such a case, the necessity of fighting against apostates is elevated to the point where "waging armed struggle against them is an individual duty . . . it is thus similar to prayer and fasting."[12] As the title of the treatise hints, the "neglect" of the duty to fight is itself a sin, at least of omission.

The argument remains difficult. It is not an impossible argument, however, and it is interesting that when more established members of the learned class, including the Shaykh al-Azhar, highest authority among the "established" *ulama* in Egypt (and, by some accounts, in the world of Sunni Islam), responded to *The Neglected Duty*, they did not criticize this argument directly.[13] Rather, they questioned its prudence, asking the author and his associates to consider that armed rebellion against the Egyptian state might well lead to widespread violence in which innocent people would be killed. Drawing on historical analogies, the Shaykh al-Azhar explicitly reminded the militants of the notorious *khawarij,* those who "seceded" from those fighting in support of 'Ali, and who in Islamic history represent the archetypal example of what might be called "excess of zeal": they are well-meaning, devoted to justice, but imprudent and thus end up causing more harm than good. The al-Azhar critique focuses less on *The Neglected Duty's* claim that a vanguard has authority to fight than on the question of whether armed resistance will violate the norms of honorable combat.

By contrast with *The Neglected Duty,* the Charter of Hamas presents the case for armed resistance as a matter of imposed war.[14] The precedents cited by the authors do not speak about the punishment of apostasy. Rather, the argument proceeds largely on the basis of an analogy with the Crusades. The actions of colonial powers in the nineteenth and twentieth centuries are interpreted as picking up where the medieval *al-faranj* left off. In the nineteenth century, missionaries set the stage with an attack on the ideological foundations of Islamic society. Military action followed in the twentieth as European powers liberated Palestine from the Turks only to assume control themselves. Struggles between Israelis and Palestinians are the flashpoint of this continuing clash, with Zionism and the Israeli state seen as a kind of Crusader outpost in the midst of historically Islamic territory. Writing in the context of the "new stage" of Palestinian resistance that followed the 1982 Israeli invasion of Lebanon, one result of which was the expulsion of Yassir Arafat and other Palestinian leaders from Beirut, the Hamas Charter reflects the thinking of activists who believe that Islam is the solution to political ills. The reasoning and claims of the text are quite different from the more secular nationalism espoused until that time by Arafat, in which Islam played a role but was not *the* solution, and in which the precedents cited were those of "people's struggles" like that of the Vietnamese against the United States in the 1960s and 1970s. The *intifada*, or uprising, by Palestinians living in the West Bank and Gaza was largely orchestrated by Hamas. Beginning in 1987 and lasting until 1990, the movement established Hamas as a continuing player in Palestinian politics.

Imperialist powers, write the authors of the Charter, "support the [Zionist] enemy with all their might, material and human . . . When Islam is manifest the unbelieving powers unite against it because the Nation of unbelief is one."[15] From this perspective, it did not (and does not) matter that non-Muslim powers were and are often engaged in power struggles among themselves, and with quite different policies regarding the state of Israel. The struggle is between a people that submits its life to God and one that does not (the nation of "faith" and the nation of "unbelief"). The modern-day crusaders (or Crusader-Zionist alliance) try to divide and conquer by picking off (or perhaps one should say buying off) those states, for example Egypt, which ought to take up the cause of defending Islam.

Most directly, the Charter conceives armed struggle as resistance to the taking of land entrusted to the Muslim community. "The Islamic Resistance Movement believes that the land of Palestine is entrusted to the Muslims until the Day of Resurrection. It is not right to give it up in whole or in part. No Arab state . . . no King or Leader . . . no organization, Palestinian or Arab, has such authority."[16] Fighting is justified, even obligatory, in the light of Crusader attempts to take land entrusted to the Muslim community. And, in accord with Shari'a precedents, the duty to fight is construed as an individual obligation.

As we have seen, however, historical precedents vary on the meaning of this idea. The Crusader analogy seems not to serve so well as the authors of the Charter believe, given that Salah al-Din was a publicly recognized authority and that, more generally, the appeal to fighting as an individual duty appears as a summons to Muslim rulers in neighboring provinces to come to the aid of their co-religionists in Syro-Palestine. The Charter is speaking of a popular resistance movement, in which leadership appears to reside with a group that includes some members of the learned class (the late Shaykh Ahmad Yassin and others like him) and ordinary Muslims able to organize local initiatives. No doubt the presence of Shaykh Yassin and other 'ulama lends an aura of public authority to the struggle. The Charter, however, does not mention this point (for example, by stipulating that its judgments about the duty to fight are formally issued by a member or members of the learned class), but rather lays heavy stress on the notion that the obligation to fight belongs to each individual Muslim: "There is no higher peak in nationalism, no greater depth of devotion than this: When an enemy makes incursions into Muslim territory then struggle and fighting the enemy becomes an obligation incumbent upon every individual Muslim and Muslimah. The woman is allowed to go fight without the permission of her husband and the slave without the permission of his master."[17] In effect, the argument is that the Muslims are in an emergency situation, in which ordinary lines of authority are suspended. The justification for armed struggle is created by the incursion of non-Muslim forces into Islamic territory. It may be that ideally the struggle should be organized and carried out by publicly constituted political leaders. Failing that, however, the duty to resist falls to each member of the Muslim community, and the right of authority belongs to anyone able to organize the resistance. Necessity, Shari'a experts say, "makes the forbidden things permitted."[18] In an emergency situation, a people cannot rely on publicly constituted leadership. There is a right, even a duty to engage in defense of the life, liberty, and property of Muslims. And that right/duty belongs to or is incumbent upon anyone who recognizes the need, and who has the available means.

Such "emergency reasoning" seems also to provide the background for the World Islamic Front *Declaration*.[19] The text is signed by leaders representing five militant groups. The most important are bin Laden, representing al-Qaʿida, the group or movement he founded in response to the decision of the royal family to allow a U.S. military presence in the Arabian Peninsula following the Gulf War of 1991; and Ayman al-Zawahiri, representing the Egyptian Islamic Group. The latter, an offshoot of Egyptian Islamic Jihad, was constituted by several of those imprisoned following the assassination of Sadat. Al-Zawahiri was one of those. The alliance between al-Qaʿida and the Islamic Group was very important in establishing bin Laden and al-Zawahiri as leaders of an international movement. As bin Laden had it, the struggle of Islam was international, and required Muslims to carry out military operations at that level. Certainly the language of the *Declaration* suggests as much:

The Arabian Peninsula has never—since God made it flat, created its desert, and encircled it with seas—been stormed by any forces like the crusader armies spreading in it like locusts, eating its riches and wiping out its fertile places. All this is happening at a time in which nations are attacking

Muslims like people fighting over a plate of food. In the light of the grave situation and the lack of support, we and you are obliged to discuss current events, and we should all agree on how to settle the matter.

Further, the summary presentation of the "three facts that are known to everyone" makes clear that the authors are speaking in terms reminiscent of imposed war. The "facts" constitute the basis for an indictment, or perhaps better, a verdict of guilt against an enemy: "these crimes and sins committed by the Americans are a clear declaration of war against God, his messenger, and the Muslims." The judgment of the authors follows the logic we have seen before:

> *'ulama'* throughout Islamic history have unanimously agreed that armed struggle is an individual duty if the enemy destroys the Muslim countries . . . The ruling to fight the Americans and their allies, civilians and military, is an individual obligation for every Muslim who can do it in any country in which it is possible to do it . . . We call on every Muslim who believes in God and wishes to be rewarded to comply with God's order to fight the Americans and plunder their money wherever and whenever they find it. We also call on Muslim *'ulama'*, leaders, youths, and soldiers to launch the raid on the adversary's U.S. troops and the satanically inspired supporters allying with them, and to displace those who are behind them so that they may learn a lesson.

It seems plain that the notion of fighting as an individual duty here is one of a popular resistance. The signatories, including Osama bin Laden, are not recognized members of the learned class, yet they consider themselves qualified to issue a formal Shari'a opinion on the duty of Muslims, including the learned. Once again, it appears that necessity establishes both a right and duty of defense, and that directive authority falls to whoever is able to organize resistance. It is instructive on this point to compare the argument of bin Laden's long 1996 *Epistle* with the 1998 *Declaration.*[20] In the earlier document he expresses disappointment in the Saudi family and more generally in the elite who make up the religio-political establishment of the Saudi state. He has not given up hope entirely, however; the *Epistle* calls on the Saudi-Wahhabi political and religious leaders, as well as on unspecified other Muslim leaders, to put aside their differences in the service of a collective or communal duty to resist American designs on Muslim territory. In this text, bin Laden writes very much in the manner of the eleventh- and twelfth-century publicists who appealed to Salah al-Din and others to do their duty and marshal their resources in defense of Islam. Bin Laden acknowledges that it is unlikely that the Saudi-Wahhabi establishment will fulfill this duty, and so goes on to appeal to the "good" political and religious leaders to assist in organizing an armed resistance that will engage in "lightning-quick" strikes at American targets in the Arabian Peninsula with the aim of convincing the Americans to withdraw their troops. Even this objective seems difficult, however, since the corrupt and impotent leadership has killed or imprisoned many of the best leaders. So leaders from outside the Peninsula, beyond the reach of the Saudi-Wahhabi establishment, should take on the task.

The alliance between al-Qaʿida and the Egyptian Islamic Group was forged by February 1998. The *Declaration* does not speak to the issue of the apostasy of current rulers that was so important in *The Neglected Duty.* Its overarching goal is to justify a popular and international armed resistance to the United States and its allies. In subsequent statements, most notably following the U.S.-led response to the September 11, 2001, attacks on New York and Washington, D.C., bin Laden noted that it is the privilege of a vanguard chosen by God to organize active resistance to the anti-Muslim forces, and thus to defend Islamic rights. Those who fight, and thus respond to the *Dec-*

laration's judgment regarding the duty of Muslims, do not need the endorsement of any established religious or political authorities, for they are responding to the call of God: "And why should you not fight in the cause of God and of those who, being weak, are ill-treated? Men, women, and children, whose cry is 'Our Lord, rescue us from this town, whose people are oppressors, and raise for us out of your beneficence one who will help!' [Qur'an 4:75]."

Given the radical nature of these claims, we might expect Muslim authorities to say that the authors of the *Declaration,* or for that matter of the Charter of Hamas and *The Neglected Duty,* are in violation of the Shari'a. The requirement that established officials authorize fighting is well founded in Islamic tradition. Nevertheless, most authorities do not raise this issue. Of course, in the case of Hamas, one might argue that there is no political establishment. When the Charter was issued, in 1988, the Palestinian National Authority was not yet in existence. Even now, that body does not have the same legal standing as the governments of recognized states. In this context, PNA officials and other Palestinian leaders not associated with Hamas or its military wing have yet to challenge the right of the group to engage in resistance.[21] Instead they appeal to prudential considerations along the lines of those articulated by the Shaykh al-Azhar in relation to *The Neglected Duty.* Similarly, and perhaps less understandably, discussion of the *Declaration* does not challenge the World Islamic Front on grounds of right authority.

In general, Muslim criticisms of militancy focus less on the problem of right authority and more on the question of means. In his rebuttal to *The Neglected Duty* the Shaykh al-Azhar asks, in effect, "Where will killing stop?" He worries about the implication of Muhammad al-Faraj's argument, for the text seems to hint that anyone participating in the affairs of the Egyptian state—say, by voting or paying taxes—might be classified as apostate. The logic of *The Neglected Duty* makes it difficult to see how al-Faraj and his associates

can avoid killing large numbers of Muslims who are doing nothing more than going about the ordinary business of citizens. "How
much blood?" is the al-Azhar question. In this sense, the leading religious authority in the Egyptian (and by some lights in the entire
Sunni world) establishment appears to be worried that the means
employed will result in damage disproportionate to the evil at which
resistance is aimed. To put it another way, those engaged in armed
resistance will violate Shari'a precedents establishing norms for honorable combat.

In the case of Hamas, arguments about such matters become clear
if we attend to the recent discussion of "martyrdom operations." On
June 19, 2002, 55 Palestinian leaders issued a joint statement in
which they argued that such operations should be stopped. The argument was pragmatic or even consequentialist: Palestinian youths
were sacrificing themselves in actions which had little or no effect on
Israel's military capacity, and which also hurt Palestinian attempts to
cultivate world opinion. Those advocating such tactics should consider that they were actually helping the most intransigent segment
of Israeli opinion (meaning the supporters of Ariel Sharon). On
June 30, 150 Palestinian leaders issued a counterstatement arguing
that resistance to oppression by any and all means is justified, and
that those willing to take action (any action) should be praised.

In the background of this exchange was the extensive debate about
Shari'a norms and martyrdom operations that took place during the
spring and summer of 2001.[22] The debate began when a prominent
Saudi scholar suggested that such operations were without precedent
in the history of Islam, and that those participating might best be
judged as "mere" suicides. The prominent scholar and television
personality Yusuf al-Qaradhawi (and many others) asserted that this
argument was incorrect. Those giving their lives in attacks against Israeli oppression were not committing suicide, said al-Qaradhawi.

They were sacrificing themselves for the sake of justice, and were therefore martyrs, worthy of praise.

Most of those making public statements agreed. Nevertheless, many wondered about the targeting of such attacks. The use of one's body as a mechanism for delivering explosives to a military target might be justified, especially under conditions of necessity. The Prophet's orders to fighters are binding, however; and these prohibit direct and intentional attacks on civilian targets. So the Shaykh al-Azhar argued that the self-sacrifice of Palestinians should be considered praiseworthy only if the intention was to kill the enemy's soldiers. Direct and intentional attacks on noncombatants were forbidden, even under conditions of necessity.

Following this opinion from al-Azhar, al-Qaradhawi spoke for the majority when he argued that "Israeli society is militaristic in nature. Both men and women serve in the army and can be drafted at any moment . . . If a child or an elderly person is killed in this type of operation, he or she is not killed on purpose, but by mistake, and as a result of military necessity. Necessity makes the forbidden things permitted."[23]

Clearly, al-Qaradhawi meant to defend martyrdom operations in terms of Shariʿa notions of honorable combat. Whether the defense is successful seems open to question. For example, al-Qaradhawi seems to have been saying that the "potential combatancy" presented by the fact that all Israelis of a certain age are eligible for military service justifies attacks in public places. Such an argument would involve a considerable stretch of, if not an outright departure from, Shariʿa precedents; perhaps that is why al-Qaradhawi ended with the statement about necessity. That is, perhaps he should be understood as arguing that extremity or emergency conditions give those engaged in resistance more latitude than would otherwise be the case. "How much latitude?" would then seem an important question, as would a set of questions concerning whether al-Qaradhawi actually meant to justify the acts of martyrs or to excuse those who carry them out, and whether he meant to provide justifications or excuses relative to particular circumstances, or for a general practice of martyrdom operations.

Both al-Qaradhawi and the Shaykh al-Azhar issued opinions against the al-Qaʿida–sponsored bombings of U.S. embassies in Kenya and Tanzania in 1998. The shaykh, for example, said: "Any explosion that leads to the death of innocent women and children is a criminal act, carried out only by people who are base cowards and traitors. A rational person with only a small portion of respect and virtue refrains from such operations."[24] Similarly, after the September 11, 2001, attacks, Qaradhawi argued that the attacks were to be considered grave sins, because they failed to distinguish between civilian and military targets, and ought to be condemned in accordance with the Qur'anic dictum (5:32) that "whoever kills a human being other than as punishment for manslaughter or acts of sowing corruption in the earth, it shall be as if that person killed all humankind." Noting that he and his associates were strongly opposed to U.S. policy with respect to Israel/Palestine, Qaradhawi nevertheless considered it important to express his judgment that the attacks of September 11 constituted a violation of Shariʿa norms.

What exactly is the difference between the activities of al-Qaʿida or the World Islamic Front and those sponsored by Hamas, Islamic Jihad, or other Palestinian organizations? The answer is not entirely clear, but we might consider the following as possible explanations: (1) the judgment is determined by the difference between fighting a "near enemy" and fighting a "far-off enemy"; (2) once one accepts the notion that any man or woman living in Israel and of a certain age should be regarded as contributing to Israel's military readiness and thus as a combatant, it is possible to distinguish targets in Israel from those in the World Trade Center. With respect to (1), the idea would be that Israeli forces constitute a clear and present military threat in ways that the New York and Washington targets do not. To continue this line of thought for a moment, it is interesting that, so far as I am aware, Qaradhawi, the Shaykh al-Azhar, and others did not condemn either the bombing of U.S. barracks in Khobar, Saudi Arabia, or the attack on the USS *Cole* off the coast of Yemen. Fighting forces located within historically Islamic territory thus pose a threat in ways that far-off targets do not.[25] With respect to (2), the point would be that the people at the World Trade Center are not immediately eligible for military service in the way that most men and women in Israel are, and thus that it is not possible to speak of the intention of those carrying out the attacks in terms that make military targets primary, and civilian damage secondary. In either case, the explanation must be joined with the obvious point that Qaradhawi and others regard the Palestinian case as special, and do not want to see the justice of that cause contaminated by association with other, less clear cases.

In the *Declaration*, we have a clear judgment that it is not only permitted but obligatory to strike at Americans (and those allied with them) without distinction between civilian and military targets. Before September 11, Osama bin Laden commented in various interviews that "indiscriminate" tactics were not only excused but justified in light of two considerations: the shared guilt of citizens in a democratic state, and the law of reciprocity. With respect to the first, the point is that democracy allows citizens freedom to express opinions contrary to the policies of their government, and to vote the scoundrels out. With respect to the second, it is simply a fact, bin Laden argued, that in the end you get what you give. Here, he appeals to a kind of law of nature; for him, this law is like gravity: one can try to overcome it, and even seem to for a while, but it expresses the direction of forces that are in the end inexorable. It is clear as well, however, that bin Laden means the law of reciprocity to function as a moral appeal. Muslim fighters are justified in killing American civilians insofar as U.S. forces kill Muslim civilians. It does not matter to him whether the latter are killed incidentally or accidentally, whether their deaths are a violation of just-war notions of discrimination or not. The law of reciprocity, here interpreted almost as a gloss on the law of retaliation, allows Muslim fighters to avenge the deaths of Muslim innocents.[26]

We have already seen that such established authorities as the Shaykh al-Azhar and Yusuf al-Qaradhawi dispute the validity of bin Laden's reasoning. Their criticisms clearly indicate a judgment that the *Declaration* is inconsistent with Shari'a notions of honorable combat. Others, including some who are otherwise quite sympathetic to bin Laden and his colleagues, share this judgment. Thus, in July 2002 the Al-Jazeera network broadcast a live interview with three Saudi dissidents, Shaykh Muhsin al-'Awaji and the scholars Safar al-Hawali and Muhammad al-Khasif.[27] None is supportive of the United States and its efforts in Afghanistan or elsewhere. The transcript of the interview/discussion begins with comments about the United States and the war on terror. The discussion then turns to bin Laden. The three agree that his popularity with the Saudi people has rested, and continues to rest, on his dedication to Islamic ideals. They agree that bin Laden is a character type the Saudi people find hard to resist. Al-'Awaji says:

> Bin Ladin is perceived to be a man of honor, a man who abstains from the pleasures of this world, a brave man, and a man who believes in his principles and makes sacrifices for them . . . What the Saudis like best about bin Ladin is his asceticism. When the Saudi compares bin Ladin to any child of wealthy parents, he sees that bin Ladin left behind the pleasures of the hotels for the foxholes of jihad, while others compete among themselves for the wealth and palaces of this world.

In the past, al-ʿAwaji indicates, especially during the resistance to the Soviet Union's incursions into Afghanistan, this affection was unqualified. But now the Saudi people have three complaints about bin Laden.

> First, bin Ladin accuses clerics and rulers of heresy, when he has no proof of this. Second, he is making the Muslim countries an arena for jihad operations. Third, he and those with him target innocent people, and I refer to the innocents on the face of the entire earth, of every religion and color, and in every region.

With respect to the first point, al-ʿAwaji and his colleagues disagree with bin Laden's judgment that the Saudi establishment is irrelevant. They want to hold out the possibility of change. On the second point, they are obviously concerned that the actions of al-Qaʿida will divide the Muslim community.

It is the third point that is of most interest to us. Al-ʿAwaji's statement is as clear a pronouncement of Shariʿa norms about targeting as one will find. Bin Laden and those associated with him violate the notion of honorable combat. Because of this, they are losing support among the Saudi people, and among Muslims more generally; one would not be wrong, I think, to understand al-ʿAwaji and his colleagues to say that they *should* lose this support.

The Al-Jazeera transcript should be read in the light of the article published by al-Qaʿida spokesman Sulayman Abu Ghayth one month earlier, in June 2002. There Abu Ghayth reiterated bin Laden's announced principle of reciprocity in support of the judgment that

> Those killed in the World Trade Center and the Pentagon were no more than a fair exchange for the ones killed in the al-ʿAmiriya shelter in Iraq, and are but a tiny part of the exchange for those killed in Palestine, Somalia, Sudan, the Philippines, Bosnia, Kashmir, Chechnya, and Afghanistan

... We have not reached parity with them. We have the right to kill four million Americans, two million of them children, and to exile twice as many and wound and cripple hundreds of thousands. Furthermore, it is our right to fight them with chemical and biological weapons, so as to afflict them with the fatal maladies that have afflicted the Muslims because of chemical and biological weapons.[28]

The three Saudi scholars, by contrast, appear to argue that even in the midst of armed combat, the norms of honor apply. Although they are as unstinting in their criticism of the United States as Abu Ghayth or bin Laden, they hold that the Shariʿa requires that armed struggle be conducted according to the directive of the Prophet: Do not mutilate anyone, nor should you kill women, children, or old men.

In late September or early October 2002, a prominent leader of Muslim resistance located in Great Britain published a short treatise on the question "Is Armed Struggle a Legitimate Means for the Establishment of Islamic Government?" The group with which the author, Shaykh ʿUmar Bakri Muhammad, is affiliated is well known for its support of Muslim resistance movements, especially in Chechnya. Further, and in ways that seemingly run counter to the views expressed in "Is Armed Struggle . . . ?," Shaykh ʿUmar's statements following the July 7, 2005, bombings in London were sufficiently provocative for the British government to require his departure. The shaykh's view, like that of bin Laden and other authors of the *Declaration*, is that Muslims are under attack around the world.[29]

In "Is Armed Struggle . . . ?," however, Shaykh Muhammad is interested in what the Shariʿa has to say concerning the legitimacy of armed struggle. In the familiar manner, he works through textual precedents in order to make the argument, first, that the establishment of just political order is a requirement for Muslims, and really for all human beings. Second, he says that the surest way to accomplish this goal is to establish a state governed by Islamic values. He does not believe the Shariʿa restricts such a state to one pattern of administration. A unified caliphate or single-ruler state is acceptable, so long as there is provision for consultation with the learned; but so is a parliamentary state in which the constitution establishes the Shariʿa as the law of the land. Third, he says that once established, such a state has an obligation to extend its influence (and thus the influence of Shariʿa) and thus to bring the blessings of justice to the entire world, or at least to as much of it as possible. According to Shariʿa precedents this mission should be accomplished first by preaching, second by diplomacy, and third by fighting, if that should be necessary. This kind of fighting deserves the name of *jihad*. It is a means authorized by God to secure human happiness. Such fighting is to be governed by Shariʿa norms, that is, by notions of honorable combat.

Such a state no longer exists. This is Shaykh Muhammad's fourth point. Since the demise of the Ottomans, no group has arisen to establish the kind of political-territorial association envisioned by Shariʿa authorities. Consequently there is no authority with competence to engage in the type of fighting deserving of the name *jihad*. Establishing such a state is essential to the well-being of the Muslims, and of the world as a whole. Muslims should strive for it. But—and this is the fifth point—it cannot be established by *jihad*, since that name is reserved for fighting conducted under the auspices of an Islamic state. Nor—sixth—can this state be established by fighting, in any case. It must be founded by agreement among the Muslims, and they are not allowed to coerce one another. Consensus must be reached as a matter of reasoned discourse, conducted according to the rules of Shariʿa inquiry.

This is a direct rebuttal of statements in bin Laden's *Epistle* indicating that Muslim forces should drive the United States and its

allies, including the Israelis, out of the region, with the aim of establishing a caliphate extending from the Arabian Peninsula to Damascus. In that sense, one might understand Shaykh Muhammad's criticism as directed at the way bin Laden's language leads to confusion
regarding the precise nature of the resisters' standing to authorize
war. As Shaykh Muhammad goes on to argue, however, there is a
kind of fighting in which such resisters not only can, but should, engage. This (in his seventh point) is to be classified as *qital* (fighting
or killing) in defense of Muslim lives, liberty, and property. Shari'a
precedents recognize a right of self-defense, he writes. And this right
is not only a matter of one's own life, liberty, and possessions. It extends to the protection of others. Such fighting is an individual duty,
in the sense that any Muslim who is able should come to the aid
of co-religionists who are under attack by nonbelievers. Thus, in
Chechnya, Saudis or others who are able should come to the aid of
those who suffer. If the Saudi government will support them, fine. If
not, there is nothing to stop individuals from coming on their own
initiative. The point, in distinction from the *Declaration,* is that the
fighting is carefully delimited in its purpose. Further, as Shaykh Muhammad concludes, it is clear that norms of honorable combat are
to govern fighters even in the emergency circumstance suggested by
the analogy with self-defense.

> From the sayings and actions of the Messenger Muhammad
> [it is clear] that non-Muslim lives are protected unless they
> are at war with the Muslims as determined by the foreign
> policy of an established Muslim state or they are violating
> the sanctity of Muslim land, honor, or life. Also, much ad-
> vice has been given by the Messenger Muhammad regarding
> armed struggle which makes it clear that this duty is pro-life
> as opposed to anti-life: Rules against killing women and
> children, the elderly or monks, not targeting trees or live-

stock, and so on. Hence although foreign forces occupying Muslim land are legitimate targets and we are obliged to liberate Muslim land from such occupation and to co-operate with each other in this process, and can even target their embassies and military bases, there is no divine evidence for us to fight against Muslims who are part of the regimes in Muslim countries as a method to establish the Islamic state. Rather we urge our Muslim brothers in Islamic movements who are engaged in this violation of Shari'a to look at the evidence and to follow that which is based on certainty. May God guide us all to the best.

The Problematic of Armed Resistance

In November 2002 bin Laden, or someone writing in his name, replied to Muslim and non-Muslim critics in a "Letter to America."[30] The document reiterated previously stated reasons why bin Laden believes attacks on civilian as well as military targets are justified in Shari'a terms. He writes that the citizens of a democratic state share responsibility for the policies of their government. Moreover, God "legislated the permission and the option to take revenge. Thus, if we are attacked, we have the right to return the attack . . . whoever has killed our civilians, we have the right to kill theirs."

Who has the better of the argument, in terms of the practice of Shari'a reasoning? Answering such a question is a matter of evaluating precedent. With respect to notions of honorable combat, established precedents are consistent on the matter of restrictions on targeting. Those critical of the judgment advanced in the *Declaration* or in bin Laden's "Letter" reflect the plain meaning of such precedents, as do those worried about the conduct of martyrdom operations in the Palestinian struggle. One can, of course, argue that the context of contemporary resistance is significantly different from those in which established precedents were crafted. In that sense, an argument like al-Qaradhawi's might be read as suggesting that the Palestinian case has special features (the "militaristic" nature of Israeli society, and the emergency conditions faced by Palestinians), and thus that those engaged in resistance should be given more latitude than suggested by historical judgments about targeting.

The argument of the *Declaration* is more opaque on these matters. It might be read as a sort of "pure" emergency appeal, along the lines of Michael Walzer's famous discussion of supreme emergencies in the context of the just-war tradition. In brief, Walzer suggests that the threat of imminent defeat by a sufficiently wicked foe justifies a temporary suspension of the ordinary rules of engagement.[31] In connection with the *Declaration*, however, such an interpretation seems forced; and bin Laden's "Letter" makes no appeal to emergency, but rather focuses on the shared guilt of citizens in a democratic state and on the Islamic version of the law of retaliation. The *Declaration*'s call for indiscriminate fighting is problematic, because the authors fail to provide an adequate argument for the overriding of precedent. Similarly, the assertions by Muhammad al-Faraj regarding the killing of apostates fail. As the Shaykh al-Azhar points out, the judgment that fighters should avoid excessive killing rests on well-established precedent, and the argument in *The Neglected Duty* provides no special reasons for overturning it.

Let us now return to arguments about the legitimacy of armed resistance per se. Muslim critiques of the *Declaration* and other militant documents do not focus on these arguments. Part of the explanation for this lack is surely the oft-cited legitimation crisis of contemporary Islamic establishments. However, the issue here is whether or not the arguments justifying armed resistance are successful, that is, in terms of the application or extension of established precedents to contemporary contexts. Two historical arguments are cited by the authors of militant texts. One refers to precedents justifying or even requiring punishment of apostasy. The other refers to precedents related to fighting imposed by foreign incursions into Islamic territory. In both cases the arguments are buttressed by the notion that under certain conditions, fighting becomes an individual rather than a collective duty. This is a way of signaling an extraordinary threat or a judgment that fighting is a response to emergency conditions. By contrast with the notion that emergency conditions justify an exception to prohibitions on the targeting of noncombatants, the idea that emergency conditions alter ordinary lines of authority seems relatively clear. An enemy is threatening Muslim lives, liberty, and property, and anyone who can assist in defending these should do so. Contemporary militant arguments stretch this reasoning a bit. Historical precedents suppose that the appeal for help is to Muslim rulers whose sphere of influence is outside the region under immediate attack, rather than to individual Muslims. What happens, though, if those rulers do not respond? The idea is that fellow Muslims are in need. If no established ruler will lend a hand, is there nothing to be done?

Advocates of armed resistance are clearly saying that something can be done. In some ways, the problematic of Shariʿa reasoning on this point may be usefully compared with Quentin Skinner's description of the dynamic of Lutheran and Calvinist discussion of the relative merits of "private law" and "constitutional" theories of resistance.[32] In the former, the right of armed resistance to tyranny is an extension of rights to defend one's life, liberty, and property. Everyone has such rights, as a private person. In the latter, the right of armed resistance is entrusted to designated public officials—the "lesser magistrates" described by Calvin in *Institutes* IV.xx. As Skinner describes it, Lutherans and Calvinists alike feared the anarchic consequences of the private-law argument. They had no satisfactory response, however, to the question "Who defends the people against tyranny, if the designated magistrates fail to follow through?"

The answer, according to those Muslims advancing justifications for armed resistance, seems to be "the people themselves" or, failing that, "a rightly guided vanguard." In terms of precedent, the argument is an innovation, but it is not implausible. Perhaps the lack of criticism aimed directly at the right of contemporary resisters to make war is as much a recognition of the strength of resistance arguments as of the legitimation crisis afflicting Islamic establishments.

In all this discussion, one available line of thought seems to be missing. The omission of appeals to the type of fighting that the learned characterized as rebellion seems odd, to say the least. This may be a result of the prima facie ways in which this set of precedents is directed at governmental response to resisters, rather than a result of the justification of resistance itself. There is an interesting line of development of rules for fighting rebels in certain Shiʿi materials, however. In particular, the late Ayatollah Khomeini's lectures on Islamic government suggest that when rulers resort to military force as a means of suppressing a nonviolent popular resistance, the rulers themselves become rebels.[33] The class of the learned, understood as the guardians of the people's rights, is then justified in calling the people to arms against the "ruling rebels." The right to resist is thereby restricted to cases in which the "deputies of the hidden Imam" provide authorization and in which the established government's tactics show that it is "no government at all." In this case, at any rate, it is still possible for religious authorities to argue against the anarchic tendencies presented in the *Declaration* and other militant texts.

Those anarchic tendencies are symptomatic of a continuing problem, however. The focus on resistance throughout the modern period indicates that Muslim societies and, with them, the practice of Shariʿa reasoning are in crisis. To say that the World Islamic Front *Declaration* advocates judgments that stretch or even violate some of the most venerable precedents in Islamic tradition is a relatively easy task. The more serious challenge is the one posed to existing political authorities. For Osama bin Laden, Ayman al-Zawahiri, and other militants, the world is out of joint. Something has gone wrong; the international system is dominated by people whose vision of order is guided less by the standards that God built into human beings at the time of creation, and more by the rule of the strong. In this context, historically Muslim societies ought to assert themselves. Their rulers profess faith in God; their legitimacy rests on a commitment to the rule of law, meaning those standards identified by Shari'a reasoning. But their witness is truncated, at best. In the militant vision, the leaders of historically Muslim lands are at best impotent, at worst corrupt; and there is no difference between them and the American and European rulers upon whom they rely for money and protection.

The crisis of Islamic societies is a matter of legitimation, and this fact affects the practice of Shari'a reasoning. In earlier centuries, recognized scholars responded to questions from the faithful. Steeped in the Qur'an and reports of the Prophet's *sunna,* knowledgeable in the rules governing the interpretation of these texts, they provided guidance in the context of societies oriented toward governance by the Shari'a. Over the last two centuries, however, a literate, professional class of devout Muslims has emerged, and some of these are not satisfied that the contemporary version of consultation between political and religious leaders yields anything approaching political justice. Indeed, for Osama bin Laden and those who stand with him, the *'ulama* are nearly as irrelevant as the leadership of historically Muslim states. At best, they are focused on splitting hairs; at worst, they publish opinions that identify Shari'a reasoning with policies of acquiescence to Europe and the United States. In either case, neither the religious or political classes provide leadership that will enable the *umma* to carry out its historical mission. This is a wrong that must be put right, not only for the sake of the Muslim community, but for the life of the world.

Arguments about resistance are thus not only a matter of the conduct of military operations. They raise questions about the location of legitimate authority. Who has the right to declare war? Who has the right to utilize power in the ordering of political life? Who has the right to bind and loose, to declare what is right or wrong in matters of political ethics? Who has the authority to issue *fatawa*, opinions based on a conscientious reading of established precedent, and thus properly commended to Muslims, and to people of good faith everywhere?

CHAPTER FIVE

MILITARY ACTION AND POLITICAL AUTHORITY

Arguments about resistance are not only about military means. They are also concerned with the way in which notions of just conduct in war connect with broader issues of political life. When the World Islamic Front *Declaration*, *The Neglected Duty*, or the Hamas Charter calls Muslims to fight, the call is embedded in assumptions about the form of political life proper to an Islamic state. Ultimately, advocates of resistance see themselves as the vanguard of a movement that will establish such a state. When they speak of "Islamic governance," they believe that notion correlates with the kind of order outlined in the story of the Prophet, the presentation of Islam as the natural religion of humanity, and with precedents identified with Islamic civilization. Advocates of resistance intend to resolve a crisis of authority within the Muslim community. In establishing an Islamic state, resistance movements will protect and defend the rights of Muslims, restore the Muslim community to a position of prominence in world affairs, and benefit all humanity.

Muslim arguments about the just war thus lead into larger questions about political authority. Evaluations of the ways resistance movements conduct themselves in the course of military action are only one part of the picture. Directly or indirectly, they also address the cause for which militants fight, and a conception of legitimate authority. Since militants claim to represent Islamic tradition, we may also ask whether there is any credible alternative to their position.

The Program of the Militants

On August 4, 2005, Ayman al-Zawahiri, al-Qaʿidaʾs second-in-command, commented on the July 7 bombings in London. His remarks were directed at citizens of the "Crusader coalition" led by the United States and the United Kingdom; no doubt he also meant to rally Muslim support for the 7/7 bombers and to inspire others to follow their example.

> As for the English, I say to them: Blair has brought destruction upon you, to the center of London, and he will have more of it, God willing. Oh peoples of the Crusader coalition! We have offered you, at least [the opportunity to] stop your aggression against the Muslims . . . The lion of Islam, the struggler, Shaykh Usama bin Ladin, may God protect him, offered you a truce, so that you will leave the lands of Islam. Did Shaykh Usama bin Ladin not tell you that you could not dream of security before we live it as a reality in Palestine and before all the infidel armies leave the land of Muhammad? But you have made rivers of blood in our countries, so we blew up volcanoes of rage in your countries. Our message to you is clear and unequivocal: You will

not be saved unless you withdraw from our land, stop stealing our oil and our resources, and cease your support of the corrupt [Muslim] rulers.

[As for the Americans,] what you have seen in New York and Washington, and the casualties you witness in Afghanistan and in Iraq, despite all the media blackout, are nothing but the casualties of the initial clashes. If you continue the same policy of aggression against the Muslims, you will see, God willing, horrors that will make you forget what you saw . . . in Vietnam . . . there is no way out of Iraq, other than immediate withdrawal, and . . . any delay in making this decision means nothing but more dead and casualties. If you do not leave today, you will definitely leave tomorrow, but with tens of thousands dead, and many more crippled and wounded. The same lies that [your leaders] said about Vietnam, they repeat today about Iraq. Did they not say that they would train the Vietnamese to manage their own affairs, and that they were defending freedom in Vietnam?[1]

Al-Zawahiri's statement was obviously a commentary on current events. But the commentary was framed by historical allusions. Of these, the most significant were "the land of Muhammad" and "our [Muslims'] land." The fighting in Afghanistan and Iraq and, more generally, the struggle with the United States and its allies were thus linked to major themes of Islamic tradition.

Al-Zawahiri's historical references also establish a link between the program of al-Qaʿida and the notion of precedent so important in the practice of Shariʿa reasoning. The August 4 statement serves as a pointed reminder that the leadership of al-Qaʿida justifies its struggle through appeals to authoritative texts. The story of Muhammad and his companions, the notion that Islam is the natural religion of humanity, and the growth of Islam as a civilization provide the backdrop for the militant program. Al-Zawahiri's remarks indicate that this program is not simply a matter of possessing territory, as though "the land of Muhammad" were Muslim "property." For al-Zawahiri, land is a trust, and good stewardship involves the establishment and maintenance of an Islamic government, in accord with the wishes of God, the creator and ultimate owner of all territory. In this, he echoes the dominant Muslim account of the way Islam became a world power. Europeans and North Americans may speak about the Islamic "conquest." Muslims speak about the "opening" of territory by which people received freedom from tyranny as *al-mujahiddin*, the strugglers in the path of God, responded to the Qur'an's depiction of the plight of the oppressed:

> Why should you not fight in God's cause and for those op-pressed—men, women, and children who cry out, "Lord, rescue us from this town whose people are oppressors! By Your grace, give us a protector and helper!"?   (Qur'an 4:75)

Muslim accounts suggest that the conquest of territory in the Middle East, North Africa, central and south Asia, and south-central Europe proceeded from the noblest of motives. The call of the op-pressed—the call of God—was for an end to tyranny. The victory of Islam provided this, removing tyrannical regimes and replacing them with something better. The liberating *mujahiddin* established patterns of administration. They collected taxes, distributed land, and performed the other functions associated with government. The new regime was also qualitatively different from the old. It involved government by Islam, the rule of Shari'a. The new regime focused on the development of a political system consonant with divine guidance, and also (since Islam is the natural religion) with the true nature of human beings.

All this has been said before, but it is worth recalling at this point. Al-Zawahiri and Osama bin Laden; the authors of *The Neglected Duty* and of the Charter of Hamas; those who carried out the attacks of 9/11/2001, of 3/11/2004, and of 7/7/2005—all these people claim the mantle of the Shari'a. They consider themselves the vanguard of Islam, blessed by God to carry out the struggle against the idols of their time. For them, the story of the Prophet is not simply a matter of historical record. It is a living narrative, through which people should interpret current events. On the day of creation, God challenged human beings to bear witness to his lordship and summoned them to walk the straight path. By means of various prophets, God reiterated the challenge to subsequent generations, offering them the way of submission as a gift and a task. As the last and greatest of the prophets, Muhammad called humanity to obedience, and his message echoes through the centuries with a force that reaches to the present. In our time, as previously, God issues a challenge, and offers human beings a gift. The challenge is for human beings, individually and collectively, to submit themselves to God. The gift is life and hope, freedom and peace. In political terms, this gift takes the form of an Islamic government, in which the purpose of the state is to establish and maintain the rule of Shari'a, so that Muslims and non-Muslims alike may know the blessings of God. Instantiated through a process of consultation between religious and political leaders, the rule of Shari'a ensures that people are properly related to one another. Men exercise oversight with respect to women, parents supervise the formation of children, and members of the Muslim community provide protection to Jews, Christians, and others living under their care.

The militants' struggle is intended to present the gift of Islamic government to all humanity. It is not, as some analyses suggest, a matter of destruction without purpose. A statement by al-Zawahiri issued in June 2005 serves to make the point:

> True reform is based on three principles: The first principle
> is the rule of Shari'a, because Shari'a, which was given by
> God, protects the believers' interests, freedom, honor, and

pride, and protects what is sacred to them. The Islamic nation will not accept any other law, after it has suffered from the anti-Islamic trends forcefully imposed on it.

The second principle of reform is the freedom of the lands of Islam. No reform is conceivable while our countries are occupied by the Crusader forces . . .

The third principle of reform is the Muslim nation's freedom to run its own affairs. This freedom will only be realized in two ways. First, freedom of the independent religious judicial system, the implementation of its rulings, and the guaranteeing of its honor, authority, and strength. Second, the freedom and right of the Islamic nation to implement the principle of "promoting virtue and preventing vice."[2]

True reform sets the Islamic community free. Once free, it may go on to bear witness to the form of order proper to all humanity. The believers must be realistic, however. They must understand that the goal will not be accomplished in a day. They must also understand that military action will be required. Finally, the believers must recognize that they will be tempted, and that they must in particular resist the siren song of democracy, with its separation of religious and political institutions. Al-Zawahiri continues:

I would also like to stress that the expulsion of the invading Crusaders and Jews from the lands of Islam will not be accomplished merely through demonstrations and hoarse throats in the streets. Reform and expelling the invaders from the lands of Islam will only be accomplished by fighting for the sake of God . . .

I salute my brothers, the lions of Islam, who are on the holy front of Islam around Jerusalem. I call upon them in the name of God not to abandon their jihad, not to throw down their weapons, not to believe the counsel of the collaborators, not to forget the lessons of history, not to trust the secularists who have sold Palestine cheaply, and not to be drawn into the secular game of elections in accordance with a secular constitution.[3]

Al-Zawahiri presents a vision of political life in which the rule of Shari'a is identified with a particular form of order. In this order, Muslims must lead. They are to be citizens of the first rank, meaning that they take leadership in the setting of policy. Further, the task of leadership is primarily a matter of implementing precedents set during Islam's classical period. For al-Zawahiri, there is little room for a sustained process of discerning divine guidance. Nor is there room for development of the type that might allow contemporary Muslims to say that they honor the precedents set by earlier generations, but that their condition requires something new. To take one example: Can the sources of Shari'a reasoning be read in ways that allow Muslims to participate in a genuinely democratic political system? Is it possible for Muslims, in good conscience, to identify the symbol of "rule by the Shari'a" with an order in which Jews, Christians, Buddhists, even people who profess no religious faith at all participate as equals, each and all having a say in the formation of policy?

For al-Zawahiri, the answer is no. He speaks as an advocate of Islamic governance. There are of course differences among militants in this regard. While most of these are tactical differences, referring to questions like "Is suicide bombing legitimate?" or "In the struggle against the U.S. and its allies, is there a meaningful distinction between civilian and military targets?," there are also differences among militants regarding the extent to which the rule of Shari'a requires ordinary believers to submit their private judgment to "right-thinking" *ulama,* or with respect to non-Muslim participation in an Islamic government.[4] Some militant authors allow for the possibility that non-Muslims might be given a role in the executive branch of government; for example, one of their number might hold the portfolio of minister of transportation or another cabinet-level post. They might even have limited representation in a consultative assembly, though this issue is more sensitive. The reason for the limitation? The commitment to rule by Shariʿa and, with it, to arrangements that safeguard the superintending role of the Islamic community requires that the legislative role of government be controlled by people of a certain character. Government must be guided by God's law rather than by a set of norms developed by human beings. Muslim leadership, in the context of rule by the Shariʿa, is basic to all militant groups. So is the rejection of democracy, with its notion of the equality of citizens. The militant vision is one in which premodern precedents are not so much interpreted as applied. To those who say that the patterns of governance illustrated in historical Islam do not fit with the needs and interests of modern persons, the militant answer is "Let the precedents stand!" If there is a problem of fit, then it is contemporary humanity that lacks understanding. The idea is to apply tried and true patterns of governance and to refashion the world in line with God's guidance.

In its appeal to premodern precedent, the militant vision of politics establishes its relationship to historical Islamic tradition. This is part of its attractiveness. Al-Zawahiri and other militant leaders speak to a widespread sense that current political arrangements are unsatisfactory. Their most direct evidence is the impotence or corruption of the existing governments of Muslim states. The World Islamic Front *Declaration on Armed Struggle against Jews and Crusaders,* the Charter of Hamas, and *The Neglected Duty* all make this point. The *Declaration*'s mention of the royal family's failure to carry through on its promise to remove U.S. troops from Saudi territory; of the inability of any Muslim government to lift United Nations–imposed sanctions on Iraq in the 1990s, and thus to relieve the suffering of Iraq; and, finally, of the lack of an effective response by

Muslim governments with respect to Israel's policies of occupation and settlement of Palestinian land—all these highlight the irrelevance of established regimes. Something is wrong, the *Declaration* suggests. There is no one able to defend Muslim interests, much less to pursue Islamically valid goals.

To this political and military evidence, other militant pronouncements add an indictment of the position of Muslims in the international economy. For example, Sulayman Abu Ghayth's "In the Shadow of the Lances" denounces the post–Cold War policies of the World Bank and the International Monetary Fund. During the 1990s these institutions' insistence that developing countries implement reforms that would make their markets attractive to international investors led states like Pakistan to privatize a number of state-owned industries. Public utilities, telephone, and other communications enterprises opened themselves to foreigners seeking profit. Abu Ghayth argues that these changes were really the work of the United States, and were a means of increasing its domination at the expense of Muslims. The fact that the new arrangements made Muslims complicit in an economic system characterized by the practice of usury presents one sort of problem; more fundamentally, the way in which change was implemented provides further evidence of the impotence of existing Muslim governments.[5]

From the militant point of view, the world is out of joint. *The Neglected Duty* asks believers to compare the current context with that of Ibn Taymiyya, who spoke of the duty to struggle against ostensibly Muslim rulers like the Mongols. Al-Zawahiri asks that they compare it also with the context of the Prophet, who in his struggle with the Quraysh typifies the eternal struggle between submission and heedlessness. The solution to humanity's problems in these historical cases was rule by the Shari'a. The same remedy applies in the current case, and believers should employ the same combination of persuasion and armed struggle as did the faithful of previous gener-

ations. Al-Zawahiri, Sulayman Abu Ghayth, and others are committed to the cause of Islamic governance. They present themselves as
the inheritors of the mantle of the Prophet and his companions; that
is, the mantle of the Shariʿa, by which God guides humanity to happiness in this world and the next.

Muslim Evaluations of Militancy

On the face of it, the claims of al-Zawahiri and other militants make
good "Islamic" sense. Their program is stated clearly, and in terms
that are basic to Islamic tradition.

Are they right?

The militants' claims are controversial, as we have seen. Some of
the most controversial points are already clear from our discussion
of the tactics employed in armed resistance. The claim of the World
Islamic Front *Declaration,* whereby fighting Americans and their allies, civilians and soldiers, is obligatory for each and every Muslim in
any country where it is possible, draws criticism from a wide assort-
ment of people. Traditional authorities like the Shaykh al-Azhar, religious personalities like Yusuf al-Qaradhawi, and prominent militants like Muhsin al-ʿAwaji alike indicate there are problems in the
argument of the *Declaration.* They point to the targeting of civilians,
the account of fighting as an individual duty, and the proper location of military operations as important issues. These criticisms go
to the heart of claims made by al-Qaʿida and like-minded groups to
represent the authentic version of Islam. Al-ʿAwaji's complaint that
bin Laden and "those with him target innocents, and I mean the innocent of every nation, of every race and religion, on the face of the
earth" counts against bin Laden's claims.[6] Similarly, when al-ʿAwaji
and his colleagues say that the model by which Saudi officials encouraged young men to go to the aid of the Muslims fighting against
Soviet forces in Afghanistan during the 1980s or to Chechnya in

more recent years corresponds more closely to the historical notion of fighting as an individual duty than does the practice of al-Qaʿida, or when al-Qaradhawi and the Shaykh al-Azhar say that military operations outside territories where one may speak of an invasion or occupation are illegitimate, they undercut the movement's authority. The militant position is rife with anarchic tendencies. Every Muslim becomes, at least potentially, judge, jury, and executioner in whatever case he deems appropriate. For this reason, in his response to the argument of *The Neglected Duty* the Shaykh al-Azhar insists that one of the things militants must consider, if they claim to serve the cause of justice, is this: Will the actions taken in the service of justice yield more harm than good? If each and every Muslim is authorized to take up arms in the context of an emergency, who will determine when the emergency is over? Even more, who will be able to enforce such a determination, so that those fighting will be willing to lay down their arms?

Given these questions, the failure to articulate a more substantial criticism of resistance movements in relation to notions of political authority seems strange. Why not insist that militants like bin Laden or al-Zawahiri cease their advocacy of military operations, or that they confine themselves to making the case for reform through normal political channels? The answer is, or seems to be, that those critics cited thus far do not in fact dissent from the militant judgment that current political arrangements are illegitimate. From al-ʿAwaji to Qaradhawi, from al-Muhajirun to the Shaykh al-Azhar, disagreements about the just war take place within a general agreement regarding the desirability of a particular kind of political structure. In its broad outlines, the militant vision articulated by al-Zawahiri is also the vision of his critics. These may complain that al-Zawahiri and Osama bin Laden lack depth or sophistication in their practice of Shariʿa reasoning; they certainly argue that the means these figures employ are wrong or counterproductive, or both. But they do not dissent from the judgment that current political arrangements are unsatisfactory, and that the cure for the ills of the world community involves the establishment of Islamic governance. Recalling the consensus among traditionally trained scholars like Rashid Rida and more popular leaders like Hasan al-Banna and Abu'l a'la Mawdudi that the abolition of the Ottoman caliphate must not mean the end of Islamic government, one should further recall that this judgment captures some of the broadest and most important tendencies in modern Islamic political thought. In this trend, Islamic government may involve a parliament or a consultative assembly. It may involve elections, so that the process of consultation, or *al-shura,* is more widely participatory than in the past. It cannot compromise on Muslim leadership, however. To do so, for example by following in the path of modern democracies, reduces the political role of Islam; it suggests that the Muslim voice should simply be one among many contributing to the making of policy. To put it another way, democracy implies a kind of moral equivalence between Islam and other perspectives. And such a situation is dangerous, not only for the standing of the Muslim community, but for the moral life of humankind.

Muslim Democrats

There are Muslims who disagree. Muslim democrats advocate a very different reading of Islamic tradition. For them, the problem of militancy is not simply a matter of objectionable tactics. The problem is the very notion of Islamic governance. Advocates of democracy read the Qur'an, the stories of the Prophet, and the history of Islamic civilization in ways that challenge the most basic assumptions of "mainstream" twentieth-century Muslim political thought. Put positively, the project of Muslim democrats involves interpreting the sources of Shari'a reasoning in ways that stress freedom of conscience and religion, and which thus require political arrangements associated with the protection of human rights. Put negatively, the democrats' argument is that the notion of a political order in which Islam is established leads inevitably to religious violence.

Democracy has been on the Muslim agenda for some time. The response to 'Ali 'abd al-Raziq's treatise, for example, had partly to do with the democratic potential of his analysis of Islamic sources. We also find writings by Muslim intellectuals asserting the compatibility of Islam and democratic values at least as far back as 'Amir 'Ali's 1891 book, *The Spirit of Islam*.[7] Frequently described as an apologia, not least because the style of presentation suggests that the argument is aimed at a British audience rather than at the author's own community of south Asian Muslims, *Spirit of Islam* nevertheless indicates ways in which a person familiar with the sources and procedures of Shari'a reasoning might develop a justification for democratic politics.

Given the prominence of militant Islam after the 9/11 attacks, or more generally since the 1978 revolution leading to the establishment of the Islamic Republic of Iran, it is perhaps understandable that the arguments of Muslim democrats are not widely distributed. They are well known in the Muslim community, however. And they are clearly regarded as a direct challenge to the conception of Islamic government. We can get a sense of the arguments and motives driving Muslim democrats by surveying the work of three figures, each currently residing in the United States, though each also has important ties to the historical territory of Islam.

Abdulaziz Sachedina, whose education in India and Iran gives him credentials in the world of traditional Islam, currently teaches in the Department of Religious Studies at the University of Virginia. He is best known in academic circles for his explorations of Twelver Shi'ism. His 2001 book, *The Islamic Roots of Democratic Pluralism*, is an extended argument in support of the view that Islamic sources require Muslims to work for a political order in which the rights of conscience are fully respected.[8]

The Islamic Roots of Democratic Pluralism discusses the relationship between Islamic tradition and international standards of human rights. Article 18 of the 1948 Universal Declaration of Human Rights, for example, states: "Everyone has the right to freedom of thought, conscience, and religion; this right includes freedom to change his religion or belief, and freedom, either alone or in community with others and in public or in private, to manifest his religion or belief in teaching, practice, worship, and observance."[9] Noting that the UN ambassador from Saudi Arabia, in particular, spoke against the adoption of this article, many scholarly treatments suggest that ideas such as freedom of conscience and freedom of religion are not particularly relevant to Islamic political thought. Militants and other advocates of Islamic government typically argue in a similar way: we have seen that in their view, all human beings have a right to hear the message of Islam, and then to convert or to come under the protection of Islam. But the freedom of non-Muslims is restricted in an Islamic state, and the freedom of Muslims is similarly restricted, not least by reason of traditional judgments against apostasy.

Sachedina argues that the Qur'an actually requires a political order in which freedom of conscience is protected. It does so by affirming a particular view of the nature of faith. At 10:99, for example, we read:

> And if your Lord had willed,
> Whoever is in the earth would have believed,
> All of them, all together.
> Would you [Muhammad] then constrain the people until
> they become believers?

The context makes clear that the proper answer to this rhetorical question is no. It was the Prophet's business to proclaim God's word.

By extension, and in a context in which Muslims were persecuted by nonbelievers (that is, the Quraysh), it was proper for Muhammad to strive to create a political order in which the right of Muslims to worship might be secure.

It was not the Prophet's task to impose faith, however. In the most fundamental sense, this *could not* be his task. For according to the Qur'an, faith is a gift of God. As Sachedina has it, Muhammad knew from bitter experience that human beings, faced with the threat of pain or death, will say or do whatever their tormentors wish. To reverse the image, people who are faced with superior power may well say, "There is no god but God," if doing so is what those in power demand. This is not a profession of faith, however. It is a profession of fear. True faith comes out of conviction; it is a matter of the heart. On Sachedina's reading, this aspect of Islamic tradition is disguised by many interpretations of Shari'a precedent. For the sake of contemporary Muslim debates, he considers it important to state the matter in a way that clarifies the issue. So he argues that Shari'a reasoning supports a political order in which persons and groups are free to hear the word of God, to accept it, and to worship according to their deeply held convictions. Shari'a reasoning also supports the converse: in order to protect the right of believers to practice their religion, it must be possible for others, nonbelievers, to hear the word of God, to reject it, and to live according to the dictates of conscience. For believers and nonbelievers alike, the Qur'an's vision of political order—the Shari'a vision—is embodied in policies that protect the right of conscience, in the context of maintaining good public order. No one may appeal to conscience in support of actions that cause unprovoked injuries to others. Nor may any person or group appeal to conscience as a way of preventing an established government from punishing those who bring about such injuries.

By contrast, the militant vision of politics holds that rights of conscience must be limited to the right of persons and groups to hear the message of Islam. The premodern consensus regarding the necessity of "protection" of non-Muslims who live in an Islamic state is relevant here. We have seen that al-Zawahiri and others argue that rule by the Shariʿa requires the "people of protection" to observe certain limits. They may not proclaim their doctrine with the intent of converting Muslims. Nor may they teach by way of outlining distinctions between their own faith and that of the Muslims, if doing so involves criticism of Islamic doctrine. Christians, for example, may meet on Sundays and, in the context of their ritual, profess their faith in the words of the Nicene Creed: "I believe in one Lord Jesus Christ, the only-begotten Son of God, begotten of the Father before all worlds, God of God, Light of Light, Very God of Very God, begotten, not made, being of one substance with the Father, by whom all things were made." They are not free to proclaim this faith to Muslims, however; further, in making clear their reasons for believing, Christians may not argue that the Muslim view, by which Jesus, son of Mary, is a prophet, but not the "son of God," is somehow incorrect. Should Christians violate this limit, they forfeit the protection of the Muslim state. Depending on the precise nature of their criticisms of Islam, Christians who proclaim their faith in the presence of Muslims may even be guilty of blasphemy.

Similarly, Muslims who hear the preaching of Christians, or who listen to the teaching of Jewish or other religious authorities, must not be allowed to convert. To do so is to "turn" from Islam, and thereby to break one's contract with God. On this point, al-Zawahiri and other militants appeal to the precedent set by Abu Bakr when, in the period immediately following his emergence as first successor, or *khalifa,* after the death of Muhammad, some of the Arabian tribes refused to pay *al-zakat,* the obligatory "tithe" that provided funds for the support of Islamic activities. We have seen that ʿulama through the centuries cited Abu Bakr's example in support of their judgment that apostasy or "turning" from Islam should be punished by the state. In debates surrounding this judgment, they made intricate distinctions regarding the types of behavior that constitute turning, and the punishment appropriate to each. Some types, at least, were punishable by death. Noting that historical authorities classified these types of apostasy as *al-hudud* (the limits) and thereby indicated that a judge has no discretion in assigning sentence, some militants suggest that a willingness to enforce this judgment is a measure of a state's dedication to rule by the Shariʿa.

Sachedina presents an alternative view. In this, the details of the process by which Abu Bakr came to his decision are as important as the judgment he reached. Reports of the incident suggest that ʿUmar ibn al-Khattab heard the news of the tribal rebellion, and wondered aloud what the leader should do. The tribe denying payment sent a message by which they specifically affirmed their faith in Muhammad as the Prophet of God, and indicated that their refusal to pay reflected their understanding that *al-zakat* was a matter of supporting Muhammad in the struggle to secure a political context in which Muslims might practice their religion. When Abu Bakr declared his intention to coerce obedience, ʿUmar questioned the decision, observing that the leader ought not make war against those who professed faith in God and God's Prophet. In reply Abu Bakr argued that his responsibility as leader was to bring the rebellious tribes to heel, because Islam involves a contract by which human beings become obligated to behave in certain ways. The report concludes with ʿUmar's statement that he understood that God had opened the heart of Abu Bakr; that is, that the leader's judgment was somehow inspired.

Sachedina argues that the "discussion" between Abu Bakr and ʿUmar is susceptible of more than one interpretation. When Abu Bakr gave reasons for fighting with the recalcitrant tribes, he specifically said that their contractual obligations did not cease with Muhammad's death. They were obligated to continue payment of *al-zakat* to him, as the successor to Muhammad. Indeed, in another context, Abu Bakr is reported to have said that the believers should take care not to speak of him as the *khalifa* of God, but as the *khalifa* of God's Prophet. Is the contract of which Abu Bakr spoke a matter of religious obligation, or is it political? If the latter, one might suppose that the Shari'a justification for Abu Bakr's policy had to do with a continuing need to secure a political order in which Muslims could feel safe. And that need might vary, according to time and place. In circumstances in which Muslims find themselves free to practice their religion, to proclaim God's word and to worship according to the dictates of their consciences, the *khalifa*, or leader, is not required to punish apostasy as a crime. Indeed, in the kind of setting envisioned by the Universal Declaration of Human Rights, the Muslim community may not need a *khalifa* of the type illustrated by the career of Abu Bakr at all. Rather, the political needs of Muslims are met by governmental institutions that ensure the rights of each and all to freedom of conscience and of religion.

Al-Zawahiri and other militants think of arguments like Sachedina's as corrupt, and say the reasoning illustrates the insidious temptation posed by the prevalence of democratic rhetoric in the contemporary world. But that response does not mean we should conclude that Sachedina is wrong. In the practice of Shari'a reasoning, the legitimacy of an argument is a matter of finding a responsible fit between precedent and contemporary life. Since reports of Abu Bakr's judgment are susceptible of more than one interpretation, Sachedina argues that Shari'a reasoning in the matter of apostasy should be led by the clear declarations of the Qur'an. These indicate that faith is a free gift of God, which no human authority may impose. Muslims do have security interests, of course, and these require a political order in which they may live and worship without fear. Legitimate security interests must not be turned into justifications for the kind of state in which others live in fear of the Muslims, however. Human beings must be free to hear God's word, and political institutions should be designed to observe certain limits. As Sachedina has it, these have to do with the fact that such institutions are not designed to take God's place in matters of faith. They are rather supposed to serve human needs. In his view, it is the militants who are wrong. Shari'a reasoning does *not* support a return to the political models with which premodern 'ulama were familiar. Instead, it requires Muslims to work for human rights, in the context of a democratic, pluralistic state.

By this logic, militants, and by extension anyone arguing for Muslim superintendence as a quintessential aspect of the political vision of Islam, commit a very basic error. The militant version of rule by the Shari'a rests on incorrect readings of historical precedent. If that is the case, then it must also be true that the militants' call to Muslims to fight lacks authority, because it would have Muslims killing and being killed for an unjust cause. In a 1990 essay, "The Development of *Jihad* in Islamic Revelation and History," Sachedina articulates his view on this matter.[10] He describes *jihad,* or struggle in the path of God, as critical to securing the right of Muslims to practice their faith. In certain cases, the aggressive nature of an enemy, for example of a government intent on limiting the right of Muslims to preach or call people to Islam, may require that Muslims take up arms. In such cases, fighting is justified as something "imposed" by the enemy. Importantly, however, the fighting has to do with security. It is not a matter of fighting to establish the hegemony of Islam over other religions, or of Muslims over other human beings. The kind of political order in which Muslims may be most secure is one in which the rights of Christians, Jews, and others, believers and nonbelievers alike, find security in observing a common or "natural" morality in which precepts designed to prevent the infliction of unprovoked injury are the proper basis for criminal law. One might imagine nonbelievers behaving in ways that would require intervention by the state—for example by attacking someone who is preaching in public—in which case believers would expect the state to act. Likewise, if believers attacked someone for his or her expression of incredulity about the claims of religion, one would again think it right for the state to intervene. The important point is that neither belief nor nonbelief justifies state action. Rather, it is the infliction of unprovoked injury that is key. In an important sense, the state is truly neutral in matters of faith. Sachedina notes that this is not the view held by most Muslims, and especially not the view of the majority of Sunni *'ulama* in the premodern period. It was the view of some Shi'i leaders, however. And in any case, it is an understanding of *jihad* that comports well with the sources and methods common to Shari'a reasoning.

Sachedina's work suggests that many of the most important questions about the goals of Islamic militants center upon the notion of religious liberty or rights of conscience. A similar idea governs the work of Abdullahi an-Na'im, who is the Charles Howard Candler Professor of Law at Emory University. An-Na'im is a Sudanese lawyer who left his home country after the 1985 execution of Mahmud Muhammad Taha, the charismatic leader of a group of reform-minded attorneys who called themselves the Republican Brothers. In the late 1970s and into the 1980s, the military regime of Ja'far Nimeiri turned increasingly to a policy of "implementing Shari'a." As became evident, this slogan meant, in the main, that Sudanese who dissented from government policies would be punished according to *al-hudud*. Thus, those convicted of stealing, beyond the realm of petty theft, would have their right hand cut off. Adulterers would be flogged, as stipulated in Qur'an 24:2 ("The woman and the man guilty of adultery or fornication: Flog each of them with a hundred stripes"). And those convicted of apostasy or blasphemy would be punished with death.

An-Na'im's work responds to this context, in which the fate of Mahmud Muhammad Taha illustrates some of the problems of a "literal" application of premodern precedents. Mahmud Taha advocated a revised account of some of the most basic themes in the history of Shari'a reasoning.[11] In particular, he argued that the relationship between the Meccan and Medinan periods in the career of the Prophet should be recast, so that precedents from the former might receive priority over those from the latter period. In some ways, this seems a good argument. The Meccan period, as reflected in the evidence of the "early" sections of the Qur'an and reports of the Prophet's life, focused on timeless aspects of his message. The great themes of Islam are played again and again: the uniqueness of God, the moral responsibilities of human beings, and the coming Judgment are emphatically and powerfully stated. The unbelief of the Quraysh is treated with sadness, and God exhorts the Prophet to bear witness and to endure.

The Medinan period is the time of communal definition and political action. Here one finds the verses on fighting; here again, one finds verses reflecting the conflict between Muslims and Jews and, to a lesser extent, between Muslims and Christians. The content of the verses is clearly related to Arabia, as are the reports of the Prophet's practice. His enemies are specific: the Quraysh, the Jewish tribes living in Medina, hypocrites among the Muslims. These are not timeless characters; they are flesh and blood, bound up with a particular social and political context.

At the same time, most interpreters of Islamic tradition have understood the Prophet's enemies as "types." Their motivation is unbelief, and this is expressed in hostility toward Muhammad and his message. The struggle is epic, connected with a tension between submission and heedlessness that runs throughout history, since the day of creation. Mahmud Muhammad Taha's interpretation was thus unusual. That it would attract the attention of more orthodox scholars and of the Nimeiri government is hardly surprising.

An-Na'im's presentation casts doubt on the notion that the Nimeiri government's interest had to do with Taha's religious teaching.[12] Rather, the point was to suppress criticisms advanced by the Republican Brothers. Taha's interpretation of the relationship between the Meccan and Medinan periods of the Prophet's career lend themselves to the judgment that Shari'a is not a settled matter. For example, punishments for specific crimes—those associated by tradition with *al-hudud*—need not be regarded as settled for all places and times. Indeed, one could argue that, in their original setting, the texts cited as establishing "the limits" were progressive. By setting limits on the punishment applied to adulterers, for example, the texts prevent ongoing feuds between the families and relatives of those hurt by the wrong of sexual infidelity. So Taha argued, and he was hardly the first to do so. The implication is that a government dedicated to the rule of Shari'a in the 1970s and 1980s should not look so much at the form of ancient texts as to the progressive spirit behind them, and that those evaluating policy alternatives should ask not only about the meaning of the Qur'an and the Prophetic *sunna*, but about what human beings have learned about crime and punishment in the thirteen centuries since.

The Nimeiri government was not interested in such niceties. Mahmud Taha was arrested, tried, and convicted of public apostasy and of blasphemy. His death in 1985 marked a watershed in the Republican Brothers' movement, which "went dormant" shortly after these events.[13]

An-Na'im's account of these events is certainly not unbiased. Whatever the precise mix of religious and political motives present in the actions of the Nimeiri government, however, there is a more general valence to the story. Where political leaders are able to classify dissenting opinion as apostasy, or where those presenting alternative views may be accused of blasphemy or heresy, those in power may well be tempted to cite Shari'a precedents as a means of maintaining the status quo. In his early work, an-Na'im's development of this point led him to suggest that contemporary Muslims should reject Shari'a.[14] Here, an-Na'im clearly accepted the definition of Shari'a advocated by the Nimeiri government, as well as by the militant authors of *The Neglected Duty* and the World Islamic Front *Declaration*. In this view, texts do not require interpretation. The meaning of the Qur'an and of the reports of Muhammad's practice is settled; to be faithful is to apply them, as strictly and forthrightly as possible. The Shari'a is therefore not a matter of finding a fit between precedent and contemporary life, but a matter of remolding contemporary life so that it is governed by historical models.

There is much evidence to show that this account of Shari'a is incorrect. The practice of *'ulama* through the centuries indicates that Shari'a reasoning works precisely by way of conscientious arguments about the fit between precedent and new contexts. One proceeds with due respect to the judgments articulated in approved texts. It must never be said that the Shari'a is closed, however. To take such a position is to deny the freedom of God. It is to render God static, whereas the voice speaking in the Qur'an, and to which the Prophet's *sunna* bears witness, is very much dynamic and living.

Given these factors, it is not strange that an-Na'im gradually began to express a different understanding of the authority of Shari'a. In his 1990 *Toward an Islamic Reformation,* for example, he argued that the conditions of contemporary political life and the lessons of history suggest that Muslims must either do away with or revise "historical" Shari'a.[15] That qualification enabled an-Na'im to maintain contact with Islamic practice while expressing his sense that the tradition was in need of reform. Nevertheless, there was still some distance between an-Na'im's account and the kind of reasoning characteristic of Islamic tradition, since the latter requires that one be instructed by precedent. In finding a fit between historical judgments and contemporary life, a conscientious Muslim must show that he or she understands why earlier generations deemed a certain way of acting as faithful to God's purposes. The fact that their judgment may not appeal to a modern person is not in and of itself a reason to set it aside. For example, it is not sufficient to say that someone instructed by the Universal Declaration of Human Rights finds traditional notions about apostasy repugnant—at least, not if one intends to be faithful to the practice of Shari'a reasoning. Instead, one must demonstrate that precedents related to apostasy no longer hold or that they do not fit the context of modern political life. The fact that many people now understand the ways in which political leaders may utilize traditional judgments for authoritarian or totalitarian purposes is relevant to the argument, as are the facts of religious pluralism, increases in literacy, and the legitimate interests of people in building an international community. Given changing contexts, one may well argue that historical precedents, conscientiously formulated, served the cause of justice at one time but do so no longer. Indeed, one might argue that certain features of contemporary life are so different from those of earlier centuries that the attempt to apply specific precedents without revision actually causes injustice.

An-Na'im's most recent work responds to these considerations, and thus presents a much stronger case for reform. His online project, *The Future of Shari'a,* promises a full-bodied version of Shari'a reasoning.[16] The form of the project is itself a model of the conversational nature of historical practice. *The Future of Shari'a* begins with the online publication of a multichapter book, available in a variety of languages, and with an invitation to interested persons around the world to respond using electronic media. In introducing the volume an-Na'im writes:

> The main objective of this book is to promote the future of Shari'a, the normative system of Islam, among believers and their communities, without the enforcement of its principles through the coercive powers of the state . . . I will chal-

lenge the dangerous illusion of an Islamic state that claims the right to enforce Shariʿa principles through the coercive power of the state [as well as the] dangerous illusion [present in] the idea that Islam can or should be kept out of the public life of the community of believers.[17]

An-Naʿim's phrase "the dangerous illusion of an Islamic state" summons up the militant vision of political order and makes clear his view that the identification of rule by the Shariʿa or of Islamic government with the kind of regime envisioned by al-Zawahiri and others is wrongheaded.

An-Naʿim's alternative involves an institutional separation of Islam and state, in which the state is religiously neutral. Such an arrangement is desirable for pragmatic and for principled reasons. With respect to the former, historical experience teaches that those who command the military, police, and taxing powers of the state, and then combine these with the power to define true religion, are easily tempted to overstep their bounds. With respect to principle, an-Naʿim argues that the types of coercion utilized by some modern states undermine the kind of practice Islam wants to encourage.

> Another main reason for insisting on the religious neutrality of the state is that it is a necessary condition for compliance with Islamic precepts and their implementation as religious obligations for individual Muslims. Such compliance must be completely voluntary because it requires pious intention *(niyah)*, which is negated by coercive enforcement of the state.[18]

What, then, of the militant argument that historical precedent establishes a particular model for political life, in which religious and political authority are intertwined? An-Naʿim argues that, aside from the example of the Prophet, the study of Islamic history actually yields a diverse set of precedents. There is no single model for Muslims seeking to fulfill their religious and political responsibilities. There is, instead, a long narrative (or set of narratives) in which Muslims try to negotiate between models involving a complete separation of religion and politics and a complete conflation or convergence of these two dimensions of life.

The Prophet's example is special, says an-Na'im. To a great extent, this is a function of his office. As the Prophet, Muhammad acts with religious authority, meaning that he claims a "superior moral authority that is not subject to the ordinary judgment of human beings."[19] To this, Muhammad joins political authority, which (according to an-Na'im) rests on human abilities, in relation to human purposes; it is therefore subject to evaluation by standards common to human beings. In his career, at least in Medina, the conflation or convergence of religious and political authority is complete, or at least it is as complete as one will ever see. In Muhammad, one finds an example in which political and military leadership accompany religious leadership, and in ways that commend themselves to believers through the centuries.

Once one moves away from the career of the Prophet, however, the picture is mixed. Even in the period of the rightly guided *khilafat,* the relationship between religious and political authority is unclear. With respect to Abu Bakr's decision to fight the tribes that refused to pay *al-zakat,* for example, the argument between Abu Bakr and 'Umar ibn al-Khattab suggests that ultimately, the former acted for political reasons. The challenge of the recalcitrant tribes was a threat to the state, or to Abu Bakr's political authority, rather than to the practice of religion or to the Muslim community's affirmation that Muhammad was God's Prophet. An-Na'im's point is that even in this very early and paradigmatic example, there are important distinctions between the religious and political responsibilities of Muslims.

Similarly with respect to later developments. Here an-Naʿim cites the *mihna*, or test, imposed by al-Maʿmun in an attempt to assert the authority of the *khalifa* in matters of religion. The refusal of Ahmad ibn Hanbal to submit to the ruler, and the support of the people for Ahmad's act, suggest that the majority of the Muslim community recognized that there must be limits on the authority of political leaders when it comes to matters of faith. In their hearts and minds, believers may approve or even long for the convergence of religious and political authority demonstrated by the Prophet. Nevertheless, they knew—and, as an-Naʿim has it, still know—that such convergence is something unique. It will not, and most likely cannot, be attained except in the presence of a leader like Muhammad. And here the notion of Muhammad as the seal of the prophets becomes important. Muhammad is not the only prophet. He is the last and greatest, however, and there can be no other after him. So Muslims affirm, and an-Naʿim argues that the political import of this affirmation is that the convergence of religion and politics one sees in Medina is an unrepeatable event.

An-Naʿim continues with further historical accounts, for example of the relation between religion and politics in Egypt during the Fatimid and Mamluk periods. The point of these examples, as of those already mentioned, is to establish that the study of history indicates that Muslims carried out their religious and political responsibilities in a variety of ways. One who engages in Shariʿa reasoning must therefore deal with a plurality of precedents. The militant vision is simply incorrect. It relies on a simplistic account of precedent as univocal. It is an illusion, because the facts of history do not support the militants' interpretation. It is dangerous, because the militants are willing to use force to achieve their ends, thus subverting the purposes of Islam, as well as causing injury to anyone with a different opinion.

The examples of an-Naʿim and Sachedina indicate that the militant vision of politics is not the only one possible for those engaged in Shariʿa reasoning. The work of Khaled Abou El Fadl extends this point, and does so in several ways. Currently the Omar and Azmeralda Alfi Professor of Law at the University of California, Los Angeles, Abou El Fadl discussed his early attraction to militant piety in Egypt and Kuwait in an interview on National Public Radio. Under the influence of his father, Abou El Fadl began to explore alternatives to militancy, and in his years of study at Yale, the University of Pennsylvania, and Princeton he came to his own distinctive understanding of Shariʿa reasoning.[20]

Some of Abou El Fadl's approach becomes clear in his nonacademic writings. For example, in *The Place of Tolerance in Islam*, Abou El Fadl comments on the precedents related to protected peoples *(ahl al-dhimma)* and their position in an Islamic state:

> When the Qur'an was revealed, it was common inside and outside of Arabia to levy poll taxes against alien groups. Building upon the historical practice, classical Muslim jurists argued that the poll tax is money collected by the Islamic polity from non-Muslims in return for the protection of the Muslim state. If the Muslim state was incapable of extending such protection to non-Muslims, it was not supposed to levy a poll tax.[21]

The comment indicates a careful and historical approach to those precedents set by premodern *ʿulama*. Shariʿa reasoning does not require blind or unthinking adherence to (or applications of) such precedents. Nor does the practice suggest that one may set historical opinions aside, as though discernment of the Shariʿa begins and ended with one's own religious and moral perceptions. Rather, one proceeds by asking about the context in which historical judgments made sense. In addition, Shariʿa reasoning requires conscientiousness in the identification of precedents. It is not enough to note that historical ʿulama justified the collection of special taxes from ahl al-dhimma. One must ascertain the reasons for their opinion, and also note any exceptions to the general rule.

Shariʿa reasoning requires that one respect the opinions of historical scholars. And yet, these opinions are not the only source to be examined. One respects historical judgments when one acts in a way that one's forebears would approve; that is, by examining the texts from which they sought direction, the Qurʾan and reports of the prophetic sunna. Even as past generations of Muslims sought to be faithful to the substance of these sources and, through them, to God, so a contemporary Muslim must examine the sources in search of divine guidance. Given this requirement, one is not surprised when Abou El Fadl continues:

> Aside from the juristic theory justifying the poll tax, the Qurʾan does not, however, pronounce an absolute and unwavering rule in favor of such an institution. Once more, attention to historical circumstance is essential. The Qurʾan endorsed a poll tax as a response to particular groups in Arabia who were persistently hostile to the early Muslims. Importantly, the Prophet did not collect a poll tax from every non-Muslim tribe that submitted to Muslim sovereignty, and in fact, in the case of a large number of non-Muslim but hostile tribes, he paid them a periodic sum of money or goods. These tribes were known as "those whose hearts have been reconciled."[22]

Further precedents indicate that ʿUmar ibn al-Khattab agreed to the request of Christians to pay al-zakat rather than the poll tax. Their point was, or seems to have been, that payment of "special" taxes degraded their participation in the Islamic polity. They preferred to be treated as citizens, and not as a special case. The point is that "there are various indicators that the poll tax is not a theologically mandated practice, but a functional solution that was adopted in response to a specific set of historical circumstances."[23] According to Abou El Fadl, Muslims have a wide variety of precedents from which to choose, and the requirements imposed by diverse contexts suggest the importance of allowing a wide latitude in working out the political dimensions of the Shari'a. One need not accept the militant judgment that arrangements associated with the period of empire constitute the sole measure of a legitimate political order.

Indeed, given specific rulings issued by 'ulama whose vision of social life appears to support that of militant spokesmen, one might strengthen this claim. It is not simply that Muslims "need not" accept the militant version of Shari'a, but that they "ought not" do so. In *Speaking in God's Name: Islamic Law, Authority, and Women*, Abou El Fadl provides a careful critique of numerous *fatawa* pronounced by contemporary scholars in response to questions related to the Shari'a and women.[24] Again and again, one sees that many of those who identify with the Wahhabi approach to Shari'a reasoning appear to work with an understanding very close to that of Osama bin Laden, al-Zawahiri, and other militants. The point here is not that all of those inclined toward this approach are associated with al-Qa'ida or would approve of the argument outlined in the World Islamic Front *Declaration*. Rather, it is that many of those trained in the tradition identified with the eighteenth-century reformer whose judgments played such a critical role in the formation of the modern Saudi state appear to hold a view that, on some of the most important questions of our day, the Shari'a position is clear. For example, with respect to the roles and responsibilities of women, the Qur'an and *sunna* provide answers that are as valid in the twenty-first as in the seventh century. Faithfulness is measured by one's willingness to apply them, without questions or reservations.

Unfortunately, the reasoning of the scholars suggests that such a view rests less on a careful examination of sources, and more on longstanding prejudices. To put it bluntly, many opinions appear to indicate a kind of intellectual laziness. In a discussion of responses to questions related to women's freedom to travel, Abou El Fadl's critique focuses on the Wahhabi scholars' selective use of sources. There are well-established precedents indicating that it is advisable for women to travel with a male escort, preferably a relative. The Wahhabi opinions under examination argue that the concern addressed in such precedents has to do with the prevention of civil strife *(al-fitna)*, which is associated with sexual temptation and immorality. The idea is that a woman who travels alone, away from the protection provided by men who are closely associated with or responsible for her welfare, poses a temptation to other men. The concern with *al-fitna* is therefore identified with the potential for illicit behavior by males; the movement of women must be restricted in order to delimit the possibility that such behavior will occur.

Thus, in response to several specific questions, Wahhabi scholars cite a report in which Muhammad says: "It is not permissible for a woman who believes in God and God's Prophet to travel beyond the distance of a day's travel without [a male escort]." That distance, they suggest, should be understood as eighty kilometers (about fifty miles).

One's understanding of this reasoning is enhanced by a consideration of the particular cases involved. This report, with the gloss indicating the distance, leads to a negative answer in response to a question from a Muslim woman: If her husband is in an accident, so that he suffers injury, and it is requested that she travel to see him, may she do so on her own, in the event that she cannot find a male relative able to travel with her? The same report is cited in connection with an opinion advising an Egyptian man who works in Saudi Arabia that it is contrary to the Shari'a for him to buy tickets for his wife and child to fly to visit him, unless they are accompanied by a male escort—even though the man specifies that he will purchase tickets for a nonstop flight! In response to this second case, one scholar notes that air travel, like other forms of travel, is susceptible of failure. Even nonstop flights may be redirected, in an emergency, with the result that the man's wife would be stranded and without protection. This lack may give rise to immorality, and so even a nonstop flight must be forbidden.

In reviewing these opinions, Abou El Fadl wonders why the scholars issuing these opinions do not see that their views of women and men are archaic, and in particular rest on an assumption that male sexuality is practically uncontrollable. As a strict matter of Shari'a reasoning, however, the first point to be made is that the report, or *hadith,* cited exists in several forms. One who examines the standard collections will find the version in which Muhammad stipulates the distance of "one day's travel" without male escort. One will also find a version that indicates Muhammad said "three days' travel." The obvious question is which one is correct, and thereby useful in discerning the guidance of God.

A second consideration is important as well. Reports of the *sunna* are evaluated not only with respect to the substance, but with respect to the chain or list of transmitters. Thus, the practice of Shari'a reasoning does not only ask *what* Muhammad said with respect to the distance a woman may travel without a male escort, but *who* passed on the report. In this case, there is some reason to doubt the soundness of the report in question, since at least one of the transmitters was considered by later generations as less than reputable—liable to make up or alter the substance of prophetic sayings.

Most decisively, however, a survey of scholarly opinion indicates that historical *'ulama* never associated the requirement that women travel with a male escort with the prevention of *al-fitna*. Rather, exemplary scholars like Malik ibn Anas and al-Shafi'i argued that the point of this requirement was the security of a woman. Further, they were of the opinion that, if safety has been secured by other means, a male escort is not required. Surveying the history of opinion on this question, Abou El Fadl writes that

> assessing the totality of evidence, including the fact that women traveled alone in the time of the Prophet when it was safe to do so, Muslim jurists separated into two camps—a camp that considered the [male escort] rule to be a religious or ethical rule that applies regardless of the social interests involved, and a camp that considered the rule to be hinged on public interest considerations. The latter camp then disagreed as to how to assess the factual circumstances before them. Some argued that older women are safe while young women are not, some that the risk has to be justifiable in light of the interest in question, and some that factual determinations as to safety need to be made on a case by case basis. The basic point is that it is inaccurate to state that Islamic law requires a [male escort] for a traveling woman in all circumstances.[25]

In the practice of Shari'a reasoning, failure to examine and report on the range of scholarly opinion, or to think critically about the use of approved sources, is as problematic as failing to examine the sources at all. With respect to the question of women's roles, as with respect to related questions about political order, the range of opinion is wide, and the set of precedents by which a contemporary Muslim may or should be instructed is diverse. Contrary to the opinions of those whose practice suggests that faithfulness to God is a matter of opening a book or two and applying self-evident texts, the matter of discerning a fit between precedent and contemporary life involves hard work.

As Abou El Fadl has it, the fundamental problem with militant versions of Shari'a reasoning is that they confuse their own views with those of the Qur'an and the *sunna*.[26] In doing so, they are encouraged by a selective or piecemeal approach to the judgments articulated by historical *'ulama*. Militants claim consistency with Islamic tradition. One is never clear just what tradition they mean, however. In the end, many end up posing as authoritarians, rather than submitting themselves to the hard and patient labor required for an understanding of authoritative texts. In Abou El Fadl's most developed scholarly work, the judgments pertaining to rebels *(ahkam al-bughat)* are the focus. In dealing with this particular subset of the more general Shari'a concern with politics and war, Abou El Fadl provides much material relevant to debates about the authority and tactics of militant resistance movements. Indeed, *Rebellion and Violence in Islamic Law* suggests that questions about political-military authority and those pertaining to tactics, though not identical, are deeply connected.[27]

Ahkam al-bughat developed out of a deep concern for political justice.[28] Abu Yusuf, al-Shaybani, and others advised the Abbasid rulers on the matter; in one instance, as we have seen, these scholars responded to Harun al-Rashid's question on the treatment of a rebel leader who failed to honor a negotiated settlement. In rendering their opinions, these early Iraqi scholars referred to the Qur'an and to the example of 'Ali ibn Abi Talib, son-in-law of the Prophet and the fourth of the rightly guided caliphs. With respect to the former, the Iraqi scholars were especially concerned with Qur'an 49:9–10:

> If two parties among the believers fight,
> Put things in order between them.
> If one of the two tries to exit [that is, violates the
> conditions of settlement],
> All of you should fight that one until it complies with the
> command of God.
> If the rebellious side complies, put things in order between
> the two sides
> By means of justice; practice fairness.

Indeed, God loves those who practice fairness.
For the believers constitute a unity; thus,
You are to put things in order between your brothers,
Being aware of God
So that you may receive mercy.

As the lines suggest, the first consideration in a case of intra-Muslim conflict is the unity of believers. Conflict is to be addressed in ways that make for reconciliation. Fighting is justified only when one of the parties is recalcitrant, and even then the restoration of harmony remains the desired goal.

Reports of the policy of 'Ali suggest a model of patience, in line with the aim of restoring peace between believers. Al-Shaybani quotes the following:[29]

[A contemporary of 'Ali said] I entered the Mosque of Kufa through the Kinda gates where I met five men who were cursing 'Ali. One of them, covered in a cloak with a hood, said: "I have made a covenant with God that I shall kill ['Ali]." I kept close until this man's companions dispersed, and then took the man to 'Ali and said: "I heard this man saying that he has made a covenant with God that he will kill you." "Bring him nearer," said [the khalifa], adding: "Woe to you; who are you?" "I am Sawwar al-Manquri," replied the man. "Let him go," said 'Ali. I replied: "Shall I let him go, despite the fact that he says he made a covenant with God to kill you?" The khalifa replied, "Shall I kill him even though he has not killed me?" I said: "He cursed you." "Then curse him or leave him," said 'Ali.

[During the Friday prayer, while 'Ali was preaching, some of his opponents] pronounced the formula: "Judgment belongs to God alone." 'Ali replied: "A word of truth, to which is given a false meaning"; [and he added] "we shall not prohibit you from entering our mosques to mention God's name, we shall not deny you a share of the booty from lawful *jihad* so long as you fight with us, nor shall we fight you until you attack us." Then he resumed his sermon.

[During the Battle of the Camel, when 'Ali fought dissidents led by A'isha, one of the most famous of Muhammad's wives, he said:] "Whoever flees shall not be chased, no prisoner of war shall be killed, none of the wounded shall be killed, no enslavement of women and children shall be allowed, and no property shall be confiscated."

[Whenever fighting ceased] 'Ali ibn Abi Talib deposited everything he had acquired [as war prizes] on the plain so that anyone who recognized something that belonged to him could take it back.

From these precedents, al-Shaybani and other early *'ulama* developed responses to questions for their own day. These responses, in their turn, guided subsequent generations in the practice of Shari'a reasoning. They suggest a serious attempt to balance several considerations. It is clear, for example, that government is considered a necessity with respect to Islamic interests. Indeed, many scholars writing on the topic saw the need as so great that believers would be well advised never to engage in rebellion. Faced with an unjust order (like the one promulgated by al-Ma'mun in connection with *al-mihna*), one should refuse to obey. But one should never take up arms against the established ruler, because doing so causes disorder. It brings division into the community, and does more harm than good.

Nevertheless, there are times when tyranny is so obvious, and oppression so severe, that justice demands that unusual measures be taken. All Muslims have a duty to oppose injustice. In some cases, this requires resort to armed force. How else is one to read Qur'an 4:75, with its challenge to fight and to provide relief to "men, women, and children whose cry is 'Our Lord! Rescue us from this town, whose people are oppressors; and raise for us from you one who will protect . . . one who will help!'" While caution is advised when it comes to outright revolt, one cannot deny the people's right to defend their interests against injustice. The option of rebellion cannot be ruled out in every case.

Should a group rise up against the government of an Islamic state, the goal should be to restore order, within a framework designed to serve justice. To begin, it is important for those in power, and in some sense for the entire community, to know why the group believes resort to military action is required. Suppose, for example, that a group located in a region that is governed by Muslims attacks a police station. Clearly, this is behavior designed to give concern to any established regime. One of the first things a group must do, if the behavior is to be considered anything but criminal, is to provide the public with justifying reasons for this act. *Ahkam al-bughat* suggests that such a justification is critical. In the opinion of premodern *'ulama,* the reasons given should demonstrate an intention to serve the cause of governance by the Shari'a. Rebels might cite the Qur'an, as did the opponents of 'Ali ibn Abi Talib. They might argue that the police service is corrupt, and that verbal appeals to appropriate officials have failed to bring relief. The government may then respond, as did 'Ali. Such citing of reasons serves to distinguish rebels from ordinary criminals. It also supports the notion of shared commitments, in the hope of increasing prospects for reconciliation.

The provision of reasons is important. It is not the only requirement in cases of rebellion, however. For the attack on the police station to count as a revolt rather than a criminal act, the behavior must be that of a representative group. The formal terminology is *al-shauka,* or strength. Scholarly opinion usually tied *al-shauka* to the size of the group, a move which suggests a concern that one is not dealing with a "private" revolt or a feud. The precise number required to satisfy this requirement is a matter of considerable debate, but the direction seems clear. The action cannot be the work of one or two people engaged in a private vendetta against the police. It must be the work of a range of people, representative of a significant portion of the citizenry.

Faced with the attack on a police station, the established regime must respond. Assuming that the perpetrators cite appropriate reasons, and that the attack is not the work of a few disgruntled citizens, the framework of *ahkam al-bughat* requires the government to listen and to offer a solution. The latter might take the form of rebutting criticisms of the police. It might also take the form of an official inquiry or of the imposition of reforms, in the spirit of the Qur'an imperative to "put things in order" between quarreling groups. If the rebels refuse a good-faith effort by the authorities, those in power have no choice but to use military force to put down the resistance. Here they must be careful, however. The goal is reconciliation, not elimination. The example of 'Ali suggests a relatively gentle approach. The rebels are treated in ways consistent with the goal. Government forces are to be scrupulous regarding targets. Prisoners are to be treated with care. Those who rely on the rebels, but are not themselves combatants, are to be spared from harm. And when fighting is over, the defeated rebels have their property restored— provided, of course, that they are willing to accept the cessation of hostilities.

One thing is missing at this point in our account of *ahkam al-bughat*. What rules of engagement govern the activities of the rebels? An answer to this question is critical. In an earlier account of the framework, Abou El Fadl argued that the "rebels are not responsible for any destruction of property or life if such destruction occurs in the course of rebellion."[30] Given the longer and more complete survey of *Rebellion and Violence in Islamic Law,* this seems an overstatement. Indeed, even the earlier account indicates that this is so. When considering specific cases, ʿ*ulama* noted that "in the course of rebellion" means that the actions of one, or even a small group of those associated with the uprising may yet be classified as crimes. For example, let us suppose that in the course of an attack on a police station, we find that a particular rebel took time to hunt down three members of a family, sons of a man with whom the rebel's father has a longstanding rivalry. Witnesses after the fact describe this behavior, noting that it involved leaving a post assigned by the leaders of the rebel forces, and that, upon return to his post, the killer took time to place a phone call to his father, saying, "It's done." Such killing is not done "in the course of the rebellion," and Abou El Fadl notes that scholarly opinion does not protect the one carrying it out from a charge of murder. Then, too, it is possible for a group to go too far. One may and should pursue governance by the Shariʿa with a hearty zeal. But can one's zeal for the Shariʿa countenance acts that themselves violate its provisions? Can a group that systematically refuses to make distinctions between military and civilian targets, for example, expect people to accept its claims to seek rule by the guidance of God?

Ahkam al-bughat certainly gives some latitude to rebel forces with respect to the conduct of military operations. In this, the framework follows the old maxim: those who fight "from below" must have room to maneuver, since the forces of the establishment typically enjoy overwhelming advantages. Yet this latitude cannot be, and is not, absolute. Rebels who claim the mantle of the Shariʿa are not free to utilize means that the Shariʿa cannot approve. If they do—if, in the quest for justice, rebels consistently utilize tactics that violate ordinary standards of right and wrong—who will trust them to take the reins of government, once conflict is over? Right conduct in the use of military force indicates something important about the intention of those fighting. In other words, a stated justification for rebellion, to the effect that the goal is rule by the Shari'a, itself imposes limits on the means rebels may employ.

As Abou El Fadl notes, the framework of *ahkam al-bughat* is not perfectly applicable to the situation of contemporary resistance groups. The most important difference is found in the implicit suggestion of the framework that rebels acknowledge that they have something in common with the established regime (even as representatives of the established regime recognize that they have something in common with the rebels). The kind of giving and taking of reasons outlined by scholars is designed to prevent, or at least to limit, the possibility that either side regards the other as "beyond the pale"; the parties remain members of a community of moral obligation. The authors of *The Neglected Duty* did not think this way. For them, rulers who fail to govern by the Shari'a (that is, as the authors understand it) are traitors to Islam. Such rulers must be killed, along with those who support them.

Similarly for the authors of the Charter of Hamas. Those who occupy Muslim land are, by reason of their location, enemies of Islam and to be treated as combatants; even so, those ostensibly Muslim leaders who would negotiate with Israel and its sponsors, giving away territory that God entrusted to the community of Muhammad, show by their behavior that they are not members of the Muslim community. Between these and the authors of the Charter, one ought not to envision a giving and taking of reasons. The Charter bears witness to the claims of God, and calls all people to repentance. If that is forthcoming, then God is merciful, and, by extension, God's servants ought to be so as well. If repentance does not occur, then fighting results, with an aim to "make God's cause succeed" (Qur'an 8:39). In Israel, we are told, there are no noncombatants except children. Military activity is not directed at these; if they are harmed, it is the fault of those who put them in a war zone.

According to the World Islamic Front *Declaration,* there is no commonality between the United States and its allies, and the fighters who struggle in God's way. Further, there is nothing to discuss or debate between the authors of the *Declaration* and the ruling authorities of historically Muslim states. Things may have been different at one time, for example in 1996, when Osama bin Laden called on the Saudi royal family to expel U.S. forces from the Arabian Peninsula, and to join his effort to eliminate or at least radically limit U.S. power in historically Islamic regions. By 1998, however, the royal family and other established Muslim elites seemed largely irrelevant. The *Declaration* makes this viewpoint clear. And in the summer of 2003, Osama bin Laden's denunciation of Muslim regimes for their failure to join in the defense of the Taliban in Afghanistan made it clear that he regarded himself less as a "rebel" in the manner envisioned by *ahkam al-bughat,* and more as a combination of leader and participant in a community struggling to be born. It is critical, bin Laden said, that Muslims (meaning those pursuing the vision he articulates) gain control of a territory within which they may implement the rule of Shari'a. Without a geopolitical expression, he stated, "the religion ceases to exist."[31] All humanity is the loser.

There are important differences between the situations envisioned by *'ulama* whose rulings constitute the framework of *ahkam al-bughat.* And yet, there is an important way in which that framework does apply, at least in terms of what one might call its deeper assumptions. For the same questions that occur in connection with the behavior of rebel groups in the course of their activities may be asked with respect to the conduct of contemporary militants. Who will trust their statements of intention, when their conduct is inconsistent with the sources to which they appeal? Militants state that their aim is to establish rule by the Shari'a. Their understanding of Shari'a is controversial, as indicated by various Muslim critiques of militant tactics, and also by the alternatives represented by scholars like Sachedina, an-Na'im, and Abou El Fadl. Leaving these contentions aside, however, one may also ask the question of intention. How is it that a group or groups that claim the mantle of the Prophet, and appeal to the Qur'an and the *sunna*, can declare a settled policy of indiscriminate fighting? This point needs care. We know that those engaged in fighting sometimes violate the rules of war. We know that no military campaign is free from tragedy or from mistakes. In the World Islamic Front *Declaration* and other statements, however, Muslim militants set forth an intention to wage indiscriminate war *as a matter of policy*. The justifications offered, to the effect that these are acts of reciprocal justice (that is, the other side killed our civilians, so we will kill theirs) or that there are no civilians in a democratic state, are unconvincing. And they are so, on Shari'a grounds. The question of intention focuses on consistency. It goes to the heart of evaluations of character. Who will trust militants to rule by the Shari'a if they themselves are unwilling to be governed by the Shari'a?

Muslim democrats are certainly engaged by the issue of militant tactics. In this they, like the Shaykh al-Azhar, Yusuf al-Qaradhawi, and Muhsin al-'Awaji, are participants in an argument regarding the militants' refusal to fight according to precedents governing the conduct of war. Muslim democrats' criticism goes further than this, however. For them, militant failings in the conduct of war raise questions about militant intentions. Indeed, the failings of the militants extend to the practice of Shari'a reasoning itself, particularly with respect to a conscientious examination of the context in which historical judgments were set. In all, the democrats' logic suggests that the practice of Shari'a reasoning does not legitimate the kind of political order the militants envision. Sachedina, an-Na'im, and Abou El Fadl provide an alternative, in the form of an Islamic rationale for democratic order. Their reasoning suggests that militants not only violate norms governing the conduct of war. They also call Muslims to kill and die in the service of a cause that is not authorized by the practice of Shariʿa reasoning. The call to *jihad* stipulated in the World Islamic Front *Declaration* and other militant texts is not simply unwise. It is unjust.

In arguing this way, Muslim democrats take a position outside the mainstream of modern Muslim political thought. They also illustrate an important point about the connections between just-war argument and political authority. The former are in some sense distinct from the latter. Human beings can deliberate about the justice of a military campaign in ways that do not engage questions about the ideal form or order of society. Muslims can and do argue about militant conceptions of justice in war without touching the differences between the alternatives represented by Islamic government and democracy.

Nevertheless, the forthright declaration of a policy of targeting noncombatants ought to provide reason for concern about the intention of militant groups. And, upon examination, we may wonder whether there is something to the Muslim democrats' notion that the very idea of Islamic government constitutes a temptation to resort to force where it ought not be used. No one familiar with the history of religions should think that this is only or especially a Muslim problem. Whenever Americans or Europeans consider these issues, the legacy of Christian intolerance is close at hand; indeed, that legacy constitutes one part of the story by which modern democracy was born. Muslim democrats are now working through that problem for their tradition. In doing so, they remind us that although judgments about war are not identical with arguments about political authority, they can be usefully related. In the context of the European wars of religion, we find the record of a rather bold peasant who asked a soldier: "Who will believe that your cause is just, when your behaviours are so unjust?"[32] The logic of Muslim democrats suggests a similar way of relating arguments about the justice of war to claims about political authority.

CHAPTER SIX

MUSLIM ARGUMENT AND
THE WAR ON TERROR

The most important weakness in the militant claim to represent true Islam is the contradiction between the end professed and the means employed. Those who seek rule by the Shariʿa should themselves be ruled by its norms. If they fail in this regard, their claim to represent the cause of justice and right is placed in doubt. Militants, it appears, are their own worst enemy.

This weakness provides an opening for those who would present an alternative. Muslim democrats argue that Islamic tradition values consultation, consensus, and freedom of conscience. Correlatively, important precedents suggest worries about the tendency of zealots to resort to violence, and thus to short-circuit processes of discussion and debate. Tradition, say the advocates of democracy, does not bind Muslims to one form of political order. Rather, it instructs them to think hard about the lessons of history, as well as about the

peculiar mix of challenges and opportunities present in diverse political contexts. For Abdulaziz Sachedina, Abdullahi an-Na'im,
Khaled Abou El Fadl, and others like them, Muslims have good reasons for judging that the most appropriate form of political order involves democratic practices that allow all citizens to exercise rights of
freedom of conscience and religion. Muslims should therefore reject
militancy and, with it, all forms of politics that rely on explicit or
implicit forms of religious coercion. They should align themselves
with Jews, Christians, and others in the promotion of democracy. In
doing so, Muslims will honor God and God's Prophet, and will pro-
mote the values embodied in the practice of Shari'a reasoning.

What are the chances that Muslim democrats will prevail? The answer depends in part on the logic of their presentation. For example,
we may ask whether the advocates of democracy make a convincing
case, whether their use of precedents identified with Abu Bakr's policy toward the "turning" of certain Arab tribes is correct. That is an
important question. It requires a careful response. Comparing the
arguments presented by Muslim democrats and those of Muslim
militants, one may at least say this: insofar as militants suggest that
the meaning of Abu Bakr's judgment is self-evident, their argument
does not fit with the historical record. In suggesting that reports of
this incident are open to interpretation, the advocates of democracy
have the weight of tradition on their side. Shari'a reasoning is a tradition of argument, in which human beings engage in the giving and
taking of reasons in hopes of ascertaining the guidance of God. One
cannot say, of course, that Shari'a reasoning knows no bounds. Participants in this practice must acknowledge the authority of the
Qur'an and the example of the Prophet. They must respond to consensual precedents established in earlier generations. They must display the rationale by which a connection between those precedents
and the context of contemporary Muslims is established. Without
such limits, there can be no Shari'a reasoning as Muslims have

known and practiced it for nearly fourteen centuries. Nonetheless, it is possible to draw the boundaries too tight, and to short-circuit the process of reasoned argument by which the practice flourishes. The militant position closes off debate. In particular, it has little use for dissenting opinions. In this respect, if in nothing else, Muslim democrats have the better of the argument.

It is important to evaluate democratic arguments in this way. But the contest between advocates of Islamic governance and Muslim democrats is not only a matter of the interpretation of texts, or of accounts of the nature of precedent. This contest has also to do with the ability of participants to articulate a fit between past and present, and to persuade others that this connection serves to enable the Muslim community to fulfill its mission of calling people to God. In this sense, democrats have always faced challenges. In an earlier time, the association of democracy with European colonialism led Muslims to think of advocates of democracy as servants of oppression. More recently, the ambiguous position of Muslims in Europe presents a challenge, with activists in the historical territory of Islam suggesting that the difficulties of North African immigrants in France or the character of opposition to Turkey's application for membership in the European Union indicates that democratic states fail to deal with Muslims in ways that suggest equal regard. The Rushdie Affair, the more recent Danish cartoon controversy and the continuing debates over women wearing *al-hijab,* the traditional headscarf, add to the mix.

In the United States, the progress of Muslims during the 1980s and 1990s appeared to suggest a more hopeful future for Muslim advocates of democracy. Since 9/11, however, stories about differential treatment of Muslims and discussions of the provisions of the Patriot Act have filled the pages of Muslim magazines. Most of all, the current debate between Muslim democrats and advocates of Islamic government is framed by the U.S.-designated war on terror. Muslims are well aware that President George W. Bush, Prime Minister Tony Blair, and other leaders of democratic states have interpreted the conflict with Muslim militants as a struggle between people who love freedom and people who do not, or between those who advocate democracy as the best form of government for humankind, and those who advocate the "Talibanization" of the Middle East. The public association of regime change in Afghanistan and Iraq with the task of bringing democracy to the Middle East has opened a wide debate among Muslims regarding the justice of war and the intentions of the great democratic powers.

Muslim argument about the just war thus extends to discussion of the war on terror. Statements and publications by militants and Muslim democrats bring the issues sharply into focus. The latter voice a concern that the conduct of the war on terror is hurting the cause of democracy among Muslims. The rhetoric of militants helps us to understand why.

The Worries of Muslim Democrats

A series of articles by Abdullahi an-Naʿim expresses a number of concerns about the war on terror. In November 2001 an-Naʿim joined in an online discussion of the question "Is This a New Kind of War? September 11 and Its Aftermath." Arguing that the attacks of 9/11 constituted a violation of international standards of human rights, an-Naʿim asserted that those who would fight the perpetrators should conduct themselves in ways that affirm those standards.[1] A just war against terrorists should therefore involve a coordinated effort focused on international institutions like the United Nations and the International Criminal Court. Further, the campaign should aim at full participation by those countries most affected by the actions of al-Qaʿida and like-minded groups. In an-Naʿim's judgment, two UN Security Council resolutions following 9/11 failed to grant clear and precise authorization for military action against al-Qaʻida bases in Afghanistan or against the Taliban regime, and the readiness of the United States and its allies to proceed without such authorization provided a poor example of democratic politics.

An-Naʻim followed this presentation with a 2002 essay, "Upholding International Legality against Islamic and American *Jihad*." As the title suggests, an-Naʻim begins with questions about the legal status of U.S. efforts in Afghanistan, as well as that of the 9/11 attacks. He then turns to a more pragmatic point. As a Muslim and advocate of democracy, an-Naʻim judges that the conduct of the war on terror is harmful to his case. Muslim democrats struggle against obstacles that are "internal" to Muslim societies, he says. These include the conservatism built into the practice of Shariʻa reasoning. Such internal obstacles can be complicated by "external" factors, and U.S. foreign policy must be regarded as one of these. The U.S. government has a right and duty to defend its citizens, but its long-term interest requires that this right be exercised in ways consistent with democratic values. In this connection, an-Naʻim writes:

> U.S. foreign policy contributes to the erosion of the internal prerequisites for social change and transformation [in Muslim societies], as well as reinforcing a sense of external threat that encourages conservative entrenchment. It also encourages strong skepticism about the validity of universal human rights . . . This recent failure of international legality severely undermines the conceptual and political premise of arguments against the traditional understanding and practice of *jihad* in Islamic society.[2]

Two essays published in 2005 continue in the same line.[3] We need not agree with an-Naʻim on all the particulars in order to appreciate his point. Many would wonder, for example, whether his arguments assign too much weight to actions by the United Nations. An-Naʻim appears to create an opening for such questions when he writes that the permanent members of the Security Council have used their position in ways that suggest an intention to advance their own power interests rather than the international rule of law. For our purposes, the more important point is the pragmatic judgment: the conduct of the United States and its allies undermines the cause of democracy in the historical territory of Islam.

The success of Muslim democrats depends not only on the logic of their arguments, but on perceptions of the behavior of democratic states. Part of the appeal of democracy in a Shari'a framework is that it embodies a process of consultation. An-Na'im's arguments suggest the worry that the conduct of the war on terror obscures the sense that democratic politics correlates with a policy process that is deliberative and involves broad participation. Ideally, such a process leads to action based on a consensus—perhaps of the majority of those affected, but if not that, at least with broad support from those in positions of responsibility. Muslim democrats envision a process in which participants engage in giving and taking reasons, citing historical examples and existing laws, and debating the facts of a current case. Democratic policymaking thus becomes an extension of procedures familiar to Muslims informed about the practice of Shari'a reasoning. This depiction is crucial to the case made by Muslim democrats. For the United States to bypass or short-circuit procedures of consultation undermines their case, because it suggests hypocrisy in the heart of a leading exemplar of democracy in action.

Comments by other Muslim democrats suggest a similar worry.[4] Will Muslims believe that democracy is legitimate, if they perceive injustice in the behavior of democratic states? An-Na'im's criticisms constitute a warning: if the United States and its allies are not careful, the conduct of the war on terror will present militants with a golden opportunity. The greatest weakness of militants involves a gap between their stated goals and the means they employ. Defenders of democracy must not give cause for Muslims to identify them with an analogous gap. The question "Who will believe that your cause is just, when your behaviours are so unjust?" may provide a rhetorical tool for militants as well as for democrats. The evidence suggests that advocates of Islamic government think this question serves them well. Some are pressing the question with great skill.

Militants and the War on Terror

All indications are that Muslim militants, or more generally advocates of Islamic governance, believe the war on terror has granted them an unprecedented opportunity to advance their political as well as their military goals. For our purposes, the most important evidence of this result lies in the way the rhetoric of leading spokesmen redirects Muslim just-war argument toward the policies of the United States and its allies. We have already seen some of this, for example in al-Zawahiri's justification of the 7/7 attacks: "You made rivers of blood in our countries, so we blew up volcanoes of rage in yours."[5] Violence deserves violence, he says, in line with al-Qaʻida's assertion of the necessity of reciprocal justice.

A more subtle piece of rhetoric comes from another, and perhaps surprising, direction. When Iranian President Mahmoud Ahmadinejad published a letter to President Bush in May 2006, most American and European commentators treated it as irrelevant. Secretary of State Condoleezza Rice led the way in this response, dismissing the letter as lacking in any serious proposals regarding the critical issue before policymakers, which was how to deal with Iran's nuclear program.

In one sense, Secretary Rice was correct. The Iranian president's letter did not address this issue, nor did it offer concrete proposals to deflect or remove international concerns about Iran's policy of supplying the Lebanese-based Hizbullah or certain Iraqi resistance groups with material support. In addition, a number of widely publicized quotes emphasizing Ahmadinejad's readiness to relate belief in the imminent appearance of the Hidden Imam, or Mahdi, to the possibility of nuclear war were not simply worrisome, but made some commentators question his mental balance.

Ahmadinejad's letter, however, is an important intervention in Muslim just-war argument. Once we place it in the context of his account of the mission of the Islamic Republic, and understand its primary audience as young Muslims rather than the U.S. president and his policy advisers, the document provides a clear example of the kind of analysis an-Na'im fears, in the context of the war on terror.

Ahmadinejad took the oath of office as president of the Islamic Republic of Iran in August 2005. An early supporter of the 1978 revolution, he has been active in the republic's political affairs since the outset. As a member of the Revolutionary Guard, Ahmadinejad served during the long war against Iraq. Estimates of Iranian casualties put the number at one million, with perhaps another million on the Iraqi side. The war began when Saddam Hussein ordered Iraqi troops to cross the border into Iranian territory in 1980. It concluded in 1988, with a peace arrangement described by the Ayatollah Khomeini as "worse than drinking poison." For Saddam, the fighting had been motivated by his desire to persuade the new Iranian government to cease a propaganda campaign aimed at Shi'i and other Iraqis dissatisfied with his government. For Khomeini and the revolutionary regime, Saddam's invasion was an attack on an Islamic state and constituted "rebellion by blasphemy against Islam."[6]

When Ahmadinejad became mayor of Tehran in 2003, he proposed moving the bodies of Iranians killed in the fighting to major squares in the city, thus emphasizing their role as martyrs for the Islamic state. In general, Ahmadinejad's political rhetoric depicts an ongoing, revolutionary struggle. "We didn't participate in the revolution for turn by turn government," he said during his campaign for the presidency. "This revolution tries to reach a world-wide govern-ment." In line with this goal, Ahmadinejad advocated better links be-tween Muslim states, and even the establishment of a kind of union between Iran and its neighbors. The arrangement would end visa re-quirements, for example, so that people could enjoy greater freedom with respect to pilgrimages—an issue particularly important to Shi'i believers, for whom the Iraqi cities of Karbala and Najjaf contain important shrines.[7]

More fundamentally, Ahmadinejad's rhetoric suggests that Islamic faith is essential to his view of the world. For him, the 1978 revolu-tion occurred in the context of God's providence. At the same time, the long struggle preceding the revolution suggests the importance of determination, and a willingness to take risks in the pursuit of goals that strike others as foolish. Speaking to a conference of Mus-lim students on October 26, 2005, now-President Ahmadinejad dis-cussed questions about current affairs, particularly those related to Israel and Palestine, in the context of an account of the Islamic revo-lution. He commended the organizers of the conference on their se-lection of the theme "The World without Zionism," saying that it takes courage to imagine the kind of change that such a phrase im-plies. As Ahmadinejad put it, the Israeli-Palestinian dispute is not simply a matter of a contest over land, or between Judaism and Is-lam. It must be seen in the context of a continuing struggle for lead-ership in world affairs, and ultimately as a matter related to the na-ture and destiny of human beings. As he put it, "The establishment of the occupying regime [in Jerusalem] was a major move by the world oppressor [the United States] against the Islamic world." Many say that the creation of Israel cannot be undone, that "it is not possi-ble to have a world without the United States and Zionism." But, Ahmadinejad said, "we" know this is not the case. The fall of the United States, of Israel, and of Zionism, "is a possible goal and slo-gan." How do "we" know this? Because of the lessons of the 1978 revolution and the subsequent history of the Islamic Republic of Iran.

> We had a hostile regime in this country that was undemo-
> cratic, armed to the teeth and which, with SAVAK, its secu-
> rity apparatus . . . watched everyone. An environment of
> terror existed. When our dear Imam [Khomeini] said that
> the regime must be removed, many of those who claimed
> to be politically well-informed said it was not possible. All
> the corrupt governments were in support of the regime
> when Imam Khomeini started his movement. All the West-
> ern and Eastern countries supported the regime . . . and
> said the removal of the regime was not possible. But our
> people resisted and it is 27 years now that we have survived
> without a regime dependant on the United States. The tyr-
> anny of the East and the West over the world must end, but
> weak people who can see only what lies in front of them
> cannot believe this.[8]

The references to "the East" in this passage mean the old Soviet Union. Ahmadinejad went on to note that the great tyranny associated with this powerful state has ended. "Who could believe that one day we could witness the collapse of the Eastern Empire?" he asked. "But we have seen its fall during our lives and it collapsed in such a way that we have to refer to libraries because no trace of it is left." Similarly, the Ayatollah Khomeini "said Saddam must go and he said he would grow weaker than anyone could imagine." Now Saddam was in chains, standing trial. Ahmadinejad's failure to mention the role of the United States and its allies in the fall of Saddam was not disingenuous. For the Iranian president, all the events mentioned have taken place within the plan of God, who may and does make use even of oppressors in bringing about the desired state of af-fairs. The United States and its allies entered Iraq under false pretenses, and with the intention of increasing their own dominance. But they too will fall. In the end, Israel will vanish, just as the Soviet Union did. Thus, Ahmadinejad urged his listeners not to compromise. Neither should they be misled by "tricks" like the 2005 withdrawal of Israeli forces from the Gaza Strip. There can be no compromise on the issue of Palestine. Ahmadinejad ended with a warning to the leaders of Muslim states: "Those who are sitting in closed rooms cannot decide for the Islamic nation and cannot allow this historical enemy to exist in the heart of the Islamic world."[9] The message of this speech affirms Ahmadinejad's faith that the Islamic Republic, and his own administration, are in line with the movement of history: "Thanks to the blood of the martyrs, a new Islamic revolution has arisen, and the Islamic revolution [of 2005, the year of his inauguration] will, if God wills, cut off the roots of injustice in the world." The "wave of the Islamic revolution . . . will reach the entire world."[10]

Ahmadinejad's approach since 2005 indicates that he sees no contradiction between such faith and the practice of power politics. The Iranian president understands, for example, that Iran's development of nuclear power changes the Islamic Republic's standing in world affairs. Although his public statements stress that Iran has no plan to turn its nuclear program toward the development of weapons, Ahmadinejad certainly knows that any state dealing with the Islamic Republic must now take the possibility of such a turn into account. Announcing that, as of November 15, 2006, Iran "possesses the full nuclear fuel cycle" is a way of asserting that the Islamic Republic has taken another step toward leadership in international affairs. In particular, such a development should be placed in the context of Ahmadinejad's criticisms of the current state of international politics, for example as embodied in the composition of the UN Security Council, whose five permanent members hold the veto power over its decisions: "It is not just for a few states to sit and veto global approvals. Should such a privilege continue to exist, the Muslim world with a population of nearly 1.5 billion should be extended the same privilege."[11] With his reference to "the Muslim world," presumably Ahmadinejad was indicating that Iran, as the leading power among Muslim states, deserves equal standing with the great powers currently holding permanent Security Council seats. Ahmadinejad's policy toward Iraq, Syria, and Lebanon indicates that he considers Iran a suitable candidate for hegemon in the historical heartland of Islam. That role correlates with the Iranian constitution's stipulation that the foreign policy of the Islamic Republic is dedicated to the protection of Muslim interests everywhere—not least, or perhaps better, as a first step, those Muslims identified with Shiʿi faith.

Ahmadinejad is not a member of the ʿulama, any more than al-Zawahiri or Osama bin Laden. And there are important differences between his understanding of Islam and the vision promulgated by these and other militant figures, as well as an important distinction in his position. As president of the Islamic Republic, Ahmadinejad is constrained by the requirements of a constitution. At the same time, he operates with considerably fewer worries about legitimacy than does the leadership of al-Qaʿida. When he speaks about the aims of an Islamic state, Ahmadinejad has the institutions of the Islamic Republic behind him.

Ahmadinejad's public statements reflect his commitment to the rule of Shariʿa. These statements also indicate that he understands Islamic government as something distinct from and superior to liberal democracy. The Iranian president perceives the crisis of our times as an opportunity to bear witness to the truth about human beings, that is, the truth of Islam. For him, there is a competition for legitimacy underway. Ahmadinejad is campaigning for Iran to assume leadership, first in the world of Islam and then in the international community. In his view, Iran's population, mineral resources, geography, and history make it destined to lead. But if it does lead, it will do so under the banner of Islam. Ahmadinejad feels no need to stress the differences between Sunni and Shi'i Muslims at this time of opportunity. The struggle with the United States is paramount, and he hopes (like the Ayatollah Khomeini before him) that others will join him, setting aside their differences for the sake of victory. In the meantime, he proceeds by calling all the nations to the path of religion, and by depicting the United States and its allies in the international community as hypocrites.

Nowhere is this approach clearer than in Ahmadinejad's public letter to President Bush.[12] In that document, Ahmadinejad raises a number of questions and ultimately invites the president to the practice of true religion, which Ahmadinejad identifies with Islam.

Ahmadinejad does not begin with assertions of the superiority of Islam. Instead, he asks President Bush how one can claim to be a follower of Jesus Christ, presenting oneself as an advocate for values everyone can approve, and yet engage in behaviors that clearly contradict religion and morality?

> Can one be a follower of Jesus Christ . . . the great
>   Messenger of God,
> Feel obliged to respect human rights,
> Present liberalism as a model civilization,
> Announce one's opposition to the proliferation of nuclear
>   weapons and WMDs,
> Make "War and Terror" his slogan,
> And finally, work towards the establishment of a unified
>   international community—a community which Christ
>   and the virtuous of the earth will one day govern;
> But at the same time, have countries attacked, the lives,
>   reputations, and possessions of people destroyed, and on

the slight chance that there are criminals in a village, city, or convoy, have the entire village, city, or convoy set ablaze?

Ahmadinejad continues with questions, wondering how a person dedicated to religious and moral ideals can justify the war in Iraq on the pretext that its government possesses weapons of mass destruction, or how such a person can waste the resources of his own country in pursuit of conflicts that achieve little. It is important, in the rhetoric of this text, that Ahmadinejad plays to the notion of Christians as followers of Jesus Christ; for him, this sort of appeal involves no contradiction, since Islam affirms Jesus as a prophet, and he chooses not to address the problematic aspects of Christian practice in this context. He is interested only in whether the U.S. president's policies are consistent with values that most Americans hold. He believes the answer is no, and, even more, Ahmadinejad believes that the hypocrisy of the Bush administration is endemic to the political system it represents. The failures of the president and those with him are failures of a civilization. That civilization, indebted to Christian sources (and thus ultimately reflecting at least something of the truth of Islam), has taken a wrong turn. Matters can be put right, but only if leaders like President Bush begin to listen and to understand the call of faith. So long as such leaders act as though they alone are the rulers of the earth, and that they have the right to make decisions for people to whom they have not listened, or with whom they have not consulted, suffering will occur. If the American president and those with him will turn from pride and acknowledge that even the powerful must live within the limits set by God, however, then it may be possible to build a better world.

In this vein, Ahmadinejad presents what he identifies as the questions of his students. These focus on specific issues in the conduct of the war on terror, including the treatment of Muslim prisoners at Guantánamo Bay, rumors of secret prisons in Europe, the relationships between the United States and Israel, and the refusal of the great powers to work with Hamas after its victory in the 2005 Palestinian elections. How, he asks, are these actions consistent with democratic or any other values? Ahmadinejad also indicates that his students wonder about U.S. policies in Latin America and Africa. They are struck, he says, by the fact that these policies appear to aim at security by means of domination. Yet the American people do not seem more secure as a result of post-9/11 policies, Ahmadinejad writes; they actually feel less secure, and the American government and media seem to conspire to make them afraid. Then he comes to his "main contention."

> Those in power have a specific time in office, and do not rule indefinitely, but their names will be recorded in history and will be constantly judged in the immediate and distant futures. The people will scrutinize our presidencies. Did we manage to bring peace, security, and prosperity for the people; or insecurity and unemployment? Did we intend to establish justice, or just to support special interest groups, and by forcing many people to live in poverty and hardship, make a few people rich and powerful . . . ? They will judge us on whether we remained true to our oath of office—to serve the people, which is our main task, and the traditions of the prophets—or not.[13]

Ahmadinejad clearly believes that the answers to these questions are in doubt, at least with respect to President Bush, and he argues that there is a better way. The way is that of Jesus, of Moses, of Muhammad, and of all the other prophets. It is the way of faith that there is only one God, and that nothing in this world—no human being or group or society—has a claim to leadership other than through or on behalf of the path ordained by God.

> History tells us that repressive and cruel governments do not survive . . . The Almighty has not left the universe and humanity to their own devices. Many things have happened contrary to the wishes and plans of governments. These tell us that there is a higher power at work and all events are determined by God.[14]

Asking President Bush to join with him in "a genuine return to the teachings of the prophets, to monotheism and justice, to preserve human dignity and obedience to the Almighty and His prophets," Ahmadinejad avers that such a return is only a matter of recognizing the direction of history. "Liberalism and western democracy have not been able to help realize the ideals of humanity. Today these two concepts have failed. Those with insight can already hear the sounds of the shattering and fall of the ideology and thoughts of the liberal democratic systems." Wishing peace to President Bush, the Iranian leader's letter concludes: "Whether we like it or not, the world is gravitating towards faith in the Almighty and justice and the will of God will prevail over all things."[15]

Ahmadinejad's letter is addressed to President Bush. More than this, however, the Iranian president presents himself as speaking *for* Muslims. In assuming this role, he also writes *to* Muslims, confirming and encouraging their sense that the advocates of democracy are on the wrong path. The questions from students may well come from Ahmadinejad's days as a university instructor. They have a wider valence than such immediate experience would suggest, however. In Ahmadinejad's letter, his students stand for young Muslims around the world. Indeed, with respect to their questions about U.S. policies in Latin America and Africa, they stand for the young of every nation on Earth, especially those with some connection to what the Ayatollah Khomeini described as *al-mustadafin,* the oppressed.

The various questions raised reflect a particular rhetorical strategy. Ahmadinejad does not begin with affirmations of the superiority of Islam, or with a discussion of the various arguments for and against democracy. At the outset, he is prepared to let President Bush's professions of value stand. When the questions begin, Ahmadinejad speaks concretely, guiding his readers even as he purports to represent their concerns. The early questions, in particular, have to do with the tactics of an administration engaged in a war on terror. While Ahmadinejad's queries engage broader issues of politics and economics as the letter proceeds, the conduct of military operations takes pride of place. We may paraphrase Ahmadinejad's questions as follows:

In the struggle against aggression, can the U.S. commit aggression?

In the fight against groups that practice lying and deception, should the United States and its allies go to war under false pretenses?

In the attempt to defeat groups who kill civilians and military personnel without discrimination, is it right for U.S. forces to cause civilian deaths—particularly in numbers that suggest excess, in terms of the value of the direct, military target of their operations?

In defense of liberty, should the United States violate the liberties of Muslims, denying them due process of law and other rights guaranteed in international conventions?

From these basic questions, Ahmadinejad moves to broader issues regarding the form of political life. His strategy is to undermine the

Bush administration's claims by exposing it as hypocritical. In effect, he encourages readers in worries about the administration's intentions. "Who will believe that your cause is just," they ask, "when your conduct belies the values of justice?"

We have engaged this type of argument earlier, with respect to criticisms of militant groups. Exposing hypocrisy is a perennial device in political debate. Nevertheless, Ahmadinejad has a point. The questions he articulates did not emerge in a vacuum. Polling data from around the world, and particularly in historically Muslim regions, record a widespread concern about American intentions.[16] These are connected with very specific practices associated with the war on terror. For example, "rendition," the practice of removing U.S. prisoners to other countries for purposes of interrogation, is defended by U.S. officials as necessary in the struggle against terror. For much of the world, however, its use and its connection with "secret" prisons raise questions about the possible use of torture as a technique for extracting information. In the context of continuing controversy about the denial of due process to prisoners interned at Guantánamo Bay, or of revelations about mistreatment of prisoners at Abu Ghraib, the debate over rendition is part of a wider concern that the states prosecuting the war on terror make use of immoral means. Similarly, data on the number of civilians killed in Iraq feed worries that, in the attempt to address problems in security, coalition forces are resorting to excessive or disproportionate tactics. And it seems clear that, however offensive and provocative the actions of Hizbullah and of a Palestinian group in kidnapping Israeli soldiers in June 2006, much of the world believes that the Israeli response was disproportionate, and that, by extension, the United States is complicit in the actions of Israel.

Most relevant to our interests is the resonance of Ahmadinejad's questions with his primary audience. For Muslims, and especially those who are young, the perception of contradictions between U.S.

values and U.S. policies is critical. These contradictions suggest that something is wrong. If the Bush administration represents democratic values, then Ahmadinejad's "students" will have nothing to do with it. For them, he says, there is a better way—the way of the prophets; the way of Islam. President Ahmadinejad's letter explicitly invites George Bush to follow Islam. Implicitly, and more importantly, the letter invites Muslims, young and old alike, to join the Iranian president in bearing witness to the more excellent way of ordering political life represented in the sources and practice of Islamic tradition. From questions about the conduct of war to issues related to intention, to judgments about democracy itself—the line of argument is not logical, in the strict sense of the word. Even were the charges of unjust conduct proven true, and the intention of the Bush administration and its major allies unsound, that outcome would not invalidate the argument of Muslim democrats with respect to democracy.

Logical proof is not Ahmadinejad's strategy, however. He seeks rather to undermine the case for democracy by showing that its most public defenders are less than forthright. That point made, he relies on his primary audience to make the connection: the weak character of democratic leaders reflects the unsound nature of democracy as a system. Immorality in the conduct of war results from the fact that democracy ignores the role of government in the formation of moral character.

We have seen that Ahmadinejad's views are influenced by the history of the Islamic Republic of Iran, and his experience of revolution and war provides the immediate background of his critique of democracy. The Ayatollah Khomeini commented on more than one occasion about the two types of government present in human history.[17] The first is a type that may be described as rule by human law. The phrase suggests government of, by, and for the people. Indeed, Khomeini's further characterizations point to the particular type of democracy that philosophers associate with the term "liberal." Governments of this type have a limited scope. They prohibit public assault, for example, and they punish those who violate others' property, but they do not consider that government has a role in the cultivation of character. The objective is to protect individual liberty. In that connection, democratic societies draw lines intended to prevent or inhibit governments from interfering in the private lives of citizens. What one does in one's home is not a concern of government, even if that entails watching television programs that exploit the violent emotions associated with physical assault, or that celebrate thieves as clever. Protections of individual liberty thus leave room for a wide variety of activities that, from many points of view, serve to undermine character by allowing people to indulge all sorts of negative passions. Since the state provides little or no guidance in these matters, rather leaving the cultivation of character up to individuals and private or voluntary associations, weaker or less hardy souls are subject to exploitation—watching lewd or exceptionally violent films may be a personal choice, but there are people ready and waiting to feed and enlarge that choice, in line with their own pursuit of wealth and the power it brings. Overall, Khomeini depicts modern democracy as a kind of abdication of responsibility before God. In the space it leaves for selfishness and other "small" forms of tyranny, human beings develop the taste for larger forms. Alternatively, one could say that left to their own devices, human beings indulge themselves in ways that leave them bereft of the moral power necessary to recognize and resist oppression. The clearest examples of this loss of moral power involve the willingness of democratic states to tolerate and even to cherish a rapacious market whereby the poor are enslaved by mountains of debt, and the immorality of the Western powers in the conduct of war.

Over against democracy or government by human law Khomeini set Islamic government, which operates in accordance with divine law. The latter does not leave human beings to wallow in the muck of their own desires. Rather, it encourages people to aspire to the model behavior of prophets and saints, whose example points toward the ultimate goal of union with God. Islamic government regulates sexual behavior, prohibits lending at usurious interest, discourages modes of dress and entertainment that awaken negative passions, and encourages people in religious observance. It recognizes the human right to own property, and in that sense is not to be identified with a socialist economy. But it does not tolerate exploitative behavior in the quest for profit, and it does not countenance immoral behavior in the conduct of war. In these matters, Khomeini's views are instantiated in the constitution of the Islamic Republic of Iran, which specifies in article 3 that fostering virtue in citizens is one of the goals of the Islamic state, and that the foreign policy of the republic is devoted to the defense of Islamic values, first in the sense of maintaining its own boundaries, and second in the sense of a readiness to intervene in cases in which Islamic interests are at stake—for example, in the struggle against tyranny.

Khomeini's critique is certainly relevant to Ahmadinejad's attempt to undermine democracy. More broadly, this set of criticisms, and the corresponding affirmation of humanity's need for forms of government that instantiate the Muslim community as the religious and moral superintendent of humanity, resonate with longstanding trends in Islamic political discourse. We have seen how, in the reaction to ʿAli ʿabd al-Raziq's treatise on Islamic government, Sunni authorities and activists suggested that the models of democracy associated with Europe and North America were not well suited to historically Islamic societies. One might argue (and some did) that the political development of these societies was not sufficient to deal with the give-and-take required by democratic practice, or that new freedoms and affirmations of equal rights would give rise to public displays of ethnic and religious animosity based on long-simmering feelings of deprivation or victimization. More importantly, though, the argument of Rashid Rida, as of more populist leaders like Hasan al-Banna or, in Pakistan, Abu'l a'la Mawdudi, suggested that democracy was not well suited to the Muslim mission. By separating religious and political institutions, and thus limiting the role of Islam in public life, democracy would inhibit the Muslim community's capacity to influence behavior. Since the Qur'an's description of and charge to the Muslims has to do with commanding right and forbidding wrong, the failure to write in a role for the Muslim community as religious and moral superintendent seems wrong. In a manner that foreshadowed Osama bin Laden and Ayman al-Zawahiri on the Sunni side, Khomeini and Ahmadinejad on the Shi'i, Rida and others argued that Muslim acceptance of this limitation would contribute to the moral slide of humanity. Did not the colonial policies of the European powers already demonstrate their willingness to use military force to suppress their subjects' attempts to secure basic rights? Did not the conduct of the First World War suggest a lack of character in democratic states? Why should the Muslims follow in the path of the West? In the 1920s and 1930s, even as in the rhetoric of Ahmadinejad or Ayman al-Zawahiri, advocacy of rule by the Shari'a suggested an Islamic model of governance that is considered superior to democracy, not least in that it addresses the human propensity toward heedlessness and tyranny.

It seems that we are moving far away from arguments about the just war. Those arguments do connect with questions of political legitimacy, however. As we have seen, judgments of the conduct of war are logically distinct from those related to resort to war; to put it another way, to say that U.S. military operations in Afghanistan or Iraq include instances in which prisoners have been abused, or that the United States and its allies resort to excessive or disproportionate force does not necessarily mean that war was immoral in the first place. Nor does it mean that President Bush did and does not enjoy standing as a legitimate authority, endowed with the power to authorize military operations with the advice and consent of the U.S. Senate. One can easily imagine a situation in which war seems necessary, but the resulting conduct of military forces involves violations of norms of discrimination or proportionality. One can also imagine cases in which military forces conduct themselves with scrupulous adherence to the rules of war, but those authorizing resort to war are unwise, wicked, usurpers of authority, or all of these.

Nevertheless, judgments about the conduct of war can be related to intention. When questionable or immoral behavior reaches a certain, difficult-to-specify point, it must be the case that people will ask: "Who will believe that your cause is just, when your behavior is so unjust?" In terms of the current debate among Muslims, the question may be put with more specificity: "Who will believe that democracy is a just cause, if the advocates of democracy fight in ways that contradict democratic values?"

Muslim Democrats and American Policy

The rhetoric of Muslim critics of the war on terror is frustrating, to say the least. Reading Ahmadinejad's litany of questions leaves an advocate of democracy wondering when she might get a hearing and demand a response to questions of her own. How can one be committed to Islamic values, a follower of Muhammad, make "peace and justice" one's slogan, and say that war is authorized only for defensive purposes while at the same time sending material support to Shi'i militia in Iraq and Lebanon, associating oneself with kidnapping and hostage-taking, and declaring that other states should be wiped off the map or vanish in the pages of time? How can one say that Islamic government is for the good of all humanity, yet oversee policies that discriminate against Jews and Bahais on the basis of religion? How can one urge that Islam regards all people as equal, yet enforce restrictions on women, dissidents, and minorities that suggest they are not?

These are widely shared concerns, with respect to the notion of Islamic governance. They are certainly the concerns of Muslim democrats, who have a great stake in participating in the continuing discourse of politics and the just-war characteristic of Islamic tradition. Muslims like Abdullahi an-Naʿim are worried that U.S. conduct in the war on terror will undermine their advocacy of democracy. Those who perceive democracy as associated with the use of excessive force or with a lack of willingness to consult with others affected by military action are not likely to listen to carefully crafted arguments in favor of the practice, no matter how convincing these are with respect to the nature and meaning of Shariʿa sources.

Why should non-Muslims listen to the concerns of Muslim democrats? The just-war argument in Islam is interesting. It sheds some light on the controversy among Muslims with respect to the tactics and aims of militant groups. But what weight do the worries of Muslim democrats have when it comes to the security of the United States and its allies? 9/11 was an attack on New York and Washington, and thus on American interests. It was not an attack on Riyadh or Cairo. Beyond this, military intervention in Afghanistan and Iraq is costing the United States and its allies dearly. The pursuit of democracy through warfare in those countries involves American losses in blood, treasure, and claims to moral superiority. Why, then, should non-Muslims listen to what Muslim democrats have to say?

Americans and Europeans have their own ways of talking about the political uses of military force. In connection with the war on terror, the just-war tradition is currently cited on all sides of a debate almost as conflicted as the one described in this book. Whether or not Iraq, in particular, should be considered as a just or an unjust war is a matter of great debate, as is the general question of how Americans and Europeans will evaluate the war on terror beyond the current terms of George Bush and Tony Blair. In this sense, the Muslim just-war argument seems to have its proper place in relation to Muslim militants, and that is of course where it is primarily directed.

Insofar as Muslims speak about the war on terror, however, there is a reason to listen and attend, even beyond those connected with simple curiosity or the hope of making more informed judgments about conduct toward one's adversaries. It is this: the war on terror is not well described as a conflict between a non-Muslim "us" and a clearly distinguishable Muslim "them." Muslims reside in every country on Earth, and the population of Muslims in Europe and North America in particular is growing. In the United States, in the United Kingdom and other European Union countries, Muslims are participants in a political process. In that sense "their" arguments about the just war are also "ours." It is reasonable to expect that Muslim participation in the public discourse of the United States and other democracies will increase in the coming decades. In the United States and Canada, for example, the percentage of Muslims holding university degrees and occupying professional positions is likely to correlate with increased financial and political influence. The election of a self-identified Muslim to the U.S. Congress in 2006 is noteworthy in this regard, as was the amount of time then-candidate George Bush and Vice-President Al Gore spent cultivating the vote in the "Detroit-Toledo corridor" in the 2000 presidential campaign. The likely increase of Muslim influence in U.S. politics correlates with the typical history of immigrant communities who move into the mainstream during the second or third generation. These are going to make their voices heard and their presence felt. With a few noteworthy exceptions, Muslims in the United States in particular seem hopeful about their integration into American political life, and desirous of operating according to the rules of democracy.

Muslim democrats help to show the way for this community, by showing that the practice of Shariʿa reasoning can legitimate democracy. In addition, they write and speak in ways that invite scrutiny from non-Muslims. The practice of democracy does not require that all participants in a public discussion agree. It does seem to require that a variety of views get a hearing, even if some are presented in ways that are disconcerting. When Muslims argue about the just war, they use sources that are unfamiliar to most Americans or Europeans. Even Muslim democrats do not cite the Hebrew Bible or the New Testament; nor do they usually engage in accounts of Roman Catholic social teaching or the code of Maimonides. They do not typically refer to John Locke or John Rawls, or even to Hugo Grotius or Francis Lieber. They do speak about right authority, just cause, and right intention, however; the prohibition of direct attacks on civilians and concerns about excessive force are recognizably present in Muslim discourse. Muslims understand the concerns of the just-war tradition, and they speak about these in terms that resonate with a billion believers around the world. Beyond this, Muslim democrats speak in ways that resonate with non-Muslims. The judgments pertaining to *jihad* and the just-war tradition have much in common, in the hands of a conscientious interpreter.

In the end, the fate of Muslim democracy may well be connected with the conduct of the war on terror. George Bush was right on that June evening in 2005; the conflict between advocates of democracy and Islamic militants is a defining moment for humanity. For Osama bin Laden, the conflict has similar import. In the current political setting, the give-and-take between Muslims and non-Muslims regarding the just war constitutes a critical aspect of democratic practice. Even as the war on terror will have an impact on the cause of Muslim democrats, so the fate of Muslim democrats is going to have an impact on the political future in the United States, the European Union, and around the world. The question Muslim democrats raise about the war on terror is a good one to consider, whenever and with whomever one engages the issues about justice and war. What is the appropriate use of military force, in connection with legitimate political goals? To ask the question is not to dictate the answer. It is, however, a way of pointing to the kind of public consultation envisioned in the practice of Shariʿa reasoning, and also of democratic politics.

NOTES

ACKNOWLEDGMENTS

INDEX

NOTES

Introduction

1. The text of President Bush's speech is available at http://www .whitehouse.gov/news/releases/2005/06/20050628-7.html; Osama bin Laden's statement may be read at www.memri.org, Special Dispatch Series Number 837.

2. See "President Bush Discusses Terror Plot upon Arrival in Wisconsin," August 10, 2006, at http://www.whitehouse.gov/news/releases/ 2006/08/20060810-3.html. See also the president's address at the American Legion National Convention, August 30, 2006, at http:// www.whitehouse.gov/news/releases/2006/08/20060831-1.html.

3. The terminology in this study reflects something of this diversity. When speaking of al-Qaʿida and like-minded groups, I most often use the term "militants," although, as readers will see, phrases like

"advocates of armed resistance" or "advocates of Islamic government" are sometimes more useful. The last, in particular, helps us to identify continuities between militant groups and a number of other, more "mainstream" writers and movements. In broad terms, these mainstream Muslims often agree with the goals espoused by militants, while expressing criticisms of the means militants employ.

4. For a recent example of theologically minded treatments of Islam in this vein, see David Dykstra, *Yearning to Breathe Free? Thoughts on Immigration, Islam, and Freedom* (Birmingham, Ala.: Solid Ground Christian Books, 2006). A standard reference (for example, cited by Dykstra) of the less theologically minded treatments mentioned is Samuel Huntington, *The Clash of Civilizations and the Remaking of World Order* (New York: Simon and Schuster, 1996).

5. In this book, transliteration of Arabic terms (for example, al-Qaʿida) follows the practice used by the *International Journal of Middle East Studies*. Thus, all diacritics are omitted except *hamza* (as in Qurʾan) and ʿ*ayn* (as in ʿ*ulama*).

6. All dates in this book are given as C.E., or common era, rather than by the Muslim, or *hijri*, calendar.

1. Sources

Epigraphs: President Bush's remarks at the Islamic Center in Washington, D.C., September 17, 2001, at http://www.whitehouse.gov/news/releases/2001/09/20010917-11.html (accessed August 21, 2006). Franklin Graham's full statement: "The God of Islam is not the same God of the Christian or the Judeo-Christian faith. It is a different God, and I believe a very evil and a very wicked religion." Graham's comments may be found at the website for *Religion and Ethics News Weekly,* December 20, 2002, at http://www.pbs.org/wnet/religionandethics/week616/cover.html (accessed August 21, 2006). Osama bin Laden, "Letter to America," *The Observer,* November 24, 2002, at http://observer.guardian.co.uk/worldview/story/0,11581,845725,00.html (accessed August 21, 2006).

1. In this, as in most matters, the *Encyclopedia of Islam,* 2d ed., 12 vols., ed. E. van Donzel, Bernard Lewis, and Charles Pellat (Leiden: E. J. Brill, 1978), is a standard reference work. On *al-islam,* see the article

by J. Jomier at 4: 171–177. Interested readers may also consult the standard Arabic-English *Dictionary of Modern Written Arabic* by Hans Wehr, 4th ed., ed. J. Milton Cowan (Ithaca, N.Y.: Spoken Language Services, 1994), 495–496; Edward William Lane, *An Arabic-English Lexicon*, 8 vols. (New York: F. Ungar, 1955–1956); and Ibn Mansur, *Lisan al-Arab*, 15 vols. (Beirut: Dar Nadir, 1992).

2. One of the best-known *ahadith*, or reports, about Muhammad puts this in terms of an encounter between Muhammad and Jibril (Gabriel), the angel of God:

> As related by 'Umar [one of the "companions" of the Prophet and, after his death, the second *khalifa*]:
> One day as we were sitting with the Messenger of God there appeared before us a man whose clothes were exceedingly white and whose hair was exceedingly black. He showed none of the signs of a traveler, though none of us had previously seen him. He walked up and sat down by the Prophet. Resting his knees against those of the Prophet, and placing the palms of his hands on the Prophet's thighs, he said: "Oh Muhammad! Tell me about Islam."
> The Messenger of God said: "Islam is to testify that there is no god but God and that Muhammad is the Messenger of God; to perform the obligatory prayers; to pay *zakat*; to fast in Ramadan; and to make the pilgrimage to the Ka'ba if one is able."
> [Gabriel] said: "You have spoken rightly. . ."

The report continues, indicating the amazement of 'Umar and others present at the seeming audacity of this stranger's testing of Muhammad. In turn, Gabriel asks Muhammad about the meaning of faith *(al-iman)*, of right action *(al-ihsan)*, and of "the Hour," meaning the Last Day. Muhammad successfully completes the test, following which his examiner leaves and Muhammad says to 'Umar: "This was Gabriel, who came to you to teach you your religion." Cf. *An-Nawawi's Forty Hadith*, trans. Ezzedin Ibrahim and Denys Johnson-Davies (Cambridge: Islamic Texts Society, 1997), 28–33.

3. Precise data are difficult to come by, not least because the U.S. Census Bureau does not collect data on religious affiliation. A source like ad-herents.com (URL http://www.adherents.com/Religions_By_Adher-

ents.html) estimates the number of Muslims at 1.3 billion but notes that in this, as with all estimates, the site's numbers go toward the high side. It is also not clear that this is a scientifically sound estimate; it is based on estimates of the percentage of Muslims in various countries, which relies on data collected and published by those countries' equivalents of the U.S. Census Bureau.

4. As related in the biography attributed to Ibn Ishaq (d. 775 C.E.), in A. Guillaume, trans., *The Life of Muhammad* (Oxford: Oxford University Press, 1955), 11. The Quraysh were one of the most prominent Arab tribes. Their great influence in Mecca established them as guardians of the Ka'ba and other holy sites. *Qurayza* indicates one of several tribes in the Arabian Peninsula associated with Judaism; these come back into the story following Muhammad's migration to Medina in 622. The genealogy with which the biography begins rests on legends in which Abraham and his son Ishmael (cf. Genesis 12–22) migrate to the Arabian Peninsula. They build the Ka'ba (at Mecca) as the first house of worship dedicated to God. In a striking (and probably deliberate) parallel to the biblical stories, Ishmael fathers twelve sons, who become the patriarchs of twelve Arabic-speaking tribes, one of which gives rise to the family of the Prophet.

5. In ancient warfare elephants were typically deployed as bearers of towers from which several archers could rain down arrows on the enemy.

6. On these points, Ignaz Goldziher, *Muslim Studies*, 2 vols., ed. S. M. Stern, trans. Stern and C. R. Barber (Albany: State University of New York Press, 1967), is still useful. But see also F. E. Peters, *Muhammad and the Origins of Islam* (Albany: State University of New York Press, 1994); Martin Hinds, *Studies in Early Islamic History* (Princeton, N.J.: Darwin, 1996); G. H. A. Juynboll, ed., *Studies on the First Century of Islamic Society* (Carbondale: Southern Illinois University Press, 1982); M. J. Kister, *Studies in Jahiliyya and Early Islam* (London: Variorum Reprints, 2002); Gordon Darnell Newby, *The Making of the Last Prophet* (Columbia: University of South Carolina Press, 1989); idem, *A History of the Jews of Arabia* (Columbia: University of South Carolina Press, 1988).

7. A. J. Arberry, trans., *The Seven Odes* (London: Allen and Unwin, 1957), 86.

8. In addition to the sources cited in note 8, see the studies of W. M.

Watt, especially *Muhammad at Mecca* (Oxford: Clarendon Press, 1956) and *Muhammad at Medina* (Oxford: Clarendon Press, 1957). These, in turn, rest on Watt's careful study of the relevant portions of al-Tabari's history of prophets and kings, now available in English translation as *The History of al-Tabari*, 39 vols., ed. Ihsan Abbas et al., with various translators (Albany: State University of New York Press, 1989–1998).

9. Guillaume, *Life of Muhammad*, 69.

10. Ibid., 80, 81.

11. Quotations from the Qur'an are influenced by the translations of Abu Yusuf, A. J. Arberry, and Muhammad A. S. Abd al-Haleem; sometimes I follow one more closely, sometimes another. The translations reflect my own sense of the Arabic text.

12. Guillaume, *Life of Muhammad*, 81.

13. Traditional biographers set Muhammad's age at twenty-nine and Khadija's at forty. On the possible relation of Muhammad's spirituality to that of Syriac Christian monks, see the older but still interesting biography by Tor Andrae, *Muhammad: The Man and His Faith*, trans. T. Menzel (New York: Harper Torchbooks, 1960).

14. Guillaume, *Life of Muhammad*, 105–106.

15. Ibid., 107.

16. Ibid., 119, 121.

17. Qur'an 3:102–110.

18. Guillaume, *Life of Muhammad*, 212–213.

19. The account of the Medina Constitution is at ibid., 231–233. At 239–269 we read of growing Jewish opposition to Muhammad; the account of the chapter of the Cow is at 247–264.

20. Ibid., 363–364, 437–439, 461–470.

21. This reflects a report of a saying of Muhammad, which may be found in *Sahih Muslim* (one of the standard collections of such reports). In the English translation by Abdulhamid Siddiqi (Delhi: Adam Publishers and Distributors, 2000), this is report 2658, which is reproduced in several versions; see 4a: 216.

22. Cf. the discussion in Abdulaziz Sachedina, "Human Viceregency: A Blessing or a Curse? The Challenge to Be God's Caliph in the Qur'an," in *Humanity before God*, ed. William Schweiker et al. (Minneapolis: Augsburg-Fortress, 2006), 31–54.

23. The Arabic term for reflection ("those who reflect," in the text

quoted) is *fikr*, thought. The term translated as "reason" is *aql*. Both cover the same idea, namely, that an ordinary human capacity lends itself to interpretation of various aspects of creation as bearing witness to the power and glory of the Creator.

24. *An-Nawawi's Forty Hadith*, 110 (report 34).

25. On this matter, as on so many others, the analysis by Marshall G. S. Hodgson is remarkably insightful. See *The Venture of Islam*, 3 vols. (Chicago: University of Chicago Press, 1974), 1: 197–199.

26. *The History of al-Tabari*, vol. 10, trans. Fred M. Donner, 1–17.

27. Ibid., vol. 9, trans. Ismail K. Poonawala, 185.

28. Ibid., 10: 55–59.

29. See the account in Fred M. Donner, *The Early Islamic Conquests* (Princeton: Princeton University Press, 1981).

30. For these later conquests, see Hodgson, *The Venture of Islam*.

31. See *The History of al-Tabari*, vol. 8, trans. Michael Fishbein, 98 ff.

32. See Ann K. S. Lambton, *State and Government in Medieval Islam* (Oxford: Oxford University Press, 1981); and E. I. J. Rosenthal, *Political Thought in Medieval Islam* (Cambridge: Cambridge University Press, 1958), which remain standard surveys of these matters. These must be supplemented by Bernard Lewis, *The Political Language of Islam* (Chicago: University of Chicago Press, 1988); and above all by Patricia Crone and Martin Hinds, *God's Caliph: Political Authority in the First Centuries of Islam* (Cambridge: Cambridge University Press, 2003).

33. See the very important studies by Khaled Abou El Fadl, *Rebellion and Violence in Islamic Law* (Cambridge: Cambridge University Press, 2001); and Michael Cook, *Commanding Right and Forbidding Wrong in Islamic Thought* (Cambridge: Cambridge University Press, 2001). Cook has produced a shorter, popular version of this work under the title *Forbidding Wrong in Islam: An Introduction* (Cambridge: Cambridge University Press, 2003).

2. Shari'a Reasoning

1. For a brief introduction to Islamic philosophy, see Marshall G. S. Hodgson, *The Venture of Islam*, 3 vols. (Chicago: University of Chicago Press, 1974), 1: 410–443. The volume edited by Seyyed Hossein

Nasr and Oliver Leaman, *History of Islamic Philosophy* (London: Routledge, 1996), contains a number of useful entries.

2. Again, Hodgson, *The Venture of Islam,* provides a good introduction at 1: 444–472. Al-Jahiz's *Book of Misers* is available in an English translation by R. B. Serjeant (New York: Garnet Education, 1998). See also *The Life and Works of al-Jahiz,* ed. Charles Pellat, trans. David Martin Hawke (Berkeley: University of California Press, 1969). Nizam al-Mulk, *The Book of Government, or, Rules for Kings,* 2d ed., trans. Hubert Darke (Boston: Routledge and Kegan Paul, 1978), provides a good example of the "mirrors of princes" genre.

3. The most important scholarly treatments have been Ignaz Goldziher, *Introduction to Islamic Theology and Law,* trans. Andreas Hamori and Bernard Lewis (Princeton: Princeton University Press, 1981); and Joseph Schacht, *The Origins of Muhammadan Jurisprudence* (Oxford: Clarendon Press, 1951); idem, *An Introduction to Islamic Law* (1964; reprint, Oxford: Clarendon Press, 1983). These older treatments are now supplemented by the various works of Wael Hallaq, among them *A History of Islamic Legal Theories* (Cambridge: Cambridge University Press, 1997), *The Origins and Evolution of Islamic Law* (Cambridge: Cambridge University Press, 2004), and *Authority, Continuity, and Change in Islamic Law* (Cambridge: Cambridge University Press, 2005). Norman J. Calder, *Studies in Early Muslim Jurisprudence* (Oxford: Oxford University Press, 1993), poses important questions about the dating of texts and, in general, the development of Shari'a discourse. A. Kevin Reinhart, "Islamic Law as Islamic Ethics," *Journal of Religious Ethics* 11, no. 2 (1983), 186–203, develops a perspective close to the one articulated here.

4. See George F. Hourani, *Islamic Rationalism: The Ethics of 'Abd al-Jabbar* (Oxford: Clarendon Press, 1971); idem, *Reason and Tradition in Islamic Ethics* (Cambridge: Cambridge University Press, 1985); Richard M. Frank, *Beings and Their Attributes* (Albany: State University of New York Press, 1978); and Josef van Ess, *The Flowering of Muslim Theology,* trans. Jane Marie Todd (Cambridge, Mass.: Harvard University Press, 2006).

5. In this early period, it appears that conversion involved adoption into one of the Arab clans. As Hodgson put it, Islam constituted the religious aspect of Arab identity; *The Venture of Islam,* 1: 206–230.

6. The various accounts of these incidents collected by al-Tabari indi-

cate how controversial the struggle was for later generations; see *The History of al-Tabari*, 39 vols., ed. Ihsan Abbas et al. (Albany: State University of New York Press, 1989–1998), vol. 15, trans. R. Stephen Humphreys, 181 ff.

7. As translated in W. M. Watt, *The Formative Period of Islamic Thought* (Edinburgh: Edinburgh University Press, 1973), 83.

8. Ibid.

9. Ibid.

10. Ibid.

11. Thus reinforcing the point that the application of such labels in the early period is problematic.

12. Watt, *Formative Period*, 75, 77–81. Watt emphasizes that al-Hasan's opposition did not extend to approval of armed uprisings. In this, al-Hasan appears to be an advocate of the position that although a citizen should "omit to obey" an unjust or irreligious order, he or she is not to take this as a right to revolt.

13. For a brief description of John's *Dialogue between a Christian and a Saracen,* see Harry Wolfson, *The Philosophy of the Kalam* (Cambridge, Mass.: Harvard University Press, 1976), 129–131. John's treatise is available in French and German translations: Jean Damascene, *Ecrits sur l'Islam*, ed. and trans. Raymond Le Cazr (Paris: Cerf, 1992), 229–251; and P. Bonafat Kotter, *Die Schriften des Johannes von Damaskos* (Berlin: W. de Gruyter, 1981), 427–438.

14. See *Al-Muwatta of Imam Malik Ibn Anas,* trans. Aisha Abdurrahman Bewley (London: Kegan Paul, 1989).

15. The "Book on the Land Tax" has been translated into French: E. Fagnan, *Le livre de l'impôt foncier* (Paris: Paul Geuthner, 1921).

16. See Majid Khadduri, trans., *The Islamic Law of Nations: Shaybani's Siyar* (Baltimore: Johns Hopkins Press, 1966), 1–74.

17. For analysis, see John Kelsay, "Al-Shaybani and the Islamic Law of War," *Journal of Military Ethics* 2, no. 1 (2003), 63–75.

18. Secs. 1419–20, in Khadduri, *The Islamic Law of Nations,* 236.

19. See *The History of al-Tabari,* vol. 30, trans. C. E. Bosworth, 125.

20. See the translation by Majid Khadduri, *Islamic Jurisprudence: Shafi'i's Risala* (Baltimore: Johns Hopkins Press, 1961).

21. As demonstrated in the various works cited in note 3, above.

22. Sec. 1, in Khadduri, *Islamic Jurisprudence,* 57–58; translation modified.

23. Sec. 10, ibid., 64, citing Qur'an 41:41–42.

24. Sec. 11, ibid., 66.

25. Secs. 12–28, ibid., 67–80.

26. Secs. 54–85, ibid., 88–108.

27. Sec. 86, ibid., 109.

28. Secs. 100–131, ibid., 123–145.

29. The collections of Muslim (d. 874) and of al-Bukhari (d. 870) are particularly favored, though those of al-Nisa'i (d. 915), Abu Da'ud (d. 888), al-Tirmidhi (d. 892), and Ibn Maja (d. 866) are used, as are works like those by Malik ibn Anas *(Al-Muwatta)* and Ahmad ibn Hanbal *(Al-Musnad)*. The "chain," as the term implies, is simply a list of names of those who "heard" and, in successive generations, related a particular report. The trustworthiness of such transmitters would become a critical issue between Sunni and Shi'i scholars. See J. Robson, "Hadith," in *Encyclopedia of Islam*, 2d ed., 12 vols., ed. E. van Donzel, Bernard Lewis, and Charles Pellat (Leiden: E. J. Brill, 1978), 3: 23–38.

30. Sec. 592, in Khadduri, *Islamic Jurisprudence*, 310.

31. As the text of *Risala* makes clear, al-Shafi'i is wary of the idea that communal consensus establishes a valid claim. For him, guidance comes from reading and applying the texts of the Qur'an and the *sunna*. He supposes that there may be cases for which he and other scholars do not know the textual precedents related to an established practice; if that practice is regarded by the entire Muslim community as valid, then there must be a text, and it has somehow been "lost." Later generations of the learned would apply the notion of consensus to the "consensual judgment" or "opinion" of the established schools of Shari'a reasoning. This is something different from the consensus mentioned by al-Shafi'i.

32. In general, see selections in H. Gerth and C. Wright Mills, eds. and trans., *From Max Weber* (New York: Oxford University Press, 1946), especially "The Social Psychology of the World's Religions" (267–301) and "Politics as a Vocation" (77–128). David Little, "Max Weber and the Comparative Study of Religious Ethics," *Journal of Religious Ethics* 2, no. 2 (1974), 5–40, informs much of my approach to the religious-ethical dimensions of religious traditions (in this case, Islam).

33. See Hodgson, *The Venture of Islam*, 1: 389–390, 473–481.

34. Given that Twelver Shi'i texts present al-Rida as the eighth Imam, it

might be appropriate to interpret al-Ma'mun as reaching out to the partisans of 'Ali, though it is still too early to speak of a developed form of Shi'i piety. Twelver doctrine would eventually mirror the positions of the Mu'tazila in the matter of the "created" Qur'an, as in most matters. See the important treatise of al-Muhaqqiq al-Hilli (d. 1277), translated by William McElwee Miller as *Al-Babu 'l-Hadi 'Ashar: A Treatise on the Principles of Shi'ite Theology* (London: Royal Asiatic Society, 1928).

35. See, among others, Hourani, *Islamic Rationalism;* H. S. Nyberg, "Al-Mu'tazila," in *Shorter Encyclopedia of Islam,* ed. H. A. R. Gibb and J. H. Kramers (Leiden: E. J. Brill, 1953); Watt, *Formative Period,* 209–253; and John Kelsay, "Religion and Morality in Islam" (Ph.D. diss., University of Virginia, 1985), 235–262.

36. See Frank, *Beings and Their Attributes;* Daniel Gimaret, *Théories de l'acte humain en théologie musulmane* (Paris: J. Vrin, 1980); Josef van Ess, *Fruhe Mu'tazilitische Haresiographe* (Beirut: Imprimerie Catholique, 1971); idem, "Early Development of *Kalam,*" in *Studies on the First Century of Islamic Society,* ed. G. H. A. Juynboll (Carbondale: Southern Illinois University Press, 1982).

37. J. R. T. M. Peters, *God's Created Speech: A Study in the Speculative Theology of the Mu'tazili Qadi l-qudat Abul-Hasan 'Abd al-Jabbar ibn al-Hamadani* (Leiden: E. J. Brill, 1976).

38. See Harry A. Wolfson, *The Philosophy of the Kalam* (Cambridge, Mass.: Harvard University Press, 1976); and the work of John of Damascus, cited above, note 13.

39. For more information on Ahmad ibn Hanbal and the controversy of the *mihna,* or test, see John Kelsay, "Divine Commands and Social Order: The Case of Classical Islam," *Annual of the Society of Christian Ethics* 10 (1990), 63–80; and, more recently, Michael Cook, *Commanding Right and Forbidding Wrong in Islamic Thought* (Cambridge: Cambridge University Press, 2001), 87–113.

40. See above, note 29.

41. Cook, *Commanding Right and Forbidding Wrong,* 113.

42. Imran Ahsan Khan Nyazee, *The Distinguished Jurist's Primer: A Translation of Bidayat al-Mujtahid,* 2 vols. (New York: Garnet Education, 1995), 1: xliii–xlxix.

43. Ibid., xiii and xiv.

44. Ibid., xlvi.

45. Ibid.

46. The work of these and others is discussed at length in Abdulaziz Sachedina, *The Just Ruler in Shi'ite Islam* (Oxford: Oxford University Press, 1988).

47. The term "designated" approximates the Arabic *al-nass,* which carries with it the notion that the object is set apart, in this case by exemplary learning and piety, and that the leader is thus "elevated" *(al-ma'sum)* so as to be divinely protected from the commission of serious sin. The doctrine of the imamate, or leadership, is perhaps the most characteristic feature of the various Shi'i groups, all of which agreed on the principle that God appoints one leader for every generation, and that it is the duty of the faithful to seek out that person and, upon finding him, to provide support. In general, see Abdulaziz A. Sachedina, *Islamic Messianism: The Idea of the Mahdi in Twelver Shi'ism* (Albany: State University of New York Press, 1981).

48. Thus grew up the distinctively Shi'i mode of scholarship known as *'ilm al-rijal,* the science of the men, whose names appear in chains of transmission. For a description of this practice, see Liyakat N. Takim, *The Heirs of the Prophet: Charisma and Religious Authority in Shi'ite Islam* (Albany: State University of New York Press, 2006).

49. See the many works purporting to explain the role of Shi'i history and doctrine in the events leading up to the Iranian revolution of 1978–79, and the establishment of the Islamic Republic of Iran. Particularly helpful are Abdulaziz A. Sachedina, "Activist Shi'ism in Iran, Iraq, and Lebanon," in *Fundamentalisms Observed,* ed. Martin M. Marty and R. Scott Appleby (Chicago: University of Chicago Press, 1994), 403–456; Said Amir Arjomand, *The Shadow of God and the Hidden Imam* (Chicago: University of Chicago Press, 1987); and Roy Mottahedeh, *The Mantle of the Prophet* (Oxford: Oneworld Publications, 2000).

50. Shi'i theology is, on most matters, consonant with the Mu'tazili position. Thus the "trust" assigned to human beings in Qur'an 33:72 is said to include a knowledge of the most basic principles of religion and morality. Further, this knowledge establishes human responsibility before God. In one sense, the affirmation of reason as a source by which humans may comprehend the Shari'a simply follows from this.

51. Spain, or *al-Andalus,* came under Islamic rule in the late seventh cen-

tury and remained so until the late Middle Ages. On al-Wansharisi's response to this episode, see Khaled Abou El Fadl, "The Legal Debates on Muslim Minorities: Between Rejection and Accommodation," *Journal of Religious Ethics* 22, no. 1 (1994), esp. 137–138.

52. On Shah Wali Allah, and also on the opinion of ʿAbd al-ʿAziz, see works by S. A. A. Rizvi, in particular *Shah Wali-Allah and His Times* (Canberra: Maʿrifat Publishing House, 1980) and *Shah ʿAbd al-ʿAziz: Puritanism, Sectarian Polemics, and Jihad* (Canberra: Maʿrifat Publishing House, 1982).

53. See the important study by Barbara Daly Metcalf, *Islamic Revival in British India: Deoband, 1860–1900* (New York: Oxford University Press, 2004).

54. On the membership and program of the former group, see Mumtaz Ahmad, "Islamic Fundamentalism in South Asia: The Jamaat-i-Islami and the Tablighi Jamaat," in Marty and Appleby, *Fundamentalisms Observed*, 457–530. For an influential account of the Taliban, see Ahmed Rashid, *Taliban: Militant Islam, Oil, and Fundamentalism in Central Asia* (New Haven: Yale University Press, 2000).

55. See, among others, Christine Moss Helms, *The Cohesion of Saudi Arabia* (Baltimore: Johns Hopkins University Press, 1980).

56. See Ann K. S. Lambton, "A Nineteenth-Century View of Jihad," *Studia Islamica* 32 (1970), 180–192.

57. See the account in Christian Troll, *Sayyid Ahmad Khan* (College Park, Md.: Prometheus, 1978).

58. See Nikki R. Keddie, *An Islamic Response to Imperialism: Political and Religious Writings of Sayyid Jamal al-Din "Al-Afghani"* (Berkeley: University of California Press, 1983). Keddie and others suggest that Jamal al-Din's place of birth and his education were in Iran, and thus that he was probably a Shiʿi Muslim of the Twelver School. This would provide a partial explanation for some of his approach, which emphasizes the correlation or complementarity between reason and revelation. If Keddie is correct, then the adaptation of al-Afghani (that is, pointing to Afghanistan as his place of birth), with its suggestion of a Sunni affiliation, would be a way of avoiding obstacles reflecting historic polemics between the two great branches of Islamic tradition.

59. See the accounts in Albert Hourani, *Arabic Thought in the Liberal Age, 1798–1939* (Cambridge: Cambridge University Press, 1983); and

Hamid Enayat, *Modern Islamic Political Thought* (Austin: University of Texas Press, 1982); as well as Malcolm Kerr, *Islamic Reform: The Political and Legal Theories of Muhammad 'Abduh and Rashid Rida* (Berkeley: University of California Press, 1966).

60. David Fromkin, *A Peace to End All Peace* (New York: Avon Books, 1990), does a good job of chronicling the political arrangements negotiated by the European powers, and thus of setting the context for Islamic developments.

61. See Muhammad Iqbal, *The Reconstruction of Religious Thought in Islam* (1929; reprint, Chicago: Kazi Publications, 1999).

62. Al-Raziq's treatise, *Al-Islam wa usul al-hukm* (Islam and the Fundamentals of Government), is available in a French translation by Abdou Filali Ansary, *L'Islam et les fondements du pouvoir* (Paris: Editions la Découverte, 1994); and in English as part of the 1928 dissertation by Charles Clarence Adams at the University of Chicago, "The Modern Reform Movement in Egypt and the Caliphate."

63. See the discussions in Hourani, *Arabic Thought in the Liberal Age;* and in Enayat, *Modern Islamic Political Thought.*

64. The best account is still Richard Mitchell's 1969 study, *The Society of the Muslim Brothers* (reprint, New York: Oxford University Press, 1993). Also see *Five Tracts of Hasan al-Banna (1906–1949),* trans. Charles Wendell (Berkeley: University of California Press, 1978).

65. See Seyyed Vali Reza Nasr, *Mawdudi and the Making of Islamic Revivalism* (New York: Oxford University Press, 1993); also, among the many writings of Mawdudi translated into English, see *First Principles of the Islamic State,* 6th ed. (Lahore: Islamic Publications, 1983); idem, *Human Rights in Islam,* trans. K. Ahmad and Ahmad Said Khan (Leicester: Islamic Foundation, 1976); and idem, *Islamic Law and Constitution,* ed. K. Ahmad (Karachi: Jamaat-e-Islami Publications, 1995).

66. On these developments, see Mottahedeh, *The Mantle of the Prophet;* also R. Allah Khomeini, *Islam and Revolution: Writings and Declarations of Imam Khomeini,* ed. and trans. H. Algar (Berkeley, Calif.: Mizan, 1981); 'Ali Shari'ati, *On the Sociology of Islam,* trans. H. Algar (Berkeley, Calif.: Mizan, 1979); Jalal Al-e Ahmad, *Plagued by the West (Gharbzadegi),* trans. Paul Sprachman (Delmar, N.Y.: Caravan Books, 1982).

67. Among the many recent treatments of Sayyid Qutb, that by Enayat in

Modern Islamic Political Thought is one of the most solid. Among Sayyid Qutb's writings, *Milestones* (Villa Park, Ill.: American Trust Publications, 1991) may be the most widely read. Also very important is his commentary *In the Shade of the Qur'an*, trans. Adil Salahi, 8 vols. to date (Leicester, U.K.: Islamic Foundation, 2005–).

68. See Muhammad al-Faraj, *The Neglected Duty*, trans. Johannes J. G. Jansen (New York: Macmillan, 1986).

3. Politics, Ethics, and War in Premodern Islam

1. This point is well made by Sohail Hashmi, "Interpreting the Islamic Ethics of War and Peace," in *The Ethics of War and Peace*, ed. T. Nardin (Princeton: Princeton University Press, 1996), 146–168. Also see John Kelsay, "And Why Should You Not Fight? The Imperative of War in Islam and Christianity," forthcoming in Linda Hogan, ed., *Religions and the Politics of Peace and Conflict* (Eugene, Ore.: Wipf and Stock, 2007).

2. *Al-Muwatta of Imam Malik Ibn Anas*, trans. Aisha Abdurrahman Bewley (London: Kegan Paul, 1989), 173–184.

3. Ibid., 173.

4. Ibid., 183.

5. On the history of the text, see Majid Khadduri's introduction in his translation of *The Islamic Law of Nations: Shaybani's Siyar* (Baltimore: Johns Hopkins Press, 1966), 1–74. For the dating of the text and its redactional history, see also Norman J. Calder, *Studies in Early Muslim Jurisprudence* (Oxford: Oxford University Press, 1993); and, more briefly, but suggestively, Khaled Abou El Fadl, *Rebellion and Violence in Islamic Law* (Cambridge: Cambridge University Press, 2001), 144–145. The earliest version of al-Shaybani's treatise available to us dates from the time of al-Sarakhsi (d. 1096), that is, two to three centuries after the death of al-Shaybani. From al-Sarakhsi's use of the treatise, it is clear that he and his contemporaries regarded it as a school text, to be used in training scholars in the Iraqi or Hanafi style of Shari'a reasoning. The text thus functioned, even at this early date, to communicate consensual precedents attributed to the earliest figures associated with its characteristic style. Although we must use the

attribution of the complete text to the "historical" al-Shaybani with care, in my judgment this constraint does not alter the book's value as an early case of systematic reasoning about the rules of war.

6. Khadduri, *The Islamic Law of Nations*, 75–77. Interestingly, given its prominence in later discussions of fighting, this report is not cited in Malik's *Muwatta*.

7. W. M. Watt, *Muhammad: Prophet and Statesman* (London: Oxford University Press, 1961), summarizes the more detailed presentations in idem, *Muhammad at Mecca* (Oxford: Clarendon Press, 1953) and *Muhammad at Medina* (Oxford: Clarendon Press, 1956).

8. According to an interpreter like Paul Ramsey, "timely resort" is the import of the last-resort criterion in any case. See Ramsey, *Speak Up for Just War or Pacifism* (University Park: Pennsylvania State University Press, 1988), 85. On just-war tradition generally, see James Turner Johnson, *Morality and Contemporary Warfare* (New Haven: Yale University Press, 1999). For formal comparisons of just-war tradition and Islamic thought, see John Kelsay, *Islam and War: A Study in Comparative Ethics* (Louisville, Ky.: Westminster/John Knox, 1993); idem, "Religion, Morality, and the Governance of War: The Case of Classical Islam," *Journal of Religious Ethics* 18, no. 2 (1990), 123–139; idem, "Bosnia and the Muslim Critique of Modernity," in *Religion and Justice in the War over Bosnia*, ed. G. Scott Davis (New York: Routledge, 1996), 117–142; Kelsay and James Turner Johnson, eds., *Just War and Jihad* (Westport, Conn.: Greenwood, 1991); James Turner Johnson and John Kelsay, eds., *Cross, Crescent, and Sword* (Westport, Conn.: Greenwood, 1990); James Turner Johnson, *The Holy War Idea in Western and Islamic Traditions* (University Park: Pennsylvania State University Press, 1997); Reuven Firestone, *Jihad: The Origin of Holy War in Islam* (Oxford: Oxford University Press, 1999); Basaam Tibi, "War and Peace in Islam," in Nardin, *The Ethics of War and Peace*, 128–145; Sohail Hashmi, "Interpreting the Islamic Ethics of War and Peace."

9. As in Khadduri, *The Islamic Law of Nations*, 218–222.

10. Ibid., 230–246 and 250–253.

11. Ibid., 195–218 and 222–229.

12. Ibid., 247–250.

13. Ibid., 96.

14. See John Kelsay, "Al-Shaybani and the Islamic Law of War," *Journal of Military Ethics* 2, no. 1 (2003), 63–75; also V. J. Parry, "Warfare," in P. M. Holt et al., *The Cambridge History of Islam*, vol. 2 (Cambridge: Cambridge University Press, 1970), 824–850.

15. Khadduri, *The Islamic Law of Nations*, 95.

16. Ibid., 86–87, 101–102.

17. Ibid., 55.

18. Ibid., 101–102.

19. Ibid., 102.

20. Portions of al-Tabari's text are translated by Yasir S. Ibrahim in "A Translation of al-Tabari's Book of the Disagreement among Muslim Jurists: The Book of Jihad (Sections 1–49)" (Master's thesis, University of Florida, 1998).

21. Al-Mawardi, *Ahkam al-Sultaniyya wa al-Wilayat al-Diniyya*, translated by Wafaa H. Wahba as *The Ordinances of Government* (Reading, U.K.: Garnet Publishing, 1996), 32, 36.

22. For example, see Ann K. S. Lambton, *State and Government in Medieval Islam* (Oxford: Oxford University Press, 1981); also E. I. J. Rosenthal, *Political Thought in Medieval Islam* (Cambridge: Cambridge University Press, 1958).

23. Wahba, *The Ordinances of Government*, 36.

24. Ibid., 37.

25. Ibid., 38–59.

26. On these matters, see Marshall G. S. Hodgson, *The Venture of Islam*, 3 vols. (Chicago: University of Chicago Press, 1974), vol. 2.

27. Wahba, *The Ordinances of Government*, 40.

28. Ibid.

29. Ibid.

30. Ibid., 41.

31. Ibid., 45.

32. Ibid.

33. Ibid.

34. For portions of the Arabic text, as well as a translation and comments, see E. Sivan, "La genèse de la Contre-Croisade: Un traité damasquin du début du XII siècle," *Journal Asiatique* 254 (1966), 197–224.

35. Wahba, *The Ordinances of Government*, 35.

36. In general, see Jane I. Smith, "Islam and Christendom," in *The Oxford History of Islam*, ed. John L. Esposito (Oxford: Oxford University Press, 1999), esp. 337–341.

37. From the Arabic text given in Sivan, "La genèse de la Contre-Croisade," 220; my translation.

38. Ibn Taymiyya, *Siyasat al-Shar'iyya*, in the translation by Omar A. Farrukh, *Ibn Taimiya on Public and Private Law in Islam* (Beirut: Khayats, 1966), 146. For a short account of Ibn Taymiyya's life and thought, see Henri Laoust's entry in the *Encyclopedia of Islam*, 2d ed., 12 vols., ed. E. van Donzel, Bernard Lewis, and Charles Pellat, vol. 3 (Leiden: Brill, 1986), 951–955. See also Michael Cook, *Commanding Right and Forbidding Wrong in Islamic Thought* (Cambridge: Cambridge University Press, 2001), 145–164.

39. Ibid., 147.

40. Ibid., 140.

41. Ibid., 141.

42. Ibid.

43. Ibid., 146.

44. Ibid., 141.

45. Ibid., 142.

46. On *al-hisba*, see the translation by M. Holland in *Public Duties in Islam* (Leicester, U.K.: Islamic Foundation, 1982). On the more general duty with which this treatise is concerned, see Cook, *Commanding Right and Forbidding Wrong*.

47. Taimiya, *Ibn Taimiya*, 145–148.

48. On these matters, see Holland, *Public Duties;* and Cook, *Commanding Right and Forbidding Wrong*, esp. 151–157.

49. Abdulaziz Sachedina, *The Just Ruler in Shi'ite Islam* (Oxford: Oxford University Press, 1988).

50. On these points, see Etan Kohlberg, "The Development of the Imami-Shi'i Doctrine of *jihad*," *Zeitschrift der Deutschen Morganlandischen Gesellschaft* 126 (1976), 64–82; al-Muhaqqiq al-Hilli, *Shara'i al-Islam fi Masa'il al-Halal wa al-Haram*, translated in 2 vols. by A. Querry as *Droit Musulman. Recueil de lois concernant les Musulmans schyites* (Paris: Imprimerie Nationale, 1871–72). A contemporary authority, the Ayatullah Murtaza Mutahhari (d. 1979), argued that at least in some cases, fighting in defense of the oppressed

244 •• NOTES TO PAGES 126-127

citizens of another country may be classified as imposed war, and seen as an even greater or higher duty than defense of one's own homeland. See his *Jihad: The Holy War of Islam and Its Legitimacy in the Qur'an,* trans. Mohammad S. Tawheedi (Albany, Calif.: Moslem Student Association [Persian Speaking Group], n.d.); and, more generally, Bruce Lawrence, "Holy War *(Jihad)* in Islamic Religion and Nation-State Ideologies," in Kelsay and Johnson, *Just War and Jihad,* 141–160.

4. Armed Resistance and Islamic Tradition

1. The *Declaration,* widely cited as "bin Laden's *fatwa*," first appeared in Arabic on February 23, 1998, in the London-based *al-Quds al-Arabi.* Five names were attached to the document, which presented itself as a pronouncement by the "World Islamic Front." As many commentators note, the name suggests an alliance among several factions, all dedicated to the project of fighting against the United States and its allies in the name or under the banner of *jihad.* Osama bin Laden represented al-Qa'ida, Ayman al-Zawahiri and Abu-Yasir Rifa'i Ahmad Taha the Egyptian Jihad Group, Mir Hamzah the Jami'at al-'ulama (Group of the Learned) in Pakistan, and Fazlar Rahman the Bangladeshi Jihad Movement. There are various English translations of the text. I find the translation at http://www.fas.org/irp/world/para/docs/980223-fatwa.htm, the website for the Federation of American Scientists, an accurate rendering of the Arabic text.

2. Muhammad al-Faraj, *Al-Faridah al-Ghaibah,* translated by Johannes J. G. Jansen as *The Neglected Duty* (New York: Macmillan, 1986). Jansen also provides an account of the publication of the Arabic text, which might also be translated as "the hidden duty." The text became widely known when the Shaykh al-Azhar published a refutation of it with the intent of refuting the reasoning of those who had assassinated President Anwar Sadat in October of that year. Parts of this refutation were excerpted in Egyptian newspapers in December 1981. Several versions of the militants' apologia appeared later in various newspapers, and a number of Islamic authorities joined their voices to the Shaykh al-Azhar's criticisms. Jansen's translation includes ma-

terials from the criticisms, as well as the militant text. Parts of the testament of al-Zawahiri, *Knights under the Prophet's Banner*, may be read in English translation at http://faculty.msb.edu/murphydd/ibd/ MiddleEast-Islam/Zawahiri's%202001%zobook20extracts.htm (checked February 23, 2007). Lawrence Wright, *The Looming Tower: Al-Qaeda and the Road to 9/11* (New York: Alfred A. Knopf, 2006), provides an overview of al-Zawahiri's journey to militancy; see esp. 32–59.

3. For a helpful account, see Christine Moss Helms, *The Cohesion of Saudi Arabia* (Baltimore: Johns Hopkins University Press, 1980).

4. On 'Abd al-'Aziz and this controversy, see S. A. A. Rizvi, *Shah 'Abd al-'Aziz: Puritanism, Sectarian Polemics, and Jihad* (Canberra: Ma'rifat Publishing House, 1982).

5. For the career of Salah al-Din, or "Saladin," see, among others, H. A. R. Gibb, *The Life of Saladin* (Oxford: Clarendon Press, 1973).

6. All quotations are from al-Faraj, *The Neglected Duty*. John Kelsay, *Islam and War: A Study in Comparative Ethics* (Louisville, Ky.: Westminster/John Knox, 1993), includes an extended discussion of this text; my discussion here shows that I have changed my mind about certain points.

7. al-Faraj, *The Neglected Duty*, 169.

8. Ibid., 169–170.

9. Ibid., 169.

10. Ibid., 191–192.

11. Ibid., 191.

12. Ibid., 200.

13. Ibid., 35–62.

14. The Charter is available in a translation by M. Maqdsi (Dallas: Islamic Association for Palestine, 1990). I have made use of Maqdsi's translation but have ultimately followed my own sense of the original.

15. Ibid., sec. 22.

16. Ibid., sec. 11.

17. Ibid., sec. 12.

18. A substantial (and widely read) discussion of this principle of Shari'a reasoning may be found at Yusuf al-Qaradhawi, *The Lawful and the Prohibited in Islam*, trans. Kamal Elhalbawy and M. Moinuddin

Siddiqi (New Delhi: Kitab Bhavan, 2006). The primary cases around which the principle developed have to do with matters of purity: for example, under some conditions, necessity may render forbidden foods permitted, or necessity may render it permissible to perform one's pre-prayer ablutions with sand rather than with water. In the current context, the principle is invoked by Qaradhawi and others to justify broader than usual participation by women and young people in military or paramilitary activities, or to justify unusual tactics like self-martyrdom (that is, "suicide bombings").

19. See http://www.fas.org/irp/world/para/docs/980223-fatwa.htm.

20. The *Epistle,* first issued on October 12, 1996, is available at http://www.washingtonpost.org.

21. Since the victory of Hamas in the 2005 parliamentary elections, the prime minister and others more typically respond to acts of violence against Israel by expressing regret for the deaths of innocents, while defending the right of Palestinians to resist oppression.

22. I describe some of this debate in "Suicide Bombers," *Christian Century* 119, no. 17 (August 14–27, 2002), 22–25.

23. See *Al-Raya* (Qatar), April 25, 2001; *Al-Ahram Al-Arabi* (Egypt), February 3, 2001; and *Al-Istiqlal,* the newspaper of the organization Palestinian Islamic Jihad, August 20, 1999, at www.memri.org, Inquiry and Analysis Series, no. 53, May 2, 2001.

24. See *Al-Quds* (Pa.), August 17, 1998, ibid.

25. This distinction seems important to the logic of the Shaykh al-Azhar's opinion justifying resistance to U.S. action in Iraq, although he seemed to be of more than one mind about such resistance during the spring of 2003; see www.memri.org, Inquiry and Analysis Series, no. 130, April 8, 2003.

26. Among other places, see the interview with John Miller of ABC from May 1998 at http://www.pbs.org/wgbh/pages/frontline/shows/binladen/who/interview.html (checked February 23, 2007).

27. The interview was primarily of Shaykh Muhsin al-'Awaji. Now based in the United Kingdom, al-'Awaji served as an imam of the Great Mosque at King Saud University in Riyadh during the late 1980s. After the Gulf War he was vocal in his opposition to Saudi policy, particularly with respect to the continuing presence of U.S. troops in the Arabian Peninsula, and served time in a Saudi prison. Safar al-Hawali and Muhammad al-Khasif are well known for similar positions and

also served prison terms. The quotations in the text are drawn from a translation of portions of the interview available at the website for the Middle East Media Research Institute, http:www.memri.org, Saudi Arabia/Jihad and Terrorism Studies, no. 400. Some of my discussion of the argument among Islamists regarding the tactics of al-Qaʿida was presented in my Templeton Lecture (October 2003) at the Foreign Policy Research Institute in Philadelphia. See http://www.fpri.org.

28. I use the translation available at www.memri.org, Special Dispatch Series, no. 388, June 12, 2002. The article was originally published (in Arabic) under a title that translates as "In the Shadow of the Lances," at http:www.alneda.com.

29. Shaykh ʿUmar Bakri Muhammad, "Is Armed Struggle a Legitimate Means for the Establishment of Islamic Government?," available at www.almuhajiroun.com.

30. First published on a website affiliated with al-Qaʿida, the document was translated by sympathetic Muslims in the United Kingdom and published in *The Observer.* See http://www.observer.co.uk/worldview/story/0,111581,845725,00.html.

31. See Michael Walzer, *Just and Unjust Wars,* 3d ed. (New York: Basic Books, 2000), 251–268.

32. See Quentin Skinner, *The Foundations of Modern Political Thought* (Cambridge: Cambridge University Press, 1978), 189–359.

33. Available, among others, in *Islam and Revolution: Writings and Declarations of Imam Khomeini,* ed. and trans. Hamid Algar (Berkeley: Mizan, 1981), 27–168. No doubt, the force of this argument is due in part to the relative strength of the *ʿulama* in Shiʿi circles.

5. Military Action and Political Authority

1. Al-Zawahiri's statement is at www.memri.org, Special Dispatches Series, No. 50, August 4, 2005.

2. Ibid.

3. Ibid.

4. Hamid Enayat, *Modern Islamic Political Thought* (Austin: University of Texas Press, 1982), stresses such diversity.

5. Abu Ghayth, "In the Shadow of the Lances" (in Arabic), at http:www.

alneda.com; translated at www.memri.org, Special Dispatch Series, no. 388, June 12, 2002.

6. With regard to insurgent or resistance activity in Iraq, Muhammad al-Maqdisi, a well-known scholar who is said by some to have been the mentor of the late Abu Musab al-Zarqawi, thought it important to write a letter to those fighting under al-Zarqawi's command warning them that attacks on civilians, particularly Muslims, were not to be countenanced, and that some of the activities in which they were thus engaged threatened their standing as *mujahiddin*. See www.memri. org, Special Dispatch Series No. 848, January 17, 2005.

7. Syed Amir Ali, *The Spirit of Islam* (1891; reprint, Kila, Mont.: Kessinger, 2004).

8. Abdulaziz Sachedina, *The Islamic Roots of Democratic Pluralism* (New York: Oxford University Press, 2001).

9. For the full text, see http://www.un.org/Overview/rights.html.

10. Abdulaziz A. Sachedina, "The Development of *Jihad* in Islamic Revelation and History," in *Cross, Crescent, and Sword*, ed. James Turner Johnson and John Kelsay (Westport, Conn.: Greenwood, 1990).

11. See Mahmud Muhammad Taha, *The Second Message of Islam*, ed. and trans. Abdullahi Ahmed an-Na'im (Syracuse: Syracuse University Press, 1987).

12. See "The Translator's Introduction," ibid., 1–30.

13. The words "went dormant" are those of Paul J. Magnarella, whose short article "Republican Brothers" provides a convenient outline of events. See John Esposito, ed., *The Oxford Encyclopedia of the Modern Islamic World* (New York: Oxford University Press, 1995), 3: 429–430.

14. See his "Translator's Introduction."

15. Abdullahi an-Na'im, *Toward an Islamic Reformation* (Syracuse: Syracuse University Press, 1990).

16. See http://people.law.emory.edu/~abduh46 (checked February 24, 2007).

17. Ibid., chap. 1, pp. 1, 3.

18. Ibid., 3.

19. Ibid., chap. 2, p. 7.

20. B.A., Yale University, 1986; J.D., University of Pennsylvania, 1989; Ph.D., Princeton University, 1999. Abou El Fadl's articles, interviews, and *fatawa* issued in response to questions submitted by Muslims are

available at http://scholarofthehouse.org/index.html (checked February 24, 2007).

21. Khaled Abou El Fadl, *The Place of Tolerance in Islam* (Boston: Beacon, 2002), 21.

22. Ibid.

23. Ibid., 22.

24. Khaled Abou El Fadl, *Speaking in God's Name: Islamic Law, Authority, and Women* (Oxford: Oneworld, 2001).

25. Ibid., 184.

26. Khaled Abou El Fadl, *And God Knows the Soldiers: The Authoritative and the Authoritarian in Islamic Discourses* (Lanham, Md.: University Press of America, 2001), esp. 37–42.

27. Idem, *Rebellion and Violence in Islamic Law* (Cambridge: Cambridge University Press, 2001).

28. Ibid. See also Khaled Abou El Fadl, "*Ahkam al-Bughat:* Irregular Warfare and the Law of Rebellion in Islam," in Johnson and Kelsay, *Cross, Crescent, and Sword,* 149–176; and John Kelsay, *Islam and War: A Study in Comparative Ethics* (Louisville, Ky.: Westminster/John Knox, 1993).

29. For discussion of these reports, see Kelsay, *Islam and War,* 77–110.

30. Abou El Fadl, "*Ahkam al-Bughat,*" 173.

31. Osama bin Laden, "A New Bin Laden Speech," www.memri.org, Special Dispatch Series No. 539, July 18, 2003.

32. See the account of James Turner Johnson in *The Holy War Idea in Western and Islamic Traditions* (State Park: Pennsylvania State University Press, 1997), 1.

6. Muslim Argument and the War on Terror

1. See http://www.crimesofwar.org/expert/paradigm-annaim.html (accessed November 11, 2001).

2. Abdullahi an-Naʿim, "Upholding International Legality against Islamic and American *Jihad,*" in *Worlds in Collision,* ed. Ken Booth and Tim Dunne (New York: Palgrave, 2002), 167.

3. Idem, "The Politics of Religion and the Morality of Globalization," in *Religion in Global Civil Society,* ed. Mark Juergensmeyer (New York:

Oxford, 2005), 23–48; idem, "Globalization and Jurisprudence: An Islamic Law Perspective," *Emory Law Journal* 54 (2005), 25–51.

4. For Abou El Fadl, see "War with Iraq: Arab TV Shows a Different Conflict," *Los Angeles Times,* April 5, 2003. Abdulaziz Sachedina focuses less on U.S. policy and more on the practical challenges a post-Saddam Iraq poses for Muslim democracy. See Sachedina, "Shia Responsibility in the Iraqi Elections," *American Muslim,* September 23, 2005, at http://theamericanmuslim.org/tam.php/features/articles/shiite_responsibility_in_the_iraqi_elections.

5. www.memri.org, Special Dispatches Series, No. 50, August 4, 2005.

6. See John Kelsay, *Islam and War: A Study in Comparative Ethics* (Louisville, Ky.: Westminster/John Knox, 1993), 57–77.

7. "Profile of Mahmoud Ahmadinejad: Friend or Foe," *Persian Mirror,* June 24, 2005, at http://persianmirror.com/community/2005/opinion/MahmoudAhmadinejad.cfm. For a good though controversial account of Ahmadinejad's life and career, with links to many of the sources cited in my discussion, readers may wish to consult http://en.wikipedia.org/wiki/Mahmoud_Ahmadinejad.

8. Translation by Nazila Fathi, *New York Times,* October 30, 2005, athttp://www.nytimes.com.2005/10/30/weekinreview/30iran.html?ex=1172552400&en=afd31f4931fbe2e8&ei=5070.

9. Ibid.

10. Ramitai Navai, "President Invokes New Islamic Wave," *The Times Online,* June 30, 2005, at http://www.timesonline.co.uk/article/0,,251–1674547,00.html.

11. "Profile of Mahmoud Ahmadinejad: Friend or Foe?" *Persian Mirror,* June 24, 2005, at http://persianmirror.com/community/2005/opinion/MahmoudAhmadinejad.cfm.

12. As translated at http://www.washingtonpost.com/wp-dyn/content/article/2006/05/09/AR2006050900878, May 9, 2006.

13. Ibid.

14. Ibid.

15. Ibid.

16. See, for example, the data presented by the Pew Research Foundation at http://people-press.org/reports/display.php3?ReportID=206.

17. As a very good example, see Ruhollah Khomeini, *Islam and Revolution: Writings and Declaration of Imam Khomeini,* trans. H. Algar (Los Angeles: Mizan, 1981), 351–364.

ACKNOWLEDGMENTS

I sometimes think I have been writing this book since the early 1980s. My debts are thus longstanding. While working on a Ph.D. at the University of Virginia, I benefited from the guidance of David Little, Abdulaziz Sachedina, and James Childress. They guided my early attempts to write about the just-war argument in Islam, and I will always be grateful. James Turner Johnson and Richard L. Rubenstein provided encouragement and good conversation as I continued my inquiries, and I thank them as well.

Since 2001, a number of people and institutions have lent support to my efforts. In the spring of that year, Paul Lauritzen extended an invitation to visit John Carroll University as the Walter and Mary Tuohy Professor. Each year, the occupant of that chair presents a series of public lectures, and in anticipation I announced the title "Islam and the Political Future." I drove my son to Boston for his first semester at the Berklee College of Music and arrived in Cleveland on September 5. Less than one week later, the topic took on meanings I had not anticipated, as all of us felt the weight of 9/11. I want to offer particular thanks to Paul, to David Mason, Mary Jane Ponyik, and others in the JCU community who made that visit so important in the development of this book.

While working at JCU, I applied for fellowships from the John Simon Guggenheim Foundation and the Princeton University Center for Human Values. It was my good fortune to receive both, and thus to benefit from the additional time for research afforded by these awards. I am grateful to the officers and staff of the Guggenheim Foundation, the faculty and staff at UCHV, and those who joined me there as Rockefeller Visiting Fellows during 2002–03. At Florida State University, Dean Donald Foss and his staff arranged things so that I could take advantage of these opportunities, and David Levenson and Barney Twiss took turns filling in as chair of the Department of Religion while I was away. I appreciate the support of my good friends Aline Kalbian, Michael Ruse, and Jeff Tatum, and the patience of Rita and our children. At Harvard University Press, Joyce Seltzer provided crucial feedback on an early outline of this project, then showed almost infinite patience as the manuscript wound its (slow!) way toward completion. In addition, two anonymous readers made useful suggestions with respect to the revision of the manuscript during the autumn of 2006, and Ann Hawthorne's wonderful copyediting helped me to bring the project to completion. I would be remiss if I did not mention the hospitality of the faculty and staff associated with the Institute of International Integration Studies at Trinity College Dublin, where an appointment as Long-Term Visiting Fellow provided time to put in place all the proposed corrections and changes. I also want to thank Matthew Hagele and Shannon Dunn for their work in compiling the index.

Whenever I think about this project, I find myself thinking most of all about my parents. They taught me to look at issues from more than one point of view. Insofar as I am able to listen to and comprehend the diverse ways in which Muslims argue about political and military affairs, my parents' teachings and example are present. I dedicate this book to Glen and Clarine Kelsay.

Some material in Chapter 3 appears in different form in John Kelsay, "Islamic Tradition and the Justice of War," in *The Ethics of War in Asian Civilizations,* edited by Torkel Brekke (New York: Routledge, 2006). I am grateful for permission to use this material.

Some of the material in Chapter 4 appears in a different form in my essay "Arguments Concerning Resistance in Contemporary Islam," in *The Ethics of War,* edited by Richard Sorabji and David Rodin (London: Ashgate, 2006). I am grateful for permission to use this material.

INDEX

Abbasids, 51, 61–62, 111–113, 121, 127, 188

Abduh, Muhammad, 81, 88

Abou El Fadl, Khaled, 182–188, 192–194, 195–196, 199, 232n33, 237n51, 240n5, 250n4

Abraham (Ibrahim), 11, 25, 27, 30–32, 230n4

Abu Bakr, 5, 35–36, 85, 118, 131, 170–172, 180, 199

Abu Ghayth, Sulayman, 127, 145, 163, 164

Abu Ghraib, 215

Abu Hanifa, 52, 114

Abu'l a'la Mawdudi, 92–94, 96, 166, 219

Abu Talib (uncle of Muhammad), 18–19, 21

Abu Yusuf, 52–54, 99, 188

al-Afghani (Jamal al-Din), 79–81

Afghanistan, 76, 144–145, 157, 164–165, 201, 202, 219, 221

African Muslims: in Europe, 200

ahkam al-bughat (judgments concerning rebels), 188, 190–195

ahkam al-jihad (judgments pertaining to armed struggle), 5–6

ahl al-dhimma ("protected people"), 39–40, 53, 76, 99, 103, 119–120, 159, 170, 182–183

Ahmadiyyat movement, 93–94

Ahmadinejad, Mahmoud, 204–216, 218–220; *See also* Iran, Islamic Republic of

Ahmad, Jalal al-e, 95

Ahmad, Mumtaz, 238n54

ʿAli, ʿAmir, 167

Andrae, Tor, 231n13

Arab tribal culture, pre-Islamic, 11–17, 21–24

Arafat, Yassir, 134

Arjomand, Said Amir, 237n49

authority, legitimate, 6, 41; and armed resistance, 131–139, 153–154; based on learning, 49–50; concept of, 110; al-Mawardi's discussion of, 110–115; in relation to just war, 101–102, 104, 113, 128, 223; and Shariʿa, 39, 121; Shiʿi discussions of just war, 123–124

al-ʿAwaji, Shaykh Muhsin, 144–145, 147, 148, 164, 165, 196

al-Awzaʿi, 50, 55

al-Azhar, Shaykh, 83, 85, 133, 139–143, 144, 150, 164–165, 196, 244n2

al-ʿAziz, ʿAbd, 75–76, 127–129, 238n52

al-Banna, Hasan, 90–92, 96, 166, 219, 239n64

bidʿa (innovation), 131–132, 152

bin Laden, Osama, 2, 3, 4, 8, 96, 127, 129, 136–139, 143–146, 147–148, 149, 153, 156, 158–159, 164, 165, 184, 195, 209, 219, 223, 244n1

Blair, Tony, 156, 200–201, 221–222

Bush, George W., 1–2, 8, 9, 200–201, 204–205, 210–216, 219–220, 221–223

Calder, Norman J., 233n3, 240n5

Charter of Hamas (1988), 129–130, 133–136, 139, 155, 158–159, 162, 194

Christianity, 10–11, 34, 41–42, 79–80, 210–211; Islamic critiques of, 25, 41–42, 65

Christians: as *ahl al-dhimma*, 40, 53, 76, 99, 102, 119–120, 159, 170; called by Muhammad, 35; challenges from the Qurʾan, 31; conversations with Muslims, 50; early conflict with Muslims, 175; interactions with Muhammad, 18, 21, 231n13; Islamic militants, 161; legacy of intolerance, 197; Muslim democrats, 173, 199; in Rashid Rida's proposed *khilafat*, 89; role in Islamic polity, 183

civilians, treatment of. *See* noncombatants

colonialism, European, 6, 75–76, 128, 200

community, Islamic concept of. *See umma.*

conquest, Islamic, 36–38, 97, 115–116, 158

conscience, freedom of, 167- 169, 172, 198, 199

Cook, Michael, 67, 232n33, 236n39, 243nn38,46,48

Crone, Patricia, 232n32

Crusades, 115–116; in militant Islamic discourse, 129, 133–135, 156, 160

Declaration on Armed Struggle against Jews and Crusaders (1998), 126, 129–130, 136–139, 143, 144, 146, 148, 150,

152–153, 155, 158–159, 162–163, 164, 177, 195–197

democracy, 2, 6–7, 87–88, 143, 160, 161–162, 166, 196, 197, 209, 210, 203–204, 213–214, 216–223. *See also* Muslim democrats

al-Din, Salah (Saladin), 129, 135, 138

discrimination, principle of, 104, 106–110, 114–115, 117–118, 123–124, 142, 143, 146, 150, 161, 164, 196, 220, 223. *See also* noncombatants

Donner, Fred, 232n29

Dykstra, David, 228n4

Egypt: assassination of Sadat, 96, 126–127, 130, 136, 244n2; Christians, 131; Egyptian Islamic Jihad, 136, 142; treaty with Israel, 130–131, 132

Enayat, Hamid, 238n59, 247n4

Ess, Joseph van, 233n4, 236n36

Evangelical Christians, 2–3, 4, 8

al-Faraj, Muhammad, 126, 131, 139–140, 150, 240n68

fatawah (legal opinions), 53, 68, 154, 184

Firestone, Reuven, 241n8

fitna (dissension; strife), 47, 71, 119, 185, 186

Frank, Richard M., 233n4, 236n36

Fromkin, David, 239n60

Gibb, H. A. R., 245n5

Gimaret, Daniel, 236n36

God (*al-lah*): human reflection on the existence of, 29–30, 31, 32; human responsibility toward, 3, 9, 28, 34, 91–92, 237n50; mercy of, 33; message of the prophets, 34

Goldziher, Ignaz, 230n6, 233n3

Guantánamo Bay, 211–212, 215

hadith (report of the Prophetic *sunna*), 45, 58–59, 64, 65–66, 98, 122, 186

Hallaq, Wael, 70, 233n3

Hamas, 134, 139, 140, 142, 211–212

Hamzah, Mir, 244n1

Hanafi school, 54–55, 105, 115

Hanbalites, 166

al-Hasan al-Basri, 49–50, 51, 234n12

Hashmi, Sohail, 240n1

al-Hawali, Safar, 144

Helms, Christine Moss, 238n55, 245n3

al-hijra, 23, 230n4

Hinds, Martin, 230n6, 232n32

Hizbullah, 204, 215

Hodgson, Marshall G.S., 232nn25, 30, 1, 233nn2,5, 235n33, 242n26

Holland, M. 243n48

Hourani, George F., 233n4, 236n35, 238n59, 239n63

al-hudud, 171, 174, 176

humanity: capable of acknowledging God, 29–30, 31, 32, 231n23; and God's will, 32; quest for security, 32; need for God's guidance, 33; "vice-regent" of God, 29

human rights, 166–167, 173, 202

Huntington, Samuel, 228n4

Husayn (son of 'Ali ibn abi Talib), 47

Hussein, Saddam, 205, 207

Ibn 'abd al-Wahhab, Muhammad, 76, 127–128

Ibn Abi Talib, 'Ali, 46–47, 63, 85, 98, 119, 133, 188–192

Ibn al-Khattab, Umar, 35–37, 45, 85, 171, 180, 183, 229n2

Ibn Anas, Malik, 50, 55, 73, 98, 186, 235n29, 241n6

Ibn Babuya, 71

Ibn Hanbal, Ahmad, 65–68, 73, 74, 181, 235n29

Ibn Ishaq, 14, 17, 18, 21, 25, 230n4

Ibn Rushd, 68–70, 74

Ibn Taymiyya, 73–74, 75, 117–122, 126–127, 163

ijtihad (effort; independent judgment), 59, 60, 110

'ilm (knowledge), 50

Imamate, 71, 122, 205, 237n47

Iqbal, Muhammad, 82

Iran, Islamic Republic of, 167, 205–209, 216, 218, 219, 237n49. See also Ahmadinejad, Mahmoud; Iranian Revolution

Iranian Revolution, 95, 206, 237n49. See also Khomeini, Ayatollah

Iraq, 70, 97, 162–163, 205, 206, 209; U.S.-led war in, 1–2, 157, 201, 204–205, 207–208, 211, 215, 219, 220, 221, 246n25

Ishmael, 30, 230n4

Islam: a living tradition, 4–5, 9, 124; opposed to culture of pre-Islamic Ara-

bia, 17; "natural religion of humanity," 10, 27–35, 44, 93, 126, 155, 157–158; Muhammad, 10, 17–27, 157–158; a world civilization, 10, 35–40, 157–158

al-islam (submission), 9–10, 25, 28, 34, 37, 100

al-isnad (chain of criticism), 59, 186; use of by Shi'i 'ulama, 71, 235n29

Israel: ancient, 25, 34; modern, 130–131, 134, 140–143, 147–148, 150, 162–163, 194, 206, 208, 211–212, 215

al-istihsan (good opinion), 54, 59

al-jahiliyya (ignorance; heedlessness), 17, 77

al-Jahiz, 43, 233n2

Jansen, Johannes J.G., 244n2

Jesus, 11, 25, 27, 34, 41–42, 210–211, 212

Jews: as ahl al-dhimma, 40, 53, 76, 99, 102, 119–120, 159, 170; called by Muhammad, 35; challenges from the Qur'an, 31; conversations with Muslims, 50; Islamic militants, 160, 161; interactions with Muhammad, 24; Muslim democrats, 173, 199; early relations to Muslims, 25, 27, 175, 231n19

Jibril (Gabriel), 229n2

jihad, 39, 41, 98, 115, 129, 147, 202; concept of, 38, 173, 174, 202; establishment of moral-social order, 147, 173; militant interpretation of, 196; Western just war tradition, 223. See also ahkam al-jihad (judgments pertaining to armed struggle)

John of Damascus, 50, 236n38

Johnson, James Turner 241n8, 249n32

Jomier, J., 228–229n1

Judaism, 10–11, 34, 41, 42, 206, 230n4; Islamic critiques of, 25, 42

just cause (in Islam), 102, 105, 220

justice: and concept of government in Islam, 84; in the Qur'an, 188–191

just war: as an aspect of the foundational narrative of Islam, 97, 99; concept of in Islam, 5, 101–102, 201, 205, 219–220, 221–222, 223; conduct (honorable combat) in war, 100–101, 104–110, 139–140, 145, 147, 148–149, 164, 219–220; "just revolution," 122; political authority, 197, 219; rebellion, 190–193; relation to the formation of an Islamic state, 102, 155–156, 165; in Western arguments, 102–103, 104, 109, 151, 221–222, 241n8

Juynboll, G.H.A., 230n6

Ka'ba, 14–15, 16, 17, 20, 30, 47, 230n4

kalam (dialectical theology), 51–52, 62

Keddie, Nikki R., 238n58

Kelsay, John, 234n17, 236nn35, 39, 240n1, 241n8, 242n14, 246n22, 246n27, 249nn28, 29, 250n6

Kerr, Malcolm, 238n59

Khadduri, Majid, 240n5, 241nn6,9, 242n15

Khadija (wife of Muhammad), 19, 21

al-khalifa (caliph; successor; leader), 5, 39, 48–49, 66–67, 83, 84–86, 101, 110–113, 171–172, 181

Khan, Sayyid Ahmad, 78–79

Kharijites, 47, 98, 118, 119

al-Khasif, Muhammad, 14

al-khilafat (caliphate), 35, 39, 48, 82, 83, 112, 121, 147–148, 166, 180; Rashid Rida's interpretation of, 89–90; al-Raziq's interpretation of, 84–86, 88

Khomeini, Ayatollah, 95, 124, 152, 205, 207, 210, 213–214, 216–219. *See also* Iran, Islamic Republic of; Iranian Revolution

Kister, M.J., 230n6

Kohlberg, Etan, 243n50

al-Kulayni, 71

Lambton, Ann K.S., 232n32, 238n56, 242n22

Laoust, Henri, 243n38

Lawrence, Bruce, 243–244n50

Lebanon, 209, 220; and Israeli invasion of (1982), 134

Lewis, Bernard, 232n32

liberal thought, 213, 223

Little, David, 235n32

madahib (schools of Islamic interpretation), 73

Magnarella, Paul J., 248n13

al-Ma'mun, 62, 65, 66–67, 181, 190

al-Maqdisi, Muhammad, 248n6

martyrdom operations, 140, 149

al-Mawardi, 110–115, 123

Metcalf, Barbara Daly, 238n53

al-mihna (test), 63, 66, 181, 190

militants, Islamic, 3, 4, 6, 124, 129, 130–

militants, Islamic *(continued)*
131, 136–138, 153, 156–166, 167, 168, 169, 179, 227–228n3; arguments for targeting noncombatants, 139–150, 151, 196; critique of democracy, 160, 161–162, 166; understanding of Shari'a, 161, 184, 187–188, 195, 196, 198; criticisms of, 164–166, 173, 187–188, 195–197, 198, 199–200, 203; and the war on terror, 129, 200–204, 221, 223;

Mitchell, Richard, 239n64

monotheism, 41, 42, 213

Moses, 11, 25, 27, 34, 212

Mottahedeh, Roy, 237n49, 239n66

Mu'awiya, 46–48, 63, 98, 119

al-Mufid, 70

al-Muhajirun, 165

Muhammad, 3, 9, 10–12, 14, 17–27, 34, 35–36, 45, 56–57, 159, 169, 185, 199, 212, 220, 229n2; agreement with Medinan tribes, 23–24; campaign against the Meccans, 26–27; interactions with Christians, 18, 21; interactions with Jews, 24; and justification of military force in Islam, 98, 100, 146, 148; as religious and political leader, 23, 84–86, 180; as the "seal" of the prophets, 93, 181

Muhammad, Shaykh 'Umar Bakri, 146–149

al-Muhaqqiq al-Hilli, 123, 235–236n34, 243n50

al-mujahiddin, 158

al-Mulk, Nizam, 233n2

al-Murtada, 70

muruwwa (manliness), 15–16, 19

Muslim Brothers (*ikhwan al-muslimin*), 90–92

Muslim democrats, 166–167, 196–197, 198–202, 216, 220–224

al-mustadafin (the oppressed), 214

Mutahhari, Ayatullah Murtaza, 243–244n50

Mu'tazila, 52, 62–63, 65, 66, 235n34, 237n50; and their teaching on *al-tawhid* (unity of God), 62–65

an-Na'im, Abdullahi, 174–182, 195–196, 199, 201–203, 205, 221

al-Nasr, Gamal 'abd, 92

Nasr, Seyyed Hossein, 232–233n1

Nasr, Seyyed Vali Reza, 239n65

Navai, Ramitai, 250n10

Neglected Duty, The (1981), 126, 129–133, 138, 139, 150, 155, 162, 163–165, 177, 194

Newby, Gordon Darnell, 230n6

Nicene Creed, 170

Nimieri, Jafar, 174–176

noncombatants, 99, 104, 106–110, 114–115, 117–118, 123–124, 139–144, 145–146, 148, 149, 151, 164, 194, 197, 214. *See also* discrimination, principle of

Nyazee, Imran Ahsan Khan, 236n42

Nyberg, H. S., 236n35

Ottoman Empire, 77, 82, 83, 127, 147, 166

Palestine, 133–135, 139, 140–142, 149–150, 156, 161, 162–163, 206, 208, 211–212, 215
Parry, V. J., 242n14
Patriot Act, 200
Peters, F. E., 230n6
Peters, J. R. T. M., 236n37
Prophet. *See* Muhammad

al-Qaʿida, 3, 127, 136–138, 142, 145, 156, 157, 164–165, 201, 202, 204, 209, 227n3, 244n1
al-Qaradhawi, Yusuf, 140–143, 144, 150, 164–165, 196, 245n18
al-qiyas (reasoning by analogy), 59–60, 69–70
Qurʾan, 4, 9, 20, 22, 25, 28, 29, 30, 32–34, 57, 153, 188, 189, 190, 196, 199; abrogation, 58; basis of religious knowledge, 51–52, 55–57, 68; "commanding good and forbidding wrong," 23, 34, 48, 219; as created speech, 64, 67, 235n34; establishment of warrior's code, 107; freedom of conscience, 168–170, 172; interpretation of, 68–69, 168, 177, 183; justification of military force, 23–24, 26, 97, 116, 117; 49; recitation of, 45
Quraysh, 14, 16, 17, 21, 22, 83, 97, 163, 169, 175, 230n4
Qutb, Sayyid, 96

Rahman, Fazlar, 244n1
Ramsey, Paul, 241n8
Rashid, Ahmed, 238n54

al-Rashid, Harun, 53–54, 188
Rashid Rida, 88–90, 91, 99, 166, 219
al-raʿy (opinion): as legitimate grounds of judgment, 54, 59
al-Raziq, ʿAli ʿabd, 83–86, 87–88, 90, 167, 218
reason (*al-ʿaql*), 231n23; in Shiʿi thought, 71–72; in the interpretation of texts, 69–70; and political obligation, 84; as providing guidance, 56–57; and social morality, 88
rebels (*al-bughat*), 99, 100, 103, 113, 152, 190–195; and apostates (*al-murtadd*), 103, 113, 118–119, 131, 132–133; rules for fighting against them, 113, 118, 120, 131, 132–133. *See* also *akham al-bughat* (judgments concerning rebels); Resistance, armed
reciprocity, 143–144, 145, 196, 204
Reinhart, Kevin A., 233n3
Republican Brothers, 174, 176
resistance, armed, 6, 130–154, 155–156, 190–195, 227n3, 234n12; in Shiʿi tradition, 152
revolution, 67, 121, 132, 190–195, 206, 208, 234n12
Rice, Condoleezza, 204
al-Rida, ʿAli, 62
al-ridda (apostasy): 36, 103, 113, 131, 133, 151, 170
righteous intention, 101–102, 105, 220, 223
Rizvi, S. A. A., 238n52, 245n4
Robson, J., 235n29
Rosenthal, E. I. J., 232n32, 242n22

Sachedina, Abdulaziz, 123, 167–174, 181–182, 195–196, 199, 231n22, 237nn46,47,49, 250n4

al-salam (peace), 9–10, 40–41

al-Sarakhsi, 240n5

Schacht, Joseph, 233n3

Sepoy Mutiny, 76

September 11, 2001, 1, 3, 138, 142–143. 158–159, 167, 200, 201–202, 212, 221

al-Shafiʻi, 55–61, 66, 68, 116, 186, 235n31

Shariʻa reasoning, 3, 4–5, 44, 49–50, 55, 67–70, 72–73, 125, 177; authorization of military force, 6, 116, 139; conduct in war 100–101, 109–110, 192–194; a conservative practice, 75, 202; and contemporary international politics, 129; counterparts in the Western just war tradition, 103, 109; and democratic politics, 6–7, 167, 203, 223–224; democratization of, 94; legitimate authority, 110–111, 121; judgments concerning rulers and subjects, 120–121; just political order, 128, 132, 146; as open practice, 77–78, 177; "the path", 3, 44, 56–57; political vision, 80, 81, 93; honorable combat, 148, 149; "rule of law," 39–40; use of reason (al-ʻaql), 72; separation from coercive state power, 178; a tradition of argument, 199

Shariʻati, ʻAli, 239n66

al-Shaybani, 52–54, 99–109, 114, 118, 123, 188–190

Shiʻa, 47–48, 71, 75–76, 94–95, 111, 206, 209, 210, 219, 220, 235n29; approach to politics and war, 122–124; Twelver Shiʻism, 71, 72, 77, 94, 122–123, 235n34, 238n58; use of reason (al-ʻaql), 72

Sivan, E., 242n34

Skinner, Quentin, 152

Smith, Jane I., 243n36

state, role of the 147, 179–181, 217–218

statecraft, 87, 112; Islamic militant vision of, 155, 158–162, 179, 200; Khomeini's vision of, 217–218

Sufism, 49, 91

al-Sulami, 115–117

sunna (traditions; practices of the Prophet), 45, 55, 57–58, 66, 68, 85, 153, 196; abrogation, 58; pre-Islamic traditions, 16; military force, 97, 101, 116, 117; Shiʻi view, 71, 122, 186

Sunnis, 48, 70, 75–76, 210, 218, 219, 235n29, 238n58; approach to politics and war, 122–124;

al-Tabari, 109, 230–231n8, 233n6, 242n20

Tablighi Jamaʻat, 76, 94

Taha, Abu-Yasir Rifaʻi Ahmad, 244n1

Taha, Mahmud Muhammad, 174–176

Takim, Liyakat N., 237n48

Taliban, 76, 78, 195, 201, 202

al-taqlid (imitation), 73–74

al-taqwa (piety; godly fear), 17

al-tawhid (unity of God), 62–65

timely resort, 103

Tobacco Revolt (1890–91), 80

Troll, Christian, 238n57

al-Tusi, 70

'*ulama* (religious specialists; "the learned"), 5, 45, 57, 70, 72, 95, 126, 137, 153, 161, 170, 177, 183–184, 187, 190, 193, 195, 209; in Shi'i tradition, 71, 80, 94–95, 123, 124

umma (community of faith), 17, 18, 35, 153,

Umayyads, 48–50, 51, 61, 85

United Nations, 162–163, 168, 201–203, 208–209

United States (and Americans), 1, 2, 3, 6, 7, 10, 131, 134, 136, 137, 138, 142–144, 146, 147–148, 149, 153, 156–157, 161, 162–163, 164, 195, 197, 200–203, 206–208, 210–216, 219–223, 244n1

Universal Declaration of Human Rights, 168, 172, 178

'Uthman, 44–45, 85

Wahba, Wafaa H. 242nn23,24,25,27,28, 29,30,31,32,33,35

Wahhabi movement, 76–77, 127; and discussions of Shari'a, 184, 185

Wali Allah, Shah, 75, 78

Walzer, Michael, 150

al-Wansharisi, 73–74

war, Islamic conception of, 99, 100, 102, 105

Waraqa (cousin of Khadija, wife of Muhammad), 21

war on terror, 7, 129, 144, 200–205, 210, 211–212, 214–215, 220–221, 223

Watt, W.M., 101, 230n8, 234nn7,12, 236n35, 241n7

Weber, Max, 62

Wolfson, Harry, 234n13, 236n38

World Islamic Front, 126, 136, 142, 152, 184, 195–197. *See also Declaration on Armed Struggle against Jews and Crusaders* (1998)

al-Zarqawi, Abu Musab, 248n6

al-Zawahiri, Ayman, 3, 127, 136, 153, 156–165, 170, 172, 179, 184, 204, 209, 219, 244n1, 244–245n2

Zionism, 134, 206